THE BOOK OF ACTS

Stanley M. Horton

THE BOOK OF ACTS

GOSPEL PUBLISHING HOUSE
SPRINGFIELD, MISSOURI
02-0317

THE BOOK OF ACTS

Library of Congress Cataloging in Publication Data

Horton, Stanley M.
The book of Acts.

(The Radiant commentary on the New Testament)
Bibliography: p.
Includes index.
1. Bible. N.T. Acts—Commentaries. I. Title.
II. Series: Radiant commentary on the New Testament.
BS2625.3.H67 226'.607 80-65892
ISBN 0-88243-317-2

4th Printing 1992

Printed in the United States of America

Contents

CONTENTS

General Outline

I. The Church Established 1:1 to 2:47
  A. The Promise of the Father 1:1-11
  B. The Witness of the Apostles 1:12-26
  C. Recognized and Empowered 2:1-42
  D. All Things Shared 2:43-47
II. Ministry in Jerusalem 3:1 to 8:3
  A. The Lame Man Healed 3:1 to 4:31
  B. Tested and Triumphant 4:32 to 5:42
  C. Seven Chosen to Serve 6:1-7
  D. Stephen Martyred 6:8 to 8:3
III. Ministry in Samaria and Judea 8:4 to 11:18
  A. Philip's Preaching 8:4 to 11:18
  B. Saul's Conversion 9:1-31
  C. Peter's Ministry Moves Out 9:32 to 11:18
IV. Antioch a New Center 11:19 to 18:22
  A. The Gospel Reaches Antioch 11:19-30
  B. Peter's Deliverance 12:1-24
  C. Paul's First Missionary Journey 12:25 to 14:28
  D. The Jerusalem Conference 15:1-35
  E. Paul's Second Missionary Journey 15:36 to 18:22
V. Ephesus a New Center 18:23 to 20:38
  A. A Better Baptism 18:23 to 19:7
  B. Revival and Riot 19:8 to 20:1
  C. Farewell to Ephesus 20:2-38
VI. The Road to Rome 21:1 to 28:31
  A. Paul's Arrest 21:1 to 23:35
  B. Appeal to Ceasar 24:1 to 26:32
  C. Voyage to Rome 27:1 to 28:15
  D. A Prisoner, Yet Free 28:16-31

Introduction

The Book of Acts is special. There is no other book like it in the Bible. We do have other historical books in the Old Testament. But they emphasize the failures, the sins, the idolatry that kept God's people from the fullness of His blessing.

In the Book of Acts that failure is in the past. Israel has learned its lesson, and idolatry is no longer a problem among them. More important, Jesus has come. His death on Calvary has put the new covenant into effect (Hebrews 9:15). By His resurrection He has brought blessing and great joy to His followers (Luke 24:51, 52). A sense of both fulfillment and the excitement of anticipation pervades the book.

Originally the book had no title. Since the middle of the second century A.D., however, it has been known as *The Acts of the Apostles.*[1] This title probably arose because the apostles are named in the first chapter (1:13). Yet, as we go through the Book we see that most of the apostles are not named again and some only barely mentioned. Peter alone is prominent in the first part of the book. Paul alone is prominent in the latter part.

Actually, the Holy Spirit is more prominent than the apostles. The Book records how Jesus himself focused attention on the Holy Spirit (1:4, 5). The outpouring of the Spirit (2:4) then sets the action of the Book in motion. Fifty-one times the Spirit is mentioned or referred to. Thus, many have suggested that *The Acts of the Holy Spirit* would be a better title.

---

[1]Because Marcion, about A.D. 144, declared that Paul was the only faithful apostle, the Muratorian list of New Testament books calls it *The Acts of All the Apostles.* See Kirsopp Lake and S. Lake, *An Introduction to the New Testament* (New York: Harper, 1937), p. 280 and F. F. Bruce, *Commentary on the Book of the Acts* (Grand Rapids: Eerdmans, 1954), p. 19.

Acts 1:1, however, suggests we might enlarge the title a little. Notice the word "began." The former treatise (Luke's Gospel) recorded what Jesus began to do and teach. The Book of Acts, therefore, records what Jesus continued to do and teach through the Holy Spirit in the growing, spreading Church. Though Jesus is now in glory at the right hand of the Father's throne, He is still doing His work in the present world. Thus, an enlarged title for the Book of Acts might well be, *The Acts of the Risen Lord by the Holy Spirit in and Through the Church.*

We must recognize, however, that just as Acts does not tell us details about all the apostles, it also does not tell the full story of the growth of the Church.[2] In many cases it gives only brief summaries of what happened.[3] The churches in Galilee and Samaria are given very little attention (9:31). Important events, such as the growth of a strong church in Egypt during the first century, are not mentioned at all. On the other hand, some events are given in great detail. (See chapters 8, 10, 11, and 28.)

It is probable that the speeches and sermons which stand out so prominently in the book are also summaries. Paul, for example, sometimes preached until midnight (20:7). Other occasions obviously required a whole synagogue service, yet what is recorded can be read in a very few minutes. It is clear, however, that these speeches reflect the style and emphases of the apostles, as well as their actual words.[4] Condensed accounts were necessary due to the limited amount of space available in an ancient papyrus book or scroll. If the entire story of the growth and development of the Early Church, with all the signs and wonders recorded in detail, were told it would more than fill up several sets of books the size of the *Encyclopedia Brittanica.* (Compare John 20:30, 31; 21:25.)

More than the limitations of space is involved, however. No one

[2]Everett F. Harrison, *Introduction to the New Testament* (Grand Rapids: Eerdmans, 1964), p. 228.

[3]See examples in 2:47; 5:42; 6:7; 8:4, 40; 9:31; 12:24; 13:49; 16:5; 18:23; 19:20; 28:30, 31.

[4]For example, early tradition says Mark got his Gospel from Peter's preaching. We do see the same emphases in Mark's Gospel as we do in Peter's preaching in Acts. In comparing Paul's sermons in Acts with his Epistles, however, keep in mind that in Acts he was speaking to people who had never heard the gospel. In the Epistles he was dealing with Christians and the problems which arose among people who already knew and believed the gospel. See Richard Heard, *An Introduction to the New Testament* (New York: Harper & Row, 1950), pp. 139, 140.

could write a history today by throwing together everything printed in the daily newspapers. The historian must choose events that he feels are significant, events that show trends, turning points, and relationships. Luke does this by following a theme suggested by the words of Jesus: "Ye shall be witnesses unto me both in Jerusalem, and in all Judea, and in Samaria, and unto the uttermost part of the earth" (1:8). The first seven chapters center around events in Jerusalem, describing the initial growth and testing of the Church. Chapters 8 through 12 reveal how the Spirit broke down barriers in Judea and Samaria. Finally, chapters 13 through 28 show how the gospel began to move toward the uttermost part of the earth. They emphasize new centers for the spread of the gospel at Antioch, Ephesus, and Rome. Luke's clarity and logical progression lead most Bible-believing scholars to agree that Luke is a first-class historian, not only because of what he included in Acts, but also because of what he left out.[5] (Bible-believing scholars agree, of course, that the Holy Spirit directed the writing of the Scriptures.)

The events which Luke does include were both significant and typical. At the time he wrote, churches in various areas were in communication with each other and were familiar with many of the events described in the book. Thus, the people who first read Acts would not have any difficulty seeing the relationship of their own local church to the course of events described in the book.[6]

Though the Book of Acts does not name its author, it is evident that Acts 1:1 refers to the same Theophilus mentioned in Luke 1:1-4. What we find in Acts is the outworking of the Gospel as recorded by Luke, though the Gospel does not name its author either. There is good evidence, however, connecting both the Gospel and Acts with the person whom Paul calls "the beloved physician" (Colossians 4:14).

One important evidence of Luke's authorship is the "we" passages in Acts 16:10-17; 20:5 to 21:18; 27:1 to 28:16. In these passages the author indicates he was with Paul on parts of the second and third missionary journeys as well as the journey to

[5]See Charles Carter and Ralph Earle, *The Acts of the Apostles* (Grand Rapids: Zondervan, 1959), p. 6. This is the view of the British historian, Sir William Ramsay.

[6]Richard Heard, *An Introduction to the New Testament* (New York: Harper & Row, 1950), p. 136.

Rome.[7] To parts of the Book of Acts, then, Luke was an eyewitness.

The fact that Luke was with Paul on his last visit to Jerusalem and also accompanied him on the journey to Rome indicates Luke was in Palestine during the two years Paul was imprisoned in Caesarea. It is evident that Luke checked his facts very carefully. Though the titles and status of Roman officials changed frequently in the first century, Luke never made a mistake. Archaeology has done a great deal to confirm what he says concerning both geography and history. It would not be wrong to assume, therefore, that Luke spent those two years checking facts and talking to eyewitnesses of the events of the Gospel and the first part of Acts.

We see, for example, that in the Gospel Luke tells the story of the birth of Jesus from Mary's viewpoint, while Matthew gives it from Joseph's. Joseph most probably was dead before Luke came to Jerusalem, but Mary was still alive. Luke tells how Mary kept the events surrounding Christ's birth in her heart (Luke 2:51). That is, she remembered them carefully. Luke also tells that Mary was present in the Upper Room on the Day of Pentecost. Paul confirmed that many who saw the risen Christ were still alive when he wrote (1 Corinthians 15:6). Luke was thus able to confirm the events which, under the guidance and inspiration of the Spirit, he included in Acts.[8]

The fact Paul calls Luke "the beloved physician" also fits what we find in Luke and Acts. Luke gives special attention to healing and often gives additional details or a more specific diagnosis. When Jesus said it was easier for a camel to go through the eye of a needle than for a rich man to enter the kingdom of heaven, the other Gospels use the common word for a sewing needle, but Luke uses the more classical Greek word which the Greeks used for a surgeon's needle. Some have tried to press this further by

[7]Eusebius (about A.D. 330) and Jerome (about A.D. 400) believed Luke was from Antioch. One ancient manuscript (Codex Beza or D) adds to Acts 11:2, "When we came together." This would indicate Luke was present in Antioch about A.D. 42.

[8]These include the miracles. Even some who have not been brought up to believe in miracles admit that the miracles are not tacked on to the Book. They are part of its very framework and structure. Take them out and the whole book falls apart. Since Luke was so meticulous in verifying everything else, we can be sure he did not fail to verify these miracles also.

finding medical terms in Luke and Acts. However, it has been shown that physicians in New Testament times used everyday language. There was no such thing then as a "medical language."[9] However, practically all Bible scholars today recognize Luke as the author of both his Gospel and Acts.

Since Acts takes us up to Paul's first imprisonment in Rome, A.D. 60, 61, that is the earliest date it could have been written. In A.D. 64 Rome burned and Nero began persecuting Christians. This brought a complete change in the relation between the Christians and the Empire. Thus, the latest date for the writing of Acts would be about A.D. 63.[10] We have in the book a record of the first generation of believers, the first thirty years of a growth of the Church that began at Pentecost.

From Pentecost on, there is an emphasis on the growth of the Church. The 120 immediately become 3,000; a little later we read of 5,000. Then there are companies of priests and even companies of Pharisees as the Lord kept adding daily to the Church. As the Church moves out there are new centers, new multitudes. In all this there is clear evidence of the guidance of the Spirit and of spiritual as well as numerical growth. Though problems arose, the Holy Spirit was sufficient for every situation.

Luke draws attention also to the way the Spirit promoted the unity of the Body as it grew. Notice how often he mentions being "in one accord." More than once the Church was in danger of being split, but the Spirit brought them together. The world tends to disrupt, divide, build barriers. The Holy Spirit broke down barriers as the Church prayed together, worked together, suffered together. Nature tends to disperse, scatter, break down. It takes a higher energy to unite, and more wisdom and power to build up than to tear down. Thus, an important theme of *The Acts of the Risen Lord Through the Holy Spirit* is church building.

Acts clearly is a Church book, giving us important teaching concerning the nature, growth, life, and purpose of the Church. Some today deny that the Acts has anything to teach us. They say we must go to the Epistles for doctrine, for Acts is only history, not

[9]Dr. Hobart in *The Medical Language of St. Luke* (1882), went too far in this direction. About 90% of his "medical terms" have been found in the works of nonmedical writers such as Josephus and even in the Septuagint version of the Old Testament.

[10]Harrison, *op. cit.,* p. 226.

doctrinal teaching. They overlook the fact, however, that the Bible does not give us history to satisfy our historical curiosity, but rather to teach truth. Even the Epistles refer to both Old and New Testament history in order to teach doctrine. When Paul wanted to explain justification by faith in Romans 4, he went back to the history of Abraham in Genesis. When he wanted to show what God's grace can do, he went back to the history of David. Acts does more than give a mere transition or "shifting of gears" between the Gospels and the Epistles. It provides a background to the Epistles and is necessary for a better understanding of the truths they teach.

Just as in the Gospels and Epistles, Jesus is central in Acts. The books complement each other and exalt Him. Acts shows that the total life of the Church continued to revolve around the living Christ, the One risen, ascended, and seated at the right hand of the Father interceding. Paul, in 1 Corinthians chapters 12 through 14, has something to say about the Holy Spirit, but in chapter 15 he returns the focus of attention to the risen Christ. So, though Acts gives teaching and shows us much of the work of the Spirit, it primarily focuses attention on Jesus. He is the Prince of Life, the One who has come, who is present through the Spirit, and who will come again. His resurrection life and power flows through the book. The Gospels, Acts, the Epistles, and the Book of Revelation are all one revelation of the Word of God. What a tragedy if any part is neglected!

One more thing should be kept in mind. Unlike many other books in the New Testament, the Book of Acts has no formal conclusion. It simply breaks off. Some suppose that this came about because Luke was martyred shortly after the Apostle Paul. However, there are several ancient traditions that he lived longer. It seems, rather, that the abrupt ending is intentional. The book had to come to an end, just as that first generation had to come to an end. But the Acts of the Risen Lord through the Holy Spirit did not end then. They continued on into the second and third centuries with the same spiritual gifts and manifestations. Further, they continue today wherever God's people gather together in one accord with an earnest desire to search His Word, seek His gifts, and do His work.

ACTS
CHAPTER
1

Did Luke plan a third volume? Some say the abrupt ending of the Book of Acts calls for this. Luke may have planned one. However, his ministry may have been cut short by martyrdom, as Gregory of Nazianzen states. At least, he stayed with Paul during Paul's second imprisonment when others deserted him to save their own lives. But the word "former" or "first" need not imply another volume. What we have in Luke's Gospel and the content of the Book of Acts complement each other perfectly. Luke's Gospel gives the good news of the life, death, and resurrection of Jesus. Acts shows the outworking of the gospel in the first generation of the Church. This work of the Holy Spirit was never intended to come to a conclusion in this age.

Theophilus ("lover of God; dear to God") was the first recipient of this book, as he was of Luke's Gospel. The Bible tells us practically nothing about him, so he has been the subject of much speculation. Was he a lawyer who was to handle Paul's case in Rome? This is unlikely. Paul rose to his own defense in all previous trials. Was he a Greek nobleman converted under Luke's ministry? Was he a philosopher searching for the truth? Was Theophilus a title or a personal name? We do not know for sure, though it was a common personal name.[1] Most likely he was a personal friend whom Luke could count on to read the book and to have copies made and circulated.

What Jesus Continued to Do and Teach (1:1)

[1]The former treatise have I made, O Theophilus, of all that Jesus began both to do and teach . . . (Acts 1:1).

[1]F. F. Bruce, *Commentary on the Book of Acts* (Grand Rapids: Eerdmans, 1974), p. 32.

The fact that Luke's Gospel dealt with what Jesus "began to do and teach" shows us two things. First, the Church had its beginning in the Gospel. Luke's Gospel ends with a convinced group of believers. Jesus "opened their understanding, that they might understand the Scriptures" (Luke 24:45). They were no longer an easily scattered group of disciples, but a commissioned body, united, worshiping, waiting to be clothed with power from on high (Luke 24:46-53). In other words, they were already the Church. As Hebrews 9:15-17 makes clear, Christ's death and the shedding of His blood put the New Covenant into effect. Thus, the believers who were daily in the Temple, especially at the hours of prayer (Acts 3:1), blessing (thanking) God, were already a New Covenant Body.

Second, the work of Jesus did not end when He ascended.[2] As has already been noted, the Book of Acts shows what Jesus continued to do and teach by the Holy Spirit through the Church.

FINAL INSTRUCTIONS (1:2, 3)

> . . . [2]until the day in which he was taken up, after that he through the Holy Ghost had given commandments unto the apostles whom he had chosen: [3]to whom also he showed himself alive after his passion by many infallible proofs, being seen of them forty days, and speaking of the things pertaining to the kingdom of God . . . (Acts 1:2, 3).

It is clear also that Jesus did not ascend until after He had given commands (injunctions, instructions) through the Holy Spirit to His chosen apostles (chosen for himself to carry out His work).[3] The word "apostles" here may not be limited to the Twelve but may include other "sent ones" commissioned by Jesus (as the 70 were in Luke 10:1). Apparently it includes those to whom Jesus showed (presented) himself (in definite ways and at definite times) after His suffering, giving many infallible proofs (positive

---

[2]"Received up" is the kind of phraseology used of Elijah's translation in the Greek Septuagint version of 2 Kings 2:9-11. It was the occasion of the beginning of Elisha's ministry, just as Christ's ascension was the occasion of the beginning of the Church's ministry.

[3]Codex Bezae (D) and some Syriac Manuscripts add that He commanded them to preach the gospel. Luke seems to assume that the command of Matt. 28:19 was known to his readers. Cf. H. B. Hackett, *A Commentary on the Acts of the Apostles* (Philadelphia: American Baptist Publication Society, 1882), p. 30.

proofs, sure signs, unmistakable and convincing evidence) that He was alive.

In these appearances He made it clear that He was not a spirit or a ghost. They touched him. He showed them His hands and His feet saying, "It is I myself" (Luke 24:28-43). During a period of 40 days He came to them again and again. These were not visions. They were objective, real, personal appearances of Jesus. They knew Him and learned from Him with real understanding the truths concerning the Kingdom (rule, royal power, and authority) of God. Now they understood how the Cross and the Resurrection were both necessary for our salvation. Both were revelations of God's mighty power and love.

Some Bible scholars see a parallel in these 40 days to the 40 days during which God dealt with Moses on Mount Sinai, giving him the Law. Certainly the teaching of Jesus was a better "law" (torah, instruction). But now the teaching was given for all, not in a restricted place like Mount Sinai, but in many places, even to as many as 500 at once (1 Corinthians 15:6). Even on the resurrection day others were with the apostles in the Upper Room (Luke 24:33) and received His instruction. A little later we see 120 were present (Acts 1:15). Thus, the final instructions of Jesus were never limited to the eleven apostles.

The Promise of the Father (1:4, 5)

. . . [4]and, being assembled together with *them,* commanded them that they should not depart from Jerusalem, but wait for the promise of the Father, which, *saith he,* ye have heard of me. [5]For John truly baptized with water; but ye shall be baptized with the Holy Ghost not many days hence (Acts 1:4, 5).

Luke's Gospel condenses the 40 days after the Resurrection and jumps to the final exhortation for the 120 to tarry (wait, sit) in Jerusalem until they receive the promise of the Father, which Jesus himself had given (Luke 24:49; John 14:16; 15:26; 16:7, 13).[4]

In Acts 1:4 Luke again goes to the time immediately preceding the Ascension. Jesus was assembled with them. The Greek indi-

[4]Cf. J. A. Alexander, *A Commentary on the Acts of the Apostles* (London: Banner of Truth Trust, reprint from 1857), I, 7.

cates He was sharing a meal with them.[5] At that time He repeated the command, emphasizing that they were not to leave Jerusalem. This was very important. The Day of Pentecost, would have had little effect if only two or three of them had remained in Jerusalem.

There is no conflict here with the command given on the resurrection day to go away into Galilee (Matthew 28:10; Mark 16:7). By comparing the Gospels we can see that Jesus initially commanded the women to tell the disciples to go to Galilee. Because they did not really believe, Peter and John went to the tomb. Two of the other disciples (not of the Twelve) decided to go home to Emmaus, while the rest stayed where they were. Jesus appeared on the evening of the resurrection day and reproved them for their unbelief. Thomas was not present when Jesus appeared, however, and refused to believe the report of His appearance. Jesus appeared again the following week and called Thomas to the place of faith. Then the disciples, along with Peter, met Jesus in Galilee. There was a delay, but Jesus needed to deal with Peter. He still carried the guilt of his denial of Jesus and needed a special humbling and a special recommissioning (John 21). There were probably other appearances in Galilee (including the one to the 500) since Jesus had spent much time there during his ministry. Then, toward the close of the 40 days the apostles and others returned to Jerusalem where Jesus gave His final teaching.

(Luke does not mention the visit to Galilee, possibly because it was described elsewhere, and his purpose was to focus attention on the coming Day of Pentecost.)

It is especially significant to the Promise of the Father that Jesus gave His instructions through the Holy Spirit (Acts 1:2). The resurrected Jesus was still full of the Spirit, as He had been during all of His previous ministry. Just as the Father bore witness to His Son when the Spirit came upon Him (and into Him) in a special way, so the Father bore witness to the faith of the believers by pouring out the promised Holy Spirit giving them power for service.

---

[5]The Greek is probably from *sun,* "together with" and *'als,* "salt." Thus, it meant originally, "eating salt with." Compare Luke 24:42, 43 and Acts 10:41. Cf. Richard B. Rackham, *The Acts of the Apostles* (Grand Rapids: Baker Book House, 1964 reprint from 1901), p. 5 and P. C. H. Lenski, *The Interpretation of the Acts of the Apostles* (Columbus, Ohio: The Wartburg Press, 1940), p. 26.

That the gift of the Spirit is called the promise of the Father also relates it to the Old Testament promises. The idea of promise is one of the bonds that unites the Old and the New Testaments. The promise to Abraham was not only for personal and national blessing, but that in him and in his seed all the families of the earth would be blessed (Genesis 12:3). When Abraham believed (trusted) God's promise, his faith was put down on the credit side of his account for righteousness (Genesis 15:6).

The story of God's dealings with His people is a step-by-step revelation: First, He promises defeat of that old serpent, the devil, through the seed of the woman (Genesis 3:15). Then He gives His promise for the seed of Abraham, of Isaac, of Jacob, of Judah, and of David. Finally, Jesus appears as David's greater Son, God's David or Beloved. (David means "beloved.")

Jesus had already promised this mighty outpouring of the Spirit to His followers (John 7:38, 39; and especially chapters 14 through 16). So had John the Baptist, whose baptism was limited to baptizing in water. Now Jesus, John promised, would baptize them in the Holy Spirit (Mark 1:8).[6] And Jesus further promised it would occur not many days hence" (after not many days).[7]

TIMES AND SEASONS (1:6, 7)

> [6]When they therefore were come together, they asked of him, saying, Lord, wilt thou at this time restore again the kingdom to Israel? [7]And he said unto them, It is not for you to know the times or the seasons, which the Father hath put in his own power (Acts 1:6, 7).

In Acts and the Epistles we find a great deal more about the Holy Spirit and the Church than we do about the Kingdom. But the Kingdom was an important part of Jesus' teaching. Mark 10:32-35 speaks both of Jesus' suffering and of James' and John's request to sit on His right hand and on His left in the Kingdom.

---

[6]"In water" is preferable to "with water." They went down into the water and came up out of the water (Matt. 3:16; Mark 1:10; Acts 8:38, 39).

[7]Note that Jesus did not add "and in fire" as John did in Matthew 3:11 when speaking to a group including hypocrites. See S. M. Horton, *What the Bible Says About the Holy Spirit* (Springfield, MO: Gospel Publishing House, 1976), pp. 84-89. Note also that Jesus had already breathed upon them and said, "Receive ye the Holy Spirit," that is, in the way we receive Him at the new birth. They had the Holy Spirit present in them, but they still needed the promised mighty outpouring and empowering. See Horton, *op. cit.,* pp. 127-133.

This shows that the cross carries with it the promise of the Kingdom.

Luke 12:32 also assured the disciples that it was the Father's good pleasure to give them the Kingdom. The word "kingdom" in the New Testament deals primarily with the king's power and rule. Righteousness, peace, and joy in the Holy Spirit are evidence that God is ruling in our lives, and that we are in His kingdom (Romans 14:17). But that does not rule out a future kingdom.

What the disciples had in mind when they questioned Jesus about the restoration of the kingdom to Israel was that future rule. They knew the prophecy of Ezekiel 36:24-27. They knew also that God's promise to Abraham included not only his seed and blessing on all nations, but also the land. All through the Old Testament the hope of God's promise to Israel is connected with the promised land. Ezekiel, in chapters 36 and 37, saw that God would restore Israel to the land, not because they deserved it, but to reveal His own holy name and character. Since Ezekiel also saw God's Spirit poured out upon a restored and renewed Israel, the promise of the Spirit would call this to mind.

Thus, it was more than mere curiosity that caused the disciples to ask about that part of God's promise.[8]

Jesus did not deny that it was still in God's plan to restore the Kingdom (the rule of God, the theocracy) to Israel. But here on earth they would never know the times (specific times) and seasons (proper occasions) of that restoration. These the Father had placed under His own authority. He is the only One who knows all things and has the wisdom to take all things into account. Therefore, the times and the seasons are His business, not ours.[9]

In Old Testament times, God did not reveal the time span between the first and second comings of Christ. Even the prophets sometimes jump from one to the other and back again in almost the same breath. Notice how Jesus stopped in the middle of Isaiah 61:2 when He was reading it at Nazareth (Luke 4:19). John the Baptist did not recognize this time difference, either. Because Jesus did not bring the judgments John foresaw, he wondered if Jesus was the Messiah or if He might be another

[8]Compare Luke 24:21, "We trusted. . . ."

[9]Cf. Lenski, *op. cit.*, p. 30.

forerunner like himself (Matthew 11:3). But Jesus did the works of the Messiah, and His disciples accepted the revelation that He is the Christ (the Messiah), the Son of the Living God (Matthew 16:16-20).

From time to time Jesus warned the disciples that no man knows the day or the hour of His return (Mark 13:32-35, for example). Then, when His own disciples on that last journey to Jerusalem supposed that the kingdom of God would immediately appear, Jesus gave them a parable to show them that it would be a long time before He would return in kingly power to rule (Luke 19:11, 12). There Jesus speaks of a nobleman going to a *far* country, thus indicating a long time. Even so, the disciples obviously had a hard time comprehending this. They did not want to accept the fact that the times and dates were none of their business.[10]

Power to Witness (1:8)

> But ye shall receive power, after that the Holy Ghost is come upon you: and ye shall be witnesses unto me both in Jerusalem, and in all Judea, and in Samaria, and unto the uttermost part of the earth (Acts 1:8).

But what was their business? Verse 8 gives the answer. They were to receive power after the Holy Spirit came upon them (the Holy Spirit having come upon them), and to be His witnesses to tell what they had seen, heard, and experienced (1 John 1:1). Beginning in Jerusalem they would carry their witness through Judea and Samaria and unto the uttermost part of the earth. This program for witnessing also gives us a virtual table of contents for the Book of Acts.[11]

God always wanted His people to be His witnesses. In Isaiah 44:8 He calls Israel to quit being afraid. But though they were commissioned to be His witnesses, fear interfered. Thus, as a whole, the nation of Israel failed to bring the witness God really wanted.

As Christians we need not fail. The baptism in the Spirit is available as an empowering experience. "Ye shall receive power"

---

[10]Cf. Donald Guthrie, *The Apostles* (Grand Rapids: Zondervan, 1975), p. 18.

[11]Galilee is not mentioned here, but there is evidence that Luke at times includes Galilee with Judea. Cf. E. F. Harrison, *Acts: The Expanding Church* (Chicago: Moody Press, 1975), pp. 40, 41.

(Greek, *dynamis,* "mighty power."). Here again, the power is related to the promise given to Abraham that all the families of the earth would be blessed. Jesus, in Matthew 24, emphasizes that they could not wait for ideal conditions before spreading the gospel to the nations. This age would be characterized by wars, rumors of wars, famines, and earthquakes. The followers of Jesus must go out and spread the gospel to all nations in the midst of all these natural calamities and political upheavals. How would this be possible? They would receive power as a result of being filled with the Spirit. This would be their secret of success in the Church Age until its final consummation when Jesus returns. Of course, this puts a great responsibility to be Christ's witnesses on all who are filled with the Spirit.[12]

THIS SAME JESUS (1:9-11)

[9]And when he had spoken these things, while they beheld, he was taken up; and a cloud received him out of their sight. [10]And while they looked steadfastly toward heaven as he went up, behold, two men stood by them in white apparel; [11]which also said, Ye men of Galilee, why stand ye gazing up into heaven? this same Jesus, which is taken up from you into heaven, shall so come in like manner as ye have seen him go into heaven (Acts 1:9-11).

Luke's Gospel is climaxed by Christ's ascension. Luke 24:50 indicates Jesus led His followers out to the Mount of Olives opposite Bethany. As He blessed them He was taken up into heaven (that is, taken gradually, not snatched away). Acts adds that this happened "as they were looking." They were not dreaming; they actually saw Him go. Then a cloud, not an ordinary cloud, but undoubtedly a glory cloud like the Old Testament Shekinah, took him up.[13] The Greek could well mean that the cloud swept under Him and He rode it up out of their sight. But not only did He leave the surface of the earth, He ascended to the right hand of the Father, and He is still bodily present in heaven. Stephen saw Him there (Acts 7:55).

After Jesus disappeared, the disciples still stood there in amazement with their gaze fixed on the heavens where He had

[12]Cf. Guthrie, *op. cit.,* p. 19.

[13]See Exodus 40:34. Compare also the cloud of the Transfiguration (Mark 9:7).

gone. Suddenly, two men stood beside them in white clothing. The white speaks of purity. Though they were not called angels here, it is generally assumed that they were. Angels are spirits, but they generally appear in the Bible as men. The white clothing also reminds us of the angels who appeared at the tomb on the resurrection day. Luke calls them men (Luke 24:4), while John refers to them as angels (John 20:12).

The angels asked why these disciples, men of Galilee (only Judas was of Judea), stood gazing into heaven. This implies they were straining their eyes as if they hoped to see into heaven where Jesus had gone. Christ's first coming was fulfilled; His work of redemption complete. It would be a long time before His return, but He would be with them as truly as He had been before (Matthew 28:20). Now, He had left them a commission, a work to do. He had given them instructions to wait in Jerusalem for the Promise of the Father and for power to be witnesses. They must obey with the assurance He would come again.

The Promise of His return is as emphatic as it could possibly be. This *same* Jesus shall *so* come in like manner (in the same way) as you have seen Him go. He had already told them He would return in the clouds (Mark 13:26). At His trial He identified himself with the Son of man of Daniel 7:13, 14 whom Daniel speaks of as coming with clouds. No wonder the fact of His return continues to be one of the most important motivations for Christian living. (See 1 John 3:2, 3.)

The Upper Room (1:12-14)

> [12]Then returned they unto Jerusalem from the mount called Olivet, which is from Jerusalem a sabbath day's journey. [13]And when they were come in, they went up into an upper room, where abode both Peter, and James, and John, and Andrew, Philip, and Thomas, Bartholomew, and Matthew, James *the son* of Alpheus, and Simon Zelotes, and Judas *the brother* of James. [14]These all continued with one accord in prayer and supplication, with the women, and Mary the mother of Jesus, and with his brethren (Acts 1:12-14).

The Gospel of Luke describes the return of Jesus' followers to Jerusalem as being "with great joy" (Luke 24:52). It was only a Sabbath day's journey (about a thousand yards) from the Mount of Olives back to the city. (Compare Exodus 16:29 and Numbers

35:5.) There, in a large upper room, the eleven apostles were staying. This may have been the same upper room of the Last Supper and of the resurrection appearances. Some believe it was the home of Mary, the mother of John Mark mentioned in Acts 12:12, though there is no proof of this.

Luke draws attention to five things here.

1. *The Eleven were in one accord.*[14] What a contrast to the jealousy exhibited before the Cross where each wanted to be the greatest (Matthew 20:24).

As was mentioned before, Jesus dealt with them all after the Resurrection, and especially Peter (John 21). Now all were restored and recommissioned, harboring no conflict, or jealousy. All were with one mind with one accord. This phrase "one accord" is one word in the Greek *(homothumadon)* and is one of Luke's favorite words. Being in one accord is surely still an important key to getting God's work done.

2. *They all continued steadfastly in prayer.* This included faithfulness to the Temple at the morning and evening hours of prayer and also persistence in the Upper Room, which was their headquarters. They kept an atmosphere of prayer and, as Luke 24:53 shows, prayer and praise was their chief occupation during these days.

3. *The women joined with them in prayer with the same steadfastness.* Actually, the women were present all along. In those days, if one man was present the masculine pronoun was used for the mixed group. Even when Peter calls them brethren (verse 16) this included the women. The Jews all understood this. But Luke wants the Gentiles to know the women were present and praying, so he mentions them specifically. They included Mary Magdalene, Salome, Joanna, Mary and Martha of Bethany, John Mark's mother, and others.

4. *Mary the mother of Jesus is given special mention.* She was present because John was fulfilling Jesus' request to take care of her. She was not there as a leader, but simply joined the others in prayer and in waiting for the promise of the Father. We may be

---

[14]Though the order is different here, the list of disciples given here is the same as that given in Luke 6:14-16 with the omission of Judas. Judas the son of James is called Thaddeus in Matthew 10:3 and Mark 3:18. Simon the Zealot was converted from a group of Jewish nationalists who believed in using force against the Romans. This group in Aramaic were called Kannaya or Kan'ana (Cananaean in Matthew 10:4; Mark 3:18).

sure she received the Spirit even though this is the last time she is mentioned in Acts. Some traditions say she died in Jerusalem. Others say she went with John to Ephesus and died there.

5. *The brothers of Jesus were present, though before the Cross they did not believe on Him* (John 7:5). Jesus, however, made a special appearance to his eldest brother, James (1 Corinthians 15:7). Both James and Jude later became leaders in the Jerusalem church. (See Acts 12:17; 15:13; 21:18; Galatians 2:9; James 1:1; Jude 1.) Now these brothers were in one accord with the others and waiting as well.[15]

Matthias Chosen (1:15-26)

[15]And in those days Peter stood up in the midst of the disciples, and said, (the number of names together were about a hundred and twenty,) [16]Men *and* brethren, this Scripture must needs have been fulfilled, which the Holy Ghost by the mouth of David spake before concerning Judas, which was guide to them that took Jesus. [17]For he was numbered with us, and had obtained part of this ministry. [18]Now this man purchased a field with the reward of iniquity; and falling headlong, he burst asunder in the midst, and all his bowels gushed out. [19]And it was known unto all the dwellers at Jerusalem; insomuch as that field is called, in their proper tongue, Aceldama, that is to say, The field of blood. [20]For it is written in the book of Psalms, Let his habitation be desolate, and let no man dwell therein: and, His bishopric let another take.

[21]Wherefore of these men which have companied with us all the time that the Lord Jesus went in and out among us, [22]beginning from the baptism of John, unto that same day that he was taken up from us, must one be ordained to be a witness with us of his resurrection. [23]And they appointed two, Joseph called Barsabas, who was surnamed Justus, and Matthias. [24]And they prayed, and said, Thou, Lord, which knowest the hearts of all *men,* show whether of these two thou hast chosen, [25]that he may take part of this ministry and apostleship, from which Judas by transgression fell, that he might go to his own place. [26]And they gave forth their lots; and the lot fell upon Matthias; and he was numbered with the eleven apostles (Acts 1:15-26).

Apparently not all of the 500 or more who saw Jesus in Galilee followed Him back to Jerusalem. Thus about 120 men and

[15]Some say these were cousins or children of Joseph by a previous marriage. However, Matthew 1:25 makes it clear that Joseph did enter into the physical marriage relation with Mary after Jesus was born. Thus, there is every reason to believe these brothers were actual children of Mary and Joseph. Mark 6:3 names them.

women returned from the Ascension and were united in this atmosphere of prayer. But they did more than pray. They also gave attention to the Scriptures.

What Peter saw in the Scriptures caused him to stand up and draw attention to the fulfillment of David's prophecy[16] spoken by the Spirit, concerning Judas who acted as a guide to those who arrested Jesus. Peter recognized that the Holy Spirit is the real author of God's Word and that what David said about his enemies applied to the enemies of Jesus, since David is a type pointing to Jesus.[17]

The tragedy was that Judas was numbered among the apostles as one of the Twelve. He received an assigned portion in their ministry. He was sent out by Jesus with authority to cast out unclean spirits and to heal all kinds of diseases and sicknesses (Matthew 10:1). Further, he was present when Jesus promised the disciples that they would sit on twelve thrones judging (ruling) the twelve tribes of Israel (Luke 22:29, 30).

In this connection Peter (or Luke) adds a parenthetical note about the death of Judas which differs from the description in the Gospels. Matthew 27:5 says Judas went away and hanged himself. Since Luke had searched out all that was written, he knew this and obviously did not see a contradiction.

Crucifixion and impalement through the middle over a sharp stake were the two common methods of hanging. Judas, of course, could not crucify himself. But he could set up a sharp stake and fall headlong over it. Peter, however, does not emphasize what Judas did as much as God's judgment. Thus he draws attention to how his body swelled and burst in its middle.

There are apparently two reasons why the field became known as Akeldama, the field of blood. Matthew 27:6-8 says that the priests bought the field. Since it was bought with the money they gave Judas, they undoubtedly bought it in Judas' name. They called the field Akeldama because the 30 pieces of silver was the price of blood, that is, of Christ's death. They also called it the

---

[16]In verse 16 Codex Bezae (manuscript D) and the Latin Vulgate have "It is necessary," thus putting the emphasis on Psalm 109:8 and the necessity of replacing Judas Iscariot.

[17]Cf. Guthrie, *op. cit.*, p. 22.

field of blood because of Judas' violent death there, since blood in the New Testament usually refers to violent death.

Peter's emphasis, however, was on Psalm 69:25 and 109:8, with special attention to the latter. "His bishopric (overseership) let another take." The Twelve were chosen as primary witnesses to the teaching of Jesus. They would have positions of authority in the coming kingdom as well (Luke 22:29, 30; Matthew 19:28). They needed someone to replace Judas. It must be someone who had been with them the whole time from Jesus' baptism to His ascension.[18] He would join them as a first-hand witness to Jesus' resurrection.

Peter laid down the conditions, but the people made the choice. Two men met the conditions best. One was Joseph, named Barsabas ("son of the Sabbath," born on the Sabbath), who like so many Jews had a Roman name, Justus. The other was Matthias. Eusebius, the third-century Church historian, says he was one of the 70 sent out by Jesus in Luke 10:1.

To make the choice between these two, the apostles first prayed, recognizing that the Lord (Jesus) knew which one He wanted as the twelfth apostle. He is the "Heart-knower" (John 2:24, 25). They also recognized that Judas fell away by his own choice and went to the place he had chosen, that is, to the place of punishment.

Then they used the Old Testament method of casting lots, probably following the precedent of Proverbs 16:33. They believed that God would overrule the laws of chance and show His choice by this means. The Book of Acts never mentions the use of this method again, however. After Pentecost they relied on the Holy Spirit for guidance.

Some modern writers question whether Peter and the others were right in doing this and say Paul should have been chosen. But he was the apostle to the Gentiles and he never anticipated ruling one of the tribes of Israel. He was an apostle equal in calling and authority to the others, but he never included himself with the Twelve (1 Corinthians 15:7, 8).[19]

---

[18]Many followed Jesus. Jesus specifically called some; others simply followed Him (John 1:35-47). Later, Jesus spent a night in prayer, and then out of the crowd of disciples chose 12 to be apostles, "sent ones." It is to this latter calling that Jesus refers in John 15:16—a choosing for a particular service.

[19]Cf. Harrison, *op. cit.*, p. 48.

Actually, the Bible states without adverse comment that Matthias was numbered with the eleven apostles. In Acts 6:2 he is still included with the Twelve. Though he is not mentioned again by name, neither are most of the other apostles.[20]

It is important to notice, however, that the fact that Judas became a lost soul made necessary his replacement. When James the brother of John was martyred, no one was chosen to take his place (Acts 12:2). James would rise again to reign with the Twelve in the coming kingdom.

[20]Cf. Hackett, *op. cit.,* pp. 40, 41.

ACTS

CHAPTER

2

The 120 continued in prayer and praise about ten days after the ascension of Jesus until the Day of Pentecost. This was a harvest festival among the Jews. In the Old Testament it was also called the Feast of Weeks (Exodus 34:22; Deuteronomy 16:16) as there was a week of weeks (seven weeks) between it and Passover. Pentecost means "fiftieth," and it was so called because on the fiftieth day after the waving of the sheaf of first fruits (Leviticus 23:15) they waved two loaves for firstfruits (Leviticus 23:17).[1]

Fully Come (2:1)

And when the day of Pentecost was fully come, they were all with one accord in one place (Acts 2:1).

Pentecost was now being completed or "fulfilled," a word that draws attention to the fact that the period of waiting was coming to an end, and Old Testament prophecies were about to be fulfilled. The 120 were still in one accord[2] and were all together in one place. None was missing. We are not told where the place was; but most take it to be the Upper Room which was their headquarters (Acts 1:13). Others, in view of Peter's statement that it was the third hour of the day (9 a.m.), believe they were in the Temple, probably in the court of the women. We have already seen that

[1]The Sadducees who controlled the Temple took the sabbath of Leviticus 23:15 to be the weekly sabbath after the Passover. This made Pentecost occur on a Sunday. Cf. Bruce, op. cit., p. 53.

[2]Codex Bezae (D) leaves out "in one accord" and simply states they were together in one place. It is clear that the majority of ancient manuscripts are right. They were, indeed, in one accord as they had been during all the preceding period.

the believers were habitually in the Temple at the hours of prayer. One of the porticoes or roofed colonnades on the edge of the court would have provided a good place for them to gather and join in worship. This would help explain the crowd that gathered after the Spirit was outpoured.[3]

Wind and Fire (2:2, 3)

[2]And suddenly there came a sound from heaven as of a rushing mighty wind, and it filled all the house where they were sitting. [3]And there appeared unto them cloven tongues like as of fire, and it sat upon each of them (Acts 2:2, 3).

Suddenly, without warning, a sound came from heaven like that of a mighty (violent) rushing wind or tornado. But it was the sound that filled the house and overwhelmed them, not an actual wind.

The wind would remind them of Old Testament divine manifestations. God spoke to Job out of a whirlwind (Job 38:1; 40:6); a mighty east wind dried out the path through the Red Sea, enabling the Israelites to escape from Egypt on dry ground (Exodus 14:21). Wind was also a frequent symbol of the Spirit in the Old Testament (Ezekiel 37:9, 10, and 14, for example). Jesus also used wind to speak of the Spirit (John 3:8).

The sound of the wind indicated to those present that God was about to manifest himself and His Spirit in a special way. That it was the sound of a wind with carrying power also spoke of the empowering Jesus promised in Acts 1:8, an empowering for service.

Just as suddenly, cloven tongues like tongues of flame or fire appeared. "Cloven" means "distributed." That is, something that looked like a mass of flames appeared over the whole group. Then it broke up[4], and a single tongue that looked like a flame of fire settled on the head of each one of them, both men and women. There was, of course, no actual fire, and no one was burned. But fire and light were common symbols of the divine

---

[3]Though the Temple is called a "house" in Acts 7:47, some believe "the whole house" cannot mean the Temple. They suggest that either the 120 left the Upper Room when the Spirit fell or else the Upper Room was open to the street. Cf. Lenski, p. 58.

[4]Cf. Hackett, *op. cit.*, p. 42.

presence, as in the case of the burning bush (Exodus 3:2), and also the Lord's appearance in fire on Mount Sinai after the people of Israel accepted the Old Covenant (Exodus 19:18).[5]

Some suppose these tongues constituted a baptism of fire bringing cleansing.[6] However, the hearts and minds of the 120 were already open to the resurrected Christ, already cleansed, already filled with praise and joy (Luke 24:52, 53), already responsive to the Spirit-inspired Word (Acts 1:16), already in one accord. Rather than cleansing or judgment, the fire here signified God's acceptance of the Church Body as the temple of the Holy Spirit (Ephesians 2:21, 22; 1 Corinthians 3:16), and, then, the acceptance of the individual believers as also being temples of the Spirit (1 Corinthians 6:19). Thus, the Bible makes clear that the Church was already in existence before the Pentecostal baptism. Hebrews 9:15, 17 shows that it was the *death* of Christ that put the New Covenant into effect. From the resurrection Day when Jesus breathed on the disciples, the Church was constituted as a new covenant Body.[7]

It is important to notice that these signs preceded the Pentecostal baptism or gifts of the Spirit. They were not part of it, nor were they repeated on other occasions when the Spirit was outpoured. Peter, for example, identified the filling of the believers at the house of Cornelius with Jesus' promise that they would be baptized in the Spirit, calling it the identical gift. (Acts 10:44-47; 11:17). But the wind and fire were not present. They seem to have been needed only once.

Filled With the Spirit (2:4)

> And they were all filled with the Holy Ghost, and began to speak with other tongues, as the Spirit gave them utterance (Acts 2:4).

Now that God had acknowledged the Church as the new Temple, the next thing was to pour out the Spirit on the members of the Body.

---

[5]Cf. J. W. Packer, *Acts of the Apostles* (Cambridge: Cambridge University Press, 1975).

[6]Rene Pache, *The Person and Work of the Holy Spirit,* rev. ed. (Chicago: Moody Press, 1966), p. 23.

[7]S. M. Horton, *What the Bible Says About the Holy Spirit* (Springfield, MO: Gospel Publishing House, 1976), pp. 140-142.

What Jesus promised as a baptism is pictured here as a filling, that is, a full, satisfying experience. Some try to make a distinction between being baptized in the Spirit and being filled.[8] Actually, the Bible uses a variety of terms. It was also a pouring out of the Spirit as Joel prophesied (Acts 2:17, 18, 33); a receiving (and active taking) of a gift (Acts 2:38); a falling upon (Acts 8:16; 10:44; 11:15); a pouring out of the gift (Acts 10:45), and a coming upon. With this variety of terms it is impossible to suppose that the baptism is any different from the filling.

Actually, since the Holy Spirit is a Person, we are talking about an experience that brings a relationship. Each term brings out some aspect of the Pentecostal experience, and no one term can bring out all the aspects of that experience.

It is clear also, since they were all together and in one accord, that when Acts 2:4 says they were all filled the entire 120 is meant. Some suppose that only the 12 apostles were filled. However, more than 12 languages were spoken. Later, when Peter spoke before a large group in Jerusalem, he said the like (identical) gift fell on the Gentiles "as it did on us who believed on the Lord Jesus Christ." This suggests that the Spirit fell in the same way, not only on the 12 but on the 120 and also on the 3,000 who believed on the Day of Pentecost. Clearly, the experience was and is for all. This, however, was a new thing. In the Old Testament only selected individuals were filled.[9]

As soon as they were filled, the 120 began to speak (and continued speaking) with other tongues (languages). "Began" is significant in that it shows, as in Acts 1:1, that what was begun was continued on other occasions, thus indicating that tongues were the normal accompaniment of the baptism in the Holy Spirit.[10] This speaking came as the Spirit gave them utterance (proceeded to give and kept on giving them to utter forth or speak out). That

---

[8]Some say that the baptism in the Spirit took place only once—on the Day of Pentecost. They call what happened after that just fillings. Peter, in Acts 11:16, however, recognizes that the gift of the Holy Spirit outpoured on the house of Cornelius also fulfilled Jesus' promise that He would baptize in the Spirit. Therefore, all believers who are filled with the Spirit can be said to be baptized in the Spirit. The Pentecostal experience today is still the baptism in the Spirit.

[9]Cf. Horton, *op. cit.*, pp. 26-29.

[10]Cf. Alexander, *op. cit.*, I, 44.

is, they used their tongues, their muscles. They spoke, but the words did not come from their minds or thinking. The Spirit gave them the utterance which they expressed boldly, loudly, and with obvious anointing and power. This was the one sign of the baptism in the Spirit that was repeated.[11]

AMAZED AND CONFUSED (2:5-13)

[5]And there were dwelling at Jerusalem Jews, devout men, out of every nation under heaven. [6]Now when this was noised abroad, the multitude came together, and were confounded, because that every man heard them speak in his own language. [7]And they were all amazed and marveled, saying one to another, Behold, are not all these which speak Galileans? [8]And how hear we every man in our own tongue, wherein we were born? [9]Parthians, and Medes, and Elamites, and the dwellers in Mesopotamia, and in Judea, and Cappadocia, in Pontus, and Asia, [10]Phrygia, and Pamphylia, in Egypt, and in the parts of Libya about Cyrene, and strangers of Rome, Jews and proselytes. [11]Cretes and Arabians, we do hear them speak in our tongues the wonderful works of God. [12]And they were all amazed, and were in doubt, saying one to another, What meaneth this? [13]Others mocking said, These men are full of new wine (Acts 2:5-13).

Jerusalem was a cosmopolitan center in that many of the Jews from the dispersion returned and settled there. "Dwelling" (verse 5) usually implies something more than a temporary stay or visit. Since it was the Feast of Pentecost we can be sure, however, that many Jews from all over the known world were there in Jerusalem.[12] These were devout, God-fearing people, sincere in

[11]Some call these tongues "ecstatic" utterance. "Ecstatic" is really an improper term and does not apply either here or in other passages where tongues are mentioned. There is no evidence that any believer spoke as if forced to do so. They retained their senses and spoke in willing cooperation with the Holy Spirit. With this in mind we must also recognize that the tongues here and the tongues in 1 Corinthians chapters 12-14 are the same. Tongues at Pentecost were a sign to unbelievers. They were used of God to draw the people together as well as to edify the believers. But when they continued in tongues, the people said they were drunk. This corresponds to what 1 Corinthians 14:23 says about uninterpreted tongues. We should also note that there are about 4,000 languages now and many more existed in past history. But in a local church, as at Corinth, there are not likely to be many foreigners present. A number of missionaries have told me of people in recent times speaking in tongues that were languages the missionaries understood but the people who were speaking did not.

[12]"All nations (peoples) under heaven" was a common idiom used to speak primarily of those in the known world or even in the Roman Empire. The word "nation" (people) was often used of the people of a Roman province.

their worship of the Lord. Actually, more of them would be in Jerusalem at this time than at Passover since travel on the Mediterranean Sea was safer at this season than earlier.[13]

As the sound of the 120 speaking in tongues rose and became heard, a crowd came from all directions. All were confounded because each one kept hearing them speak in his own language. *Own* is emphatic, his very own language that he used as a child. Tongue here means a distinct language. They were not speaking merely in a variety of Galilean or Aramaic dialects but in a variety of entirely different languages.[14]

The result was total amazement. They were astonished. They were filled with awestruck wonder, for they recognized, probably by their clothing, that the 120 were Galileans. They could not understand how it was that each one heard them speaking his own language in which he was born.

Some take verse 8 to mean that the 120 were all really speaking the same language and by a miracle of hearing the multitude were made to hear it in their mother tongue. But verses 6 and 7 are too specific for that. Each man heard them *speak* in his own dialect without any Galilean accent.[15] There would have been no surprise if the 120 spoke in Aramaic or Greek.

Some others have supposed that the 120 really spoke in tongues, but no one understood them. They propose that the Spirit interpreted unknown tongues in the ears of the hearers into their own language. But verses 6 and 7 rule that out, too. They spoke in real languages which were actually understood by a variety of people from a variety of places.[16] This gave witness to the universality of the Gift and to the universality and unity of the Church.[17]

The places named where these godly Jews were born were in all directions, but they also follow a general order (with exceptions) beginning in the northeast. Parthia was east of the Roman Empire

[13]Cf. Ralph Earle, *The Acts of the Apostles* (Kansas City: Beacon Hill Press, 1965), p. 273.

[14]Cf. Lenski, *op. cit.,* p. 65.

[15]Hackett, *op. cit.,* pp. 42, 43 points out that these were clearly unacquired languages different from the native language of these Galileans, which was Aramaic. (They also knew Greek.)

[16]Cf. Alexander, *op. cit.,* I, 45; Earle, *op. cit.,* p. 278.

[17]Many see a reversal of what happened at the tower of Babel here, but this can only be applied to the age to come.

between the Caspian Sea and the Persian Gulf; Media was east of Assyria;[18] Elam was north of the Persian Gulf in the southern part of Persia; Mesopotamia was the ancient Babylonia, mostly outside the Roman Empire. Babylon had a large Jewish population in New Testament times and later became a center for orthodox Judaism (1 Peter 5:13).

Judea is mentioned because Jews there still spoke Hebrew and would have been amazed at the lack of Galilean accent. It is also possible that Luke includes with Judea all of Syria, in fact, all the territory of David and Solomon from the Euphrates River to the River of Egypt (Genesis 15:18).[19] Cappadocia was a large Roman province in the central part of Asia Minor; Pontus was a Roman province in northern Asia Minor on the Black Sea; Asia was the Roman province comprising the western third of Asia Minor; Phrygia was an ethnic district, part of which was in the province of Asia and part in Galatia. Paul later founded many churches in this area.

Pamphylia was a Roman province on the south coast of Asia Minor; Egypt to the south had a large Jewish population. The Jewish philosopher Philo said in A.D. 38 that there were about a million Jews there, many in Alexandria. Cyrene was a district in Africa west of Egypt on the Mediterranean coast (Acts 6:9; 11:20; 13:1).

Others present in Jerusalem were strangers (sojourners, temporary residents) in Jerusalem, citizens of Rome, including both Jews and proselytes (Gentile converts to Judaism).[20] Still others were from the island of Crete and from Arabia, the district east and southeast of Palestine.

All these kept hearing in their own languages the wonderful works (the mighty, magnificent, sublime deeds) of God. This may have been in the form of ejaculations of praise to God for these wonderful works. No discourse or preaching is implied, though

---

[18]Some of the exiles from the 10 northern tribes were settled in Media (2 Kings 17:6). There is evidence that these and others of the 10 tribes joined in with the synagogues of the Jews, so that all 12 tribes were represented among the Jews of the Dispersion.

[19]Cf. Earle, *op. cit.*, p. 279 (citing Lake and Cadbury).

[20]Full proselytes took circumcision, a self-baptism, and offered a sacrifice to declare their purpose to keep the Jewish Law and live as Jews. Some believe verse 10 means that both Jews and proselytes were found among all 15 nations. Cf. Earle, *op. cit.*, p. 280.

preaching would surely have brought the salvation of some (1 Corinthians 1:21). There is no record here or elsewhere, however, of the gift of tongues being used as a means of preaching or teaching the gospel.

Instead, the hearers were amazed (astounded) and in doubt (perplexed, at a loss, completely unable to understand) what this was all about. "What meaneth this" is literally, "What will this be?" It expresses their total confusion as well as their extreme amazement. They understood the meaning of the words, but not the purpose. This is why they were confused by what they heard.

Others in the crowd, who apparently did not understand any of the languages, took it all as something unintelligible. Then, because they could not understand the meaning, they jumped to the conclusion that it has no meaning.[21] Therefore, they proceeded to mock and show great scorn, saying that these men (these people, including both men and women) were full of (filled, saturated with) new wine (sweet wine). New wine here is the Greek *gleukous* from which we get our word glucose for grape sugar. It is not the ordinary word for new wine and probably represents an intoxicating wine made from a very sweet grape. It would be some time until the grape harvest started in August and grape juice would again be available.

The Greek indicates there were mocking gestures as well as words. Some drinkers become noisy and this may be what the mockers were thinking of. We must not suppose there was any sign of the kind of frenzy that marked heathen drunken debauchery. Their chief emotion was still joy. They had been thanking and praising God in their own language (Luke 24:53), and now the Holy Spirit had given them new languages to praise God in. We can be sure their hearts were still going out to God in praise, even though they did not understand what they were saying.

Peter Explains (2:14-21)

[14]But Peter, standing up with the eleven, lifted up his voice, and said unto them, Ye men of Judea, and all *ye* that dwell at Jerusalem, be this known unto you, and hearken to my words: [15]for these are not drunken, as ye suppose, seeing it is *but* the third hour of the day. [16]But this is that

[21]Cf. Guthrie, *op. cit.,* p. 27.

which was spoken by the prophet Joel; [17]And it shall come to pass in the last days, saith God, I will pour out of my Spirit upon all flesh: and your sons and your daughters shall prophesy, and your young men shall see visions, and your old men shall dream dreams: [18]and on my servants and on my handmaidens I will pour out in those days of my Spirit; and they shall prophesy: [19]and I will show wonders in heaven above, and signs in the earth beneath; blood, and fire, and vapor of smoke: [20]the sun shall be turned into darkness, and the moon into blood, before that great and notable day of the Lord come: [21]and it shall come to pass, *that* whosoever shall call on the name of the Lord shall be saved (Acts 2:14-21).

When Peter and the eleven other apostles (including Matthias) stood to their feet, the 120 immediately ceased speaking in tongues. Then the whole crowd gave their attention to him. Still anointed by the Spirit, he raised his voice and proceeded to "utter forth" or speak out to them. The word used for this speaking is from the same verb used of the utterance in tongues in Acts 2:4. It suggests that Peter spoke in his own language (Aramaic) as the Spirit gave utterance.[22] In other words, what follows is not a sermon in the ordinary sense of the word. Certainly, Peter did not sit down and figure out three points. Rather, this is a spontaneous manifestation of the gift of prophecy (1 Corinthians 12:10; 14:3).[23]

Peter's address was directed to the Jewish men and the inhabitants of Jerusalem. This was a polite way to begin and followed their custom, but it does not rule out the women. The same would be true of verses 22 and 29.

Apparently, as the 120 continued to speak in tongues, the mocking increased until most were mocking. Even some of those who understood the languages may have joined them. Peter did not draw attention to the fact some did understand. He answered only those who mocked.

These people were not drunk as the crowd supposed, for it was only the third hour of the day, about nine o'clock in the morning. Actually, even the sweet wine was not very strong. In those days they had no way of distilling alcohol or fortifying drinks. Their strongest drinks were wine and beer and they made it a practice to dilute the wine with several parts of water. It would have taken a

---

[22]Cf. Kirsopp Lake and H. J. Cadbury, *The Beginnings of Christianity,* Part I, IV, 21, cited in Earle, *op. cit.,* p. 282.

[23]Cf. Horton, *op. cit.,* p. 144.

great deal to get them drunk that early in the morning. We can be sure also that anyone drinking would not be in a public place at that hour. Thus the words of the mockers were shown to be absurd.

Peter then declared that what they saw and heard (2:33) was a fulfillment of Joel 2:28-32 (Joel 3:1-5 in the Hebrew). Because the context in Joel goes on to deal with the coming judgment and the end of the age, some today believe that Joel's prophecy had a fulfillment on the Day of Pentecost. One writer actually says Peter did not really mean "This is that," but rather, "This is something like that." In other words, the Pentecostal outpouring was only similar to what will happen when Israel is restored at the end of the age.[24]

Peter, however, did say, "This is that!" Joel, like the other Old Testament prophets, did not see the time span between the first and second comings of Christ. Even Peter himself probably did not see how long it would be. He did see, however, that the Messianic Age was coming, and probably hoped it would be soon.

Peter makes one apparent change in the prophecy. Under the inspiration of the Spirit he specified what the word "afterward" in Joel 2:28 means: the outpouring is "in the last days." Thus he recognized that the last days began with the ascension of Jesus (Acts 3:19-21). From this we can see that the Holy Spirit recognizes the entire Church Age as "last days." We are in the last age before the Rapture of the Church, the restoration of Israel, and Christ's millennial reign on earth, the last age before Jesus comes in flaming fire to take vengeance on those who know not God and reject the gospel (2 Thessalonians 1:7-10).

The first part of the quotation from Joel has an obvious application to the 120. The many languages highlight God's purpose to pour out His Spirit on all flesh. In the Hebrew "all flesh" usually means all mankind, as in Genesis 6:12. Flesh can also speak of frailty, and this fits in with the fact that the baptism in the Spirit is an empowering experience. The Spirit wants to give us power and make us strong.

Whether any dreams or visions were seen while they were speaking in tongues, we do not know. Perhaps there were. But the

---

[24]A. C. Gabelein, *The Holy Spirit in the New Testament* (New York: Our Hope, n.d.), p. 34.

repeated emphasis (verses 17 and 18) is on the pouring out of the Spirit so that those filled would prophesy. Evidently, Peter, through the Spirit, saw that tongues when understood are the equivalent of prophecy (1 Corinthians 14:5, 6). In the Bible to prophesy means to speak for God as His spokesman or "mouth." (Compare Exodus 7:1 and Exodus 4:15, 16.)

"All flesh" is then broken down to sons and daughters. There would be no distinction in the Pentecostal experience with regard to sex. This is another indication that all 120 were baptized in the Spirit, including the women.[25]

Young men would see visions and old men dream dreams. No division with respect to age would exist. Nor does there seem to be any real distinction here between dreams and visions. The Bible often uses the words interchangeably. Here they are at least parallel. (See Acts 10:17; 16:9, 10; and 18:9 for examples of visions.)

Even upon male and female slaves (which is what servants and handmaids actually means) God would pour out His Spirit. In other words, the Spirit would pay no attention to social distinctions. Though there were probably no slaves among the 120, the Roman Empire had many areas where slaves comprised as high as 80 percent of the population. The fulfillment would come.

It is also possible to take verse 18 as a summary statement: "upon my church of slaves," parallel to the Israelite slaves delivered from Egypt by God's mighty power. All the Epistles refer to the believers as servants (literally, slaves) rather than disciples. They asked nothing for themselves, claimed no rights, and gave everything in the service of their Master and Lord. Even the brothers of Jesus, James and Jude, call themselves servants (slaves) of the Lord Jesus (James 1:1; Jude 1).

Many interpret verses 18 and 19 symbolically.[26] Others suppose they were somehow fulfilled during the three hours of darkness while Jesus hung on the cross. It seems, rather, that the mention of the signs indicates that the outpouring and the prophesying would continue until these signs come at the end of the age. Peter also means that these signs can just as confidently be expected.

We may see also the gift of the Spirit as the first-fruits of the age

---

[25]Cf. Harrison, *op. cit.,* p. 58.

[26]A. W. Pink, *The Holy Spirit* (Grand Rapids: Baker Book House, 1970), p. 41.

to come (Romans 8:23). The unregenerate human heart and mind has no conception of the things God has prepared for those who love Him. But God "has revealed them unto us by His Spirit" (1 Corinthians 2:9, 10). The inheritance that will be fully ours when Jesus comes is no mystery to us. We have already experienced it, at least in a measure. As Hebrews 6:4, 5 points out, all who have tasted (really experienced) the heavenly gift and are made partakers of the Holy Spirit have already experienced the good word (promise) of God and the powers (mighty powers, miracles) of the world (age) to come.[27]

Some also see in the fire and smoke a reference to the signs of God's presence at Mount Sinai in Exodus 19:16-18; 20:18 and look at Pentecost as the giving of a new law or the renewing of the new covenant. However, as Hebrews 9:15-18, 26, 28 indicates, the death of Christ put the new covenant into effect and there was no need for anything further.

The signs here also include blood (verse 19) and refer to the increasing bloodshed, wars, and smoke from wars that will cover the sun and make the moon appear red. These things will happen before the great and notable (manifest) day of the Lord. They are part of this present age. The Day of the Lord in the Old Testament includes both the judgments on the present nations of the world and the restoration of Israel with the establishment of the Messianic kingdom. But Peter is not concerned with these prophecies as such here. He wants his hearers to understand that the Pentecostal power of the Spirit will continue to be poured out throughout this present age. The age of the Church is the age of the Holy Spirit; the gift of the Spirit will still be available even in the midst of coming wars and bloodshed.

Verse 21 gives the purpose of the outpouring. Through its empowering the convicting work of the Spirit will be done in the world, not just in the end, but throughout the age right down to the great day of the Lord. All during this period, whoever calls (for help for his need, that is for salvation) on the name of the Lord will be saved. The Greek is strong: "all whoever." No matter what happens or what forces oppose the Church, the door of

---

[27]Jans Conzelmann, *An Outline of the Theology of the New Testament,* trans. John Bowden (New York: Harper & Row, c1969), p. 37.

salvation will remain open. The Greek also indicates that we can expect many to respond and be saved.

Jesus Exalted (2:22-36)

[22]Ye men of Israel, hear these words; Jesus of Nazareth, a man approved of God among you by miracles and wonders and signs, which God did by him in the midst of you, as ye yourselves also know: [23]him, being delivered by the determinate counsel and foreknowledge of God, ye have taken, and by wicked hands have crucified and slain: [24]whom God hath raised up, having loosed the pains of death: because it was not possible that he should be holden of it. [25]For David speaketh concerning him, I foresaw the Lord always before my face; for he is on my right hand, that I should not be moved: [26]therefore did my heart rejoice, and my tongue was glad; moreover also my flesh shall rest in hope: [27]because thou wilt not leave my soul in hell, neither wilt thou suffer thine Holy One to see corruption. [28]Thou hast made known to me the ways of life; thou shalt make me full of joy with thy countenance.

[29]Men *and* brethren, let me freely speak unto you of the patriarch David, that he is both dead and buried, and his sepulchre is with us unto this day. [30]Therefore being a prophet, and knowing that God had sworn with an oath to him, that of the fruit of his loins, according to the flesh, he would raise up Christ to sit on his throne; [31]he, seeing this before, spake of the resurrection of Christ, that his soul was not left in hell, neither his flesh did see corruption. [32]This Jesus hath God raised up, whereof we all are witnesses. [33]Therefore being by the right hand of God exalted, and having received of the Father the promise of the Holy Ghost, he hath shed forth this, which ye now see and hear. [34]For David is not ascended into the heavens: but he saith himself, The Lord said unto my Lord, Sit thou on my right hand, [35]until I make thy foes thy footstool. [36]Therefore let all the house of Israel know assuredly, that God hath made that same Jesus, whom ye have crucified, both Lord and Christ (Acts 2:22-36).

The main body of Peter's message centers, not around the Holy Spirit, but around Jesus. The Pentecostal outpouring was intended to bear powerful witness to Jesus (Acts 1:8; John 15:26, 27; 16:14).

Peter first drew attention to the fact that the inhabitants of Jerusalem knew the *man* of Nazareth, Jesus,[28] and they knew how God had approved Him for their benefit by miracles (mighty works, mighty powers), and wonders, and signs. These are the three words used in the Bible for supernatural miracles. They

[28]Nazareth in Hebrew is derived from the word "branch" used in Isaiah 11:1 of the greater Son of David, the Messiah.

refer to the variety of miracles Jesus did, especially in the Temple at the feast times (John 2:23; 4:45; 11:47).[29]

This Jesus, Peter says, you by wicked hands (the hands of lawless men, men outside the Law; that is, the Roman soldiers) crucified and slew (nailed up and slew). Peter did not hesitate to make the people of Jerusalem responsible for the death of Jesus, though he also made it clear that Jesus was delivered up (given over) to them by the determinate counsel (the designated will) and foreknowledge of God. Compare Luke 24:26, 27, 46. If they had understood the prophets they would have known the Messiah had to suffer. Peter does not intend, however, to lessen their guilt by saying this.

It should be emphasized also that Peter was speaking here to Jerusalem Jews, many of whom were involved in the cry, "Crucify Him!" The Bible never puts this kind of responsibility on the Jews in general. For example, in Acts 13:27-29, Paul, speaking to Jews in Pisidian Antioch, is careful to attribute the crucifixion to the dwellers in Jerusalem and says "they," not "you."

Quickly Peter adds, "whom God raised up." The resurrection took away the stigma of the cross and reversed the decision of the Jerusalem leaders, while also indicating God's acceptance of Jesus' sacrifice. By the resurrection also, God released Jesus from the pains (pangs) of death because it was not possible for Him to be held by it. "Pangs" here usually means "birthpangs," so that the death here is perceived as labor. Just as labor pains are relieved by the birth of a child, so the resurrection brought an end to the pains of death.

Since the wages of sin is death (Romans 6:23), some say the reason death could not hold Him was because He had no sin of His own for death to claim. However, Peter does not reason that way at this point. He bases his whole argument on the Word of God, the prophetic Scriptures. Under the inspiration of the Spirit he says that David was speaking of Jesus in Psalm 16:8-11. Jewish tradition of the time also applied this to the Messiah.

The central point is the promise that God would not leave (abandon) His soul in hell (Greek, Hades, the place of the after

[29]Bruce, *op. cit.*, p. 69, points out that the early apostolic preaching involved four parts: (1) The last days are here. (2) the story of Jesus' ministry, death, resurrection, and ascension. (3) Old Testament Scriptures proving Jesus is the Messiah. (4) a call to repentance.

life, translating the Hebrew word, Sheol), and that He would not permit His Holy One to see corruption (putrifaction).

Peter declares that it was proper for him to say boldly (freely and openly) of the patriarch (chief father or ancestral ruler) David that the psalm could not possibly apply to him. He not only died and was buried, his tomb was still there in Jerusalem. Obviously David's flesh did see corruption. But Jesus' did not. Though Peter did not say it, he clearly implies that Jesus' tomb was empty.

Because David was a prophet (a speaker of God), and because he knew God had sworn an oath that of the fruit of his loins One would sit on his throne, he foresaw and spoke of the resurrection of the Christ (the Messiah, God's Anointed One). The reference here is to the Davidic covenant. In it God promised David there would always be a man from his seed for the throne. This was first given with respect to Solomon (2 Samuel 7:11-16). But it recognized that if David's descendants sinned they would have to be punished just as anyone else. God, however, would never turn His back on David's line and substitute another as He had in the case of King Saul. This covenant was reaffirmed in Psalm 89:3, 4; 132:11, 12.

Because the kings of David's line did not follow the Lord, God finally had to bring an end to their kingdom and send them into Babylonian exile. His purpose in doing this was to rid Israel of idolatry. But the promise to David still stood. There would yet be One to sit on David's throne and make it eternal.

Peter thus declares that Jesus is the Messianic King. Because God raised Him up, He was not left (abandoned) in Hades, nor did His flesh see corruption. Moreover, Peter and the 120 were all witnesses to His resurrection.

Christ's resurrection, however, was only part of a process whereby God, by His right hand of power, raised Jesus to an exalted position of power and authority at His right hand. (Both "by" and "at" His right hand are indicated.) This is also the place of triumph and victory. Paying the full price, Jesus won the battle against sin and death for us. Thus He remains at God's right hand throughout this age. (See Mark 16:19; Romans 8:34; Ephesians 1:20, 21; Colossians 3:1; Hebrews 1:3; 8:1; 10:12; 12:2; 1 Peter 3:22.)

In Christ, we also are seated at the right hand of God (Ephesians 2:6). Because this is our position in Christ we do not need our own works of righteousness to claim His promise. Nothing we could do could give us a higher position than we already have in Christ.

Next Peter uses Christ's exalted position to explain the Pentecostal experience. Now at the Father's right hand, He received from the Father the promise of the Holy Spirit and poured forth the Spirit, the results of which the crowd now saw and heard—the 120 speaking in other tongues.

Jesus had said it was necessary for Him to go away in order for the Comforter to come (John 16:7). Thus, though the baptism in the Holy Spirit is the promise of the Father, Jesus is the One who pours it forth. We see here also a clear distinction between the Persons of the Triune God. God is the Giver, but Jesus is the Baptizer.

The outpouring of the Spirit was also evidence that Jesus actually was exalted at the Father's right hand. This means something to us who now believe and receive the baptism in the Spirit. This baptism becomes evidence to us personally that Jesus is there at the right hand of the Father even now interceding for us. Thus we can be first-hand witnesses to where Jesus is and what He is doing.

That none of this could apply to David is further evidenced by another quotation from the Scripture. David did not ascend into the heavens as Jesus did, but he prophesied that exaltation in Psalm 110:1. Again, David could not be speaking of himself, for he says, "The Lord said unto my Lord, Sit thou at my right hand, until I make thine enemies thy footstool (indicating complete and final defeat as in Joshua 10:24). Jesus also referred to this in Luke 20:41-44, recognizing that David calls his greater Son Lord. (See also Matthew 22:42-45; Mark 12:36, 37.)

The conclusion Peter draws is that all the house of Israel needed to know assuredly that God has made this Jesus, whom the Jerusalem residents crucified, both Lord and Christ (Messiah).

From this also we see that, in fulfillment of Joel's prophecy, Jesus is the Lord on whom all must call for salvation. Paul also recognizes that God has highly exalted Him and given Him a name above every other name (Philippians 2:9). "The Name" in the Old Testament Hebrew always means the Name of God. (The Hebrew has other ways of referring to the name of a human being without using the word "the.") The Name stands for the authority, person, and especially the character of God in His righteousness, holiness, faithfulness, goodness, love, and power. "Lord" was used in the New Testament for the Name of God. Mercy, grace, and love are part of the holiness, the holy Name by which Jesus is recognized as Lord, the full revelation of God to man. The assurance is here also that Jesus is in heaven, and in control. God will see to it that His plan is carried out whatever happens in this world.

Three Thousand Added to the Church (2:37-42)

[37]Now when they heard *this,* they were pricked in their heart, and said unto Peter and to the rest of the apostles, Men *and* brethren, what shall we do? [38]Then Peter said unto them, Repent, and be baptized every one of you in the name of Jesus Christ for the remission of sins, and ye shall receive the gift of the Holy Ghost. [39]For the promise is unto you, and to your children, and to all that are afar off, *even* as many as the Lord our God shall call. [40]And with many other words did he testify and exhort, saying, Save yourselves from this untoward generation. [41]Then they that gladly received his word were baptized: and the same day there were added *unto them* about three thousand souls. [42]And they continued steadfastly in the apostles' doctrine and fellowship, and in breaking of bread, and in prayers (Acts 2:37-42).

The response to this prophetic Word was immediate. They were pricked in (pierced to) the heart. No longer were they saying, "What does this mean?" Peter's words from the Holy Spirit stung their consciences. They cried out to him and to the other apostles (who were evidently still standing with him), Brothers, what shall we do?

They did not feel completely cut off, however. Peter had called them brothers, and they responded by calling the apostles brothers. Their sin in rejecting and crucifying Christ was great, but their very cry shows that they believed there was hope, there was something they could do.

Peter answered by calling on them to repent, that is, change their minds and fundamental attitudes by accepting the will of God revealed in Christ. As in Romans 12:1, 2, this change required a renewing of their minds with an accompanying change in attitude toward sin and self. The person who truly repents abhors sin (Psalm 51). He humbles himself, recognizes his dependence on Christ, and realizes he has no good thing in himself by which he can stand before God.

The repentant ones could then declare that change of mind and heart by being baptized in the name (Greek, upon the name) of Jesus Christ, that is, upon the authority of Jesus. Luke does not explain further, but he often does not explain what is made clear elsewhere. The authority of Jesus points to His own command given in Matthew 28:19. Thus, the actual baptizing was done into the name (into the worship and service) of the Father, the Son, and the Holy Spirit.

This baptism would also be "unto" the remission (forgiveness) of their sins. How marvelous! What earthly king has forgiven a traitor? But Christ did and does. This is pure grace and matchless love. (See Romans 5:8, 10.) "Unto the remission of your sins" is, however, better translated "because of the release from and forgiveness of your sins." Our sin and guilt is removed as far from us as the east is from the west (Psalm 103:12). They are not only forgiven, they are really gone, out of existence, never to be brought up against us any more.

"Because of" is better than "unto" since it is the same type of Greek construction used where John baptized people in water "unto" repentance (Matthew 3:11). It is clear that John baptized no one to produce repentance. When the Pharisees and Sadducees came to him he demanded that they produce fruit worthy of repentance (demonstrating true repentance). That is, they had to repent first, then he would baptize them. We are saved by grace through faith, not through baptism (Ephesians 2:8). After repentance, water baptism becomes the answer or testimony of a good conscience that has already been cleansed by the blood and by the Spirit's application of the Word concerning Christ's resurrection (1 Peter 3:21; Romans 10:9, 10).

Some argue wrongly that there was not enough water in Jerusalem to baptize 3,000 by immersion. However, the pool of Bethesda alone was a large double pool, and remains of other pools have been excavated. In fact, the facilities for baptism by immersion were much greater in Jerusalem then than now.

Next Peter spoke of the Promise. Believers would also receive the Holy Spirit as a distinct gift after the forgiveness of their sins. This gift of the Holy Spirit is, of course, the baptism in the Holy Spirit. It must be distinguished from the gifts of the Spirit which are given *by* the Spirit (1 Corinthians chapters 12-14). The *gift* of the Spirit is given by Jesus, the mighty Baptizer.

Peter goes on to emphasize that this promise of the baptism in the Spirit was not limited to the 120. It would continue to be available, not only to them, but also to their children (including all their descendants), and to all who are far away, even to as many as the Lord our God shall call to himself. Thus, the only condition for receiving the Promise of the Father is repentance and faith. It is therefore still available to us today.

The "calling" may refer to Joel 2:32, but cannot be limited to the Jews. In Isaiah 57:19 God speaks peace to him that is far off, and Ephesians 2:17 applies this to the preaching of the gospel to the Gentiles. Acts 1:8 also speaks of the uttermost part of the earth. Though Peter may not have understood this fully until his experience at the house of Cornelius, it is clear that the Gentiles are included. It is clear also that as long as God is calling men and women to himself, the promised baptism in the Spirit is available to all who come to Him.

Luke does not record the rest of Peter's witness and exhortation. But in this exhortation Peter may have been exercising another of the gifts of the Spirit (Romans 12:8). Peter became the instrument through which the Holy Spirit carried out the work foretold by Jesus in John 16:8.

The essence of Peter's exhortation was that they should save themselves (rather, be saved) from this untoward (perverse, crooked) generation. Namely, they should turn away from the perversity and corruptness of those around them who were rejecting the truth about Jesus. (See the words of Jesus in Luke 9:41; 11:29; and 17:25.) There is no other antidote to the perversity and corruptness of contemporary society.

Those who received (welcomed) Peter's word (message) then testified to their faith by being baptized in water.

Again, Luke does not always specify details that are clear elsewhere. He does not have the space to do it in this one book. Therefore, though Luke does not mention it, we can be sure that all 3,000 who were added to the Church received the Promise of the Father as Peter said they would and were filled with the Spirit, speaking in other tongues as in Acts 2:4.

By the Spirit they also had been baptized into the Body of Christ (1 Corinthians 12:13). God never saves us to wander off by ourselves. Thus, the 3,000 did not scatter but remained together, continuing steadfastly in the apostles' doctrine (teaching) and fellowship, and in the breaking of bread, and in the prayers.

From this we see that the further evidence of their faith was this persistent desire for teaching. Their acceptance of Christ and the gift of the Spirit opened up to them a whole new understanding of God's plan and purpose. With joy, they became hungry to learn more. This shows also that the apostles were obeying Jesus and teaching (making disciples) as He commanded in Matthew 28:19. It also shows that discipleship includes this kind of eager desire to learn more of Jesus and of God's Word.

Fellowship was experienced in the teaching. It was more than just getting together. It was a partnership in the purposes of the Church and a sharing in its message and work. As in 1 John 1:3, the Word, as witnessed to by the teaching of the apostles, brought this fellowship, a fellowship not only with the apostles but also with the Father and with the Son.

The breaking of bread some take to mean only the Lord's Supper, but it also includes table fellowship. They could not observe the Lord's Supper in the Temple, so this was done in homes, at first in connection with a meal (since Jesus instituted it at the close of the Passover meal).

Their prayers would include daily gathering in the Temple at the hours of prayer, which they all still continued, plus prayer meetings in homes.

A Growing Church (2:43-47)

[43]And fear came upon every soul: and many wonders and signs were done by the apostles. [44]And all that believed were together, and had all things common; [45]and sold their possessions and goods, and parted them to all *men,* as every man had need. [46]And they, continuing daily with one accord in the temple, and breaking bread from house to house, did eat their meat with gladness and singleness of heart, [47]praising God, and having favor with all the people. And the Lord added to the church daily such as should be saved (Acts 2:43-47).

The continuing witness of the apostles to the resurrection of Christ brought a reverential fear (including a sense of awe in the presence of the supernatural) on every soul (every person) who heard. This was further enhanced by the many wonders and signs done by the apostles. (That is, done by God through the apostles.

The Greek indicates secondary agency. God really did the work. Compare 1 Corinthians 3:6.)

Later God gave miracles through many others. But here the apostles had the teaching from Jesus and the background of His encouragement of their faith. The miracles were not for display, but rather to confirm the Word, the teaching. (See Mark 16:20.) They also helped the faith of the new Pentecostal church members to be established in the Word and in the power of God. (See 1 Corinthians 2:4, 5.)

The believers remained together and had things common (shared). Many sold pieces of land they owned and personal property as well; the money was distributed to whomever had need. "Every man had need" is a key statement: They did not sell property until there was a need.

This was not communism in the modern sense, or even communal living. It was just Christian sharing. They all realized the importance of becoming established in the apostles' teaching (which we have in the written Word). Some of those from outside Jerusalem soon ran out of money, so those who were able simply sold what they could to make it possible for them to stay. Later Peter made it clear that no one was under any compulsion to sell anything or give anything (Acts 5:4). But the fellowship, joy, and love made it easy to share what they had.

The picture, then, is of a loving Body of believers meeting daily in the Temple with one accord, one mind, one purpose, and sharing table fellowship in their homes ("from house to house" means by households.) Each house became a center of Christian fellowship and worship. Mark's mother's home was one such center. Undoubtedly, the home of Mary and Martha in Bethany was another. Jerusalem was not able to hold such a multitude, and many certainly stayed in surrounding villages.

The table fellowship was also very important. They took their food with rejoicing (delight and great joy) and with simplicity of heart. There was no jealousy, no criticism, no wrangling, just joy and hearts full of praise to God. We can be sure that the praise found expression also in psalms, hymns, and spiritual songs coming from their hearts (Colossians 3:16).

The result was that they found favor with the whole of the people (of Jerusalem). Thus the Lord kept adding (together, to the Church) day by day those who were being saved. These the Church joyfully accepted, we may be sure.

It should be noted here that no predestination of individuals is intended by the last part of verse 47. The Greek is a simple statement that every day some were being saved and the saved ones were added to the Church. Notice, too, that no great pressure was placed on others. The people saw the joy and the power and they opened their hearts to the Word, the truth about Jesus.

ACTS

CHAPTER

3

Luke often makes a general statement and then gives a specific example. Acts 2:43 states that many wonders and signs were done through the apostles. Now Luke proceeds to give one example to illustrate this and at the same time show how this brought further growth to the Church.

On this occasion Peter and John were going up the Temple hill into the Temple to join the others for the hour of evening prayer, the ninth hour (about 3 p.m.). Sacrifice and incense were being offered by the priests at the same time.

A Gift of Healing (3:1-10)

[1]Now Peter and John went up together into the temple at the hour of prayer, *being* the ninth *hour.* [2]And a certain man lame from his mother's womb was carried, whom they laid daily at the gate of the temple which is called Beautiful, to ask alms of them that entered into the temple; [3]who, seeing Peter and John about to go into the temple, asked an alms. [4]And Peter, fastening his eyes upon him with John, said, Look on us. [5]And he gave heed unto them, expecting to receive something of them. [6]Then Peter said, Silver and gold have I none; but such as I have give I thee: In the name of Jesus Christ of Nazareth rise up and walk.

[7]And he took him by the right hand, and lifted him up: and immediately his feet and ankle bones received strength. [8]And he leaping up stood, and walked, and entered with them into the temple, walking, and leaping, and praising God. [9]And all the people saw him walking and praising God: [10]and they knew that it was he which sat for alms at the Beautiful gate of the temple: and they were filled with wonder and amazement at that which had happened unto him (Acts 3: 1-10).

Between the Court of the Gentiles and the Court of the Women was a beautiful carved, Corinthian style, bronze gate with gold and silver inlays. It was worth more than if it had been made of solid gold.[1]

At the Gate Beautiful Peter and John were confronted by a man lame from birth who daily was carried and laid outside it to ask alms (a gift of charity). Later we read that the man was over 40 years old. Jesus passed this way many times, but apparently the man never asked Him for healing. Possibly also, Jesus, in divine providence and timing, left this man so that he could become a greater witness when he was healed later.

When this man asked to receive an alms, Peter, together with John, fastened his eyes on him. What a contrast this is to the jealousy the disciples once showed toward each other (Matthew 20:24). Now they act together in complete unity of faith and purpose. Then Peter as the spokesman said, "Look on us." This riveted the man's full attention on them and aroused an expectation that he would receive something.

Peter, however, did not do the expected. What money he had was probably already given to needy believers. But he did have something better to give. His statement, "Silver and gold have I none; but such as I have give I thee" took faith on Peter's part. He undoubtedly said it under the prompting of the Holy Spirit who had given him a gift of healing for this man (1 Corinthians 12:9, 11).[2]

As a positive command, Peter then said, "in the name of Jesus Christ of Nazareth [the Nazarene], rise up and walk."[3] At the same time Peter put his own faith into action by taking hold of the man's right hand and lifting him up. Immediately the man's feet and ankle bones received strength (were made firm). It is quite possible also that the man's faith was stirred at the mention of Jesus Messiah of Nazareth. Perhaps some of the 3,000 saved at Pentecost had already witnessed to him. He surely had heard of others healed by Jesus.

When strength went into the man's feet and ankles, Peter no longer had to lift. The man jumped to his feet, stood for a moment, and began to walk. Since he was lame from birth, he had

---

[1]The court of the Gentiles was as far as the Gentiles could go. The Court of the Women was as far as women could go. Men would go on into the Court of Israel and could take a part in the offering of the sacrifices (Leviticus 1:2-5).

[2]See Horton, *op. cit.*, pp. 273, 274.

[3]A few ancient manuscripts omit "rise up and"; but the Greek word even in these is clearly implied, so "rise up" is a proper reading.

never learned to walk. No amount of psychology could have accomplished this.

Now that the man was healed he could go into the Temple. Since cripples were not allowed to enter, this would be the first time in his life. He went in, walking normally, with Peter and John, and every few steps leaping for pure joy, shouting God's praises continually. He had been touched by God and could not hold in the joy and praise.

Verse 11 indicates he still held on to Peter's hand and took hold of John's as well. What a scene this must have been as the man came walking and jumping in the Temple court, dragging Peter and John along with him.

All the people saw him and recognized him as the man who was born lame and was always sitting asking alms at the Beautiful Gate. His healing, therefore, filled them with wonder (not the ordinary word, but one that is related to awe) and amazement (implies also bewilderment). They were astonished and overwhelmed.

The Prince of Life (3:11-21)

[11]And as the lame man which was healed held Peter and John, all the people ran together unto them in the porch that is called Solomon's, greatly wondering. [12]And when Peter saw *it,* he answered unto the people, Ye men of Israel, why marvel ye at this? or why look ye so earnestly on us, as though by our own power or holiness we had made this man to walk? [13]The God of Abraham, and of Isaac, and of Jacob, the God of our fathers, hath glorified his Son Jesus; whom ye delivered up, and denied him in the presence of Pilate, when he was determined to let *him* go. [14]But ye denied the Holy One and the Just, and desired a murderer to be granted unto you; [15]and killed the Prince of life, whom God hath raised from the dead; whereof we are witnesses. [16]And his name, through faith in his name, hath made this man strong, whom ye see and know: yea, the faith which is by him hath given him this perfect soundness in the presence of you all.

[17]And now, brethren, I wot that through ignorance ye did *it,* as *did* also your rulers. [18]But those things, which God before had showed by the mouth of all his prophets, that Christ should suffer, he hath so fulfilled. [19]Repent ye therefore, and be converted, that your sins may be blotted out, when the times of refreshing shall come from the presence of the Lord; [20]and he shall send Jesus Christ, which before was preached unto you: [21]whom the heaven must receive until the times of restitution of all things, which God hath spoken by the mouth of all his holy prophets since the world began (Acts 3:11-21).

By this time the healed cripple, still holding the hands of Peter and John, was in Solomon's Porch, a roofed portico on one side of the Temple court. From all over the Temple courts the people ran together to see them there. There could easily have been 10,000 people in the Temple at the hour of prayer.

This was Peter's opportunity, and he was quick to answer the unspoken questions on their wondering faces. His message follows the same general pattern given by the Spirit on the Day of Pentecost, but adapted to this new situation.

Addressing them as Israelite men (This was the custom, even though there were women in the crowd.), he asked them why they marveled at this and why they fastened their eyes on him and John as if the man's ability to walk had its source in their own power or holiness (godliness).

Peter continually bore witness to Jesus. The One the Scriptures describe as the God of Abraham, Isaac, and Jacob, the God of their fathers (Exodus 3:6, 15), had glorified His Son (Servant) Jesus.[4]

Again he reminds them that they were the ones who were responsible for arresting Jesus and denying him before Pilate, even when Pilate had decided to release Him. The One they denied was the Holy and just (righteous) One. Again, this is a reference to the suffering Servant in Isaiah (Isaiah 53:11; cf. Zechariah 9:9). But they had turned from Him so completely that they asked for a murderer to be released to them instead. (See Luke 23:18, 19, 25.)

They were guilty of killing the Prince of life. What a contrast! They gave death to the One who gave them life. Prince (Greek, *archegon*) is a word that usually means originator, author, founder. In Hebrews 2:10 it is translated captain; in Hebrews 12:2 it is translated author. It speaks of Jesus' part in the creation. As John 1:3 says of Jesus, the living Word, "All things were made by (through) him; and without Him was not anything made that was

[4]The Greek word here *(paida)* is not the ordinary word for son and is not used of Jesus when the emphasis is on His divine sonship. The word may mean servant or child. Here Peter undoubtedly has in mind the identification of Jesus with the suffering Servant in Isaiah 52:13 to 53:12. The Servant of the Lord is the one who does the Lord's work. This healing was the result of the fulfillment of Isaiah's prophecy. That prophecy spoke of the sufferings of Jesus in our behalf. Cf. Lenski, *op. cit.*, p. 133; Harrison, *op. cit.*, pp. 72, 73; Earle, *op. cit.*, p. 293.

made." In other words, the preincarnate Jesus was the living Word who spoke the worlds into existence, and through Him God breathed life into the man He had formed (Genesis 2:7). This Jesus, the very source of life, and therefore of healing, they had killed. But God raised Him from the dead. Peter and John were witnesses to this. The man's healing was also a witness that Jesus was alive.

Notice the repetition of the Name in verse 16. By faith (on the ground of faith, on the basis of faith) in His Name this man who you see and know, His Name has made strong. And the faith that is by (through) Him (Jesus) has given him this freedom from bodily defect in the presence of you all.

The Name, of course, refers to the character and nature of Jesus as the Healer, the great Physician. The healing came on the ground of faith in Jesus for what He is. But it was not their faith as such that brought the healing. It was the Name, that is, the fact that Jesus is true to His nature and character. He is the Healer. Faith did have a great part, of course, but it was the faith that was through Jesus. The faith Jesus himself had imparted (not only to Peter and John, but to the man) gave complete freedom from defect to this lame man before their very eyes.[5] Jesus had healed the lame; He was still healing the lame through His disciples.

Peter adds that he knew that through ignorance they and their rulers killed Jesus. Paul later confessed that he persecuted the Church because of ignorance and unbelief (1 Timothy 1:13). This implies that they did not really know Jesus was the Messiah, nor did they know He was God's Son. This ignorance did not lessen their guilt. Yet even in the Old Testament there was always forgiveness available for sins done in ignorance. Jesus himself cried out, "Father, forgive them; for they know not what they do" (Luke 23:34).[6]

The sufferings and death of Jesus were also the fulfillment of prophecies God had revealed by the mouth of all His prophets, that is, by the body of prophets as a whole. Their message, taken

[5]"Perfect soundness" is the same term used of the freedom from defect necessary for animals used in the sacrifices.

[6]Some today claim that when the Jews had Jesus crucified, God cut them off forever. But the Bible says: "God hath not cast away His people which He foreknew" (Romans 11:2).

as a whole, had for a focal point the death of Christ. Even so, this did not lessen the guilt of the Jerusalemites either.

As on the Day of Pentecost, Peter then called on them to repent, to change their minds and attitudes about Jesus. Let them be converted (turn to God) so that their sins (including the sin of rejecting and killing Jesus) might be blotted out (wiped away, obliterated) when (literally, in order that) times (seasons, occasions) of refreshing from the presence (face) of the Lord might come. And to you who repent, He will send the appointed-for-you Messiah Jesus, whom the heavens must receive until the times of restoration (reestablishment) of all things which were spoken by God through the mouth of His holy prophets from the beginning of the age (or from of old). "Since the world began" is a paraphrase which could mean "from eternity" or "from the beginning of time." The sense is "all the prophets ever since there were prophets."

From this passage we see that repentance and turning to God not only brings the obliteration of sins but seasons of refreshing from the Lord. Nor do we have to wait until Jesus comes back before we can enjoy these times. It indicates, especially in the Greek, that we can have them now and until the time Jesus comes.

Too many put all their emphasis on the warnings of perilous times to come and on the statement that there will be a falling away (2 Timothy 3:1; 2 Thessalonians 2:3). These things will come. The falling away, of course, may mean spiritual falling away, though the Greek word ordinarily means revolt or revolution and war. Though the warnings are necessary, the Christian does not need to make this the focus of his attention. Repentance (a change of mind and attitude) and a turning to God will still bring seasons of refreshing from the presence of God. The day of spiritual blessing, the day of miracles, the day of revival is not past. In the midst of perilous times we can still get our eyes on the Lord and receive mighty, refreshing outpourings of His Spirit.

The times of restitution refer to the coming age, the Millennium. Then God will restore and renew and Jesus will reign personally on the earth. The restitution prophesied includes a further outpouring of the Spirit on the restored kingdom.

Some take the restitution of all things out of context and try to make it include even the salvation of Satan. But "all things" must be taken with "which God has spoken." Only those things prophesied to be restored will be restored.

The prophets also show the kingdom must be brought in through judgment. Daniel 2:35, 44, 45 pictures the Babylon image which represents the whole world system from Babylon until the end of the age. Not until it is hit in the feet (in the last days of this age) will the present world system be destroyed and crushed to powder. Even the good in the present world system will have to be destroyed to make way for the better things of the coming kingdom which will fill the earth after Jesus comes again.

We do not know when that will be. But the important thing is that we do not have to wait for the Kingdom to come before we experience God's blessings and power. The Holy Spirit brings us an earnest, a first installment of things to come. And we can have these promised seasons of refreshing even now if we will fulfill the conditions of repentance and turning to God.

A Prophet Like Moses (3:22-26)

> [22]For Moses truly said unto the fathers, A Prophet shall the Lord your God raise up unto you of your brethren, like unto me; him shall ye hear in all things whatsoever he shall say unto you. [23]And it shall come to pass *that* every soul, which will not hear that Prophet, shall be destroyed from among the people. [24]Yea, and all the prophets from Samuel and those that follow after, as many as have spoken, have likewise foretold of these days. [25]Ye are the children of the prophets, and of the covenant which God made with our fathers, saying unto Abraham, And in thy seed shall all the kindreds of the earth be blessed. [26]Unto you first God, having raised up his Son Jesus, sent him to bless you, in turning away every one of you from his iniquities (Acts 3:22-26).

Peter next goes back to Moses and quotes from Deuteronomy 18:18, 19 where God promises to raise up a prophet like Moses. (See also Leviticus 26:12; Deuteronomy 18:15; Acts 7:37.) This was the promise the people had in mind also when they asked John the Baptist if he were "that prophet" (John 1:21, 25). Some feel Deuteronomy calls for a partial fulfillment in Joshua (a man in whom is the Spirit; Numbers 27:18), Samuel, and the line of Old Testament prophets. But it had a complete fulfillment in Jesus.[7]

[7]Cf. Earle, *op. cit.,* p. 296.

In what way was Jesus like Moses? God used Moses to bring in the Old Covenant; Jesus brought in the New Covenant. Moses led the nation of Israel out of Egypt and brought them to Sinai where God brought them to himself (into a covenant relation with himself). (See Exodus 19:4.) Jesus became the new and living way whereby we can enter into the very holiest presence of God. Moses gave Israel the command to sacrifice a Lamb; Jesus is the Lamb of God. Moses was used by God to perform great miracles and signs; Jesus performed many more miracles and signs, but most were signs of love rather than of judgment. (See Hebrews 3:3-6 which proclaims the superiority of Christ to Moses.)

Moses warned the people they would be cut off if they did not receive and obey this Prophet. Thus, though God is good, there is a penalty involved for those who do not repent. Peter emphasized the meaning of Moses' warning. They would be destroyed from among the people. That is, God will not destroy His people as a whole, but individuals can lose out.

Samuel was the next great prophet after Moses (1 Samuel 3:20). From that time on, all the prophets foretold of these days, that is the days of God's work through Christ. Some may not have given specific prophecies in their writings, but all of them gave prophecies which led up to or prepared for these days.

The Jews Peter was addressing were the literal descendants of the prophets, heirs also of the Abrahamic covenant with its promise that in Abraham's seed (Christ) all the families of the earth will be blessed (Genesis 22:18; Galatians 3:16).

That blessing promised to all the families of the earth came first to these Jerusalem Jews. What a privilege! Yet this was not favoritism on God's part. It was their opportunity to receive the blessing by repenting and by turning from their sins (evil or malicious acts). It was also an opportunity for service.

Actually, someone had to be first to carry the message. (Compare Romans 1:16; 2:9, 10; 3:1, 2.) Paul always went to the Jew first because they had the Scriptures and the background and knew about the Promise. But they could not carry the message and the blessing to others without first repenting and experiencing the blessing for themselves. God had prepared the Jews for this. All the first evangelists (spreaders of the Good News) were Jews.

ACTS
CHAPTER
4

While Peter and John were still speaking,[1] the priests (chief priests), the captain of the Temple (the priest next in rank to the high priest) who commanded the Temple guard of chosen Levites, and a group of their Sadducee supporters came up on them suddenly and unexpectedly. As verse 3 indicates, it was now evening (about sundown), and since the miracle took place about 3 p.m., Peter and John had continued to talk to the crowd about three hours. Undoubtedly they explained the full gospel further and probably had time to answer questions from the crowd.

Peter and John Arrested (4:1-4)

[1]And as they spake unto the people, the priests, and the captain of the temple, and the Sadduccees, came upon them, [2]being grieved that they taught the people, and preached through Jesus the resurrection from the dead. [3]And they laid hands on them, and put *them* in hold unto the next day: for it was now eventide. [4]Howbeit many of them which heard the word believed; and the number of the men was about five thousand (Acts 4:1-4).

The high priest was a Sadducee, as were many of the priests in Jerusalem. They claimed to be religious but did not accept the traditions of the Pharisees and did not consider the Old Testament prophetical books or the Writings (the third division of the Hebrew canon) to be on the same level as the Law (the Torah, the Pentateuch).[2] They also denied the existence of angels and spirits

[1]"They" refers to Peter and John, and the verb "spake" is a plural participle indicating continuous action. It shows also that John did some speaking and that more was said than Luke had space to record. Cf. Harrison, *op. cit.*, p. 79.

[2]Cf. Harrison, *op. cit.*, p. 80.

and said there was no resurrection (Acts 23:8; Matthew 22:23).

They were not excited about the miracle, but they were disturbed because there was such a great crowd around Peter and John. Then they were grieved (upset, greatly troubled, deeply annoyed) because the apostles preached (proclaimed) through (in) Jesus the resurrection from (out from) the dead.

Peter was preaching a resurrected Jesus, and they understood that this was evidence for the truth of the resurrection of all believers. Because this teaching was against their doctrine, the Sadducees felt they could not tolerate it.

They therefore laid hands on Peter and John (arrested them) and threw them in jail overnight. It was evening, too late to call the Sanhedrin together. But it was too late, also, to stop the gospel from having its effect. Many who heard the Word believed. We can be sure they were soon baptized in water (probably the next day) as well as in the Holy Spirit. The number is given as about 5,000 men. The Greek may be "became about 5,000," so some take this to mean the total number of believers was now up to 5,000. But the way it is stated here indicates the number was so large that they counted only men. There must have been a large number of women who believed also. Acts 3:9 says all the people saw the lame man, and 4:1, 2 indicates they were teaching the whole people, both men and women.

It is clear that though the officials were no longer indifferent to what the apostles were doing, the apostles were still held in high esteem by the people.

Brought to Trial (4:5-12)

[5]And it came to pass on the morrow, that their rulers, and elders, and scribes, [6]and Annas the high priest, and Caiaphas, and John, and Alexander, and as many as were of the kindred of the high priest, were gathered together at Jerusalem. [7]And when they had set them in the midst, they asked, By what power, or by what name, have ye done this? [8]Then Peter, filled with the Holy Ghost, said unto them, Ye rulers of the people, and elders of Israel, [9]if we this day be examined of the good deed done to the impotent man, by what means he is made whole; [10]be it known unto you all, and to all the people of Israel, that by the name of Jesus Christ of Nazareth, whom ye crucified, whom God raised from the dead, *even* by him doth this man stand here before you whole. [11]This is the stone which was set at nought of you builders, which is become the head of the corner. [12]Neither is there salvation in any other: for there is

none other name under heaven given among men, whereby we must be saved (Acts 4:5-12).

The next day the rulers (the executives or official members of the Sanhedrin, the Jewish Senate and Supreme Court)[3] with the elders and scribes (teachers of the Law, experts in the Law) who were in Jerusalem assembled. With them, specifically, came Annas, Caiaphas, John, Alexander, and all the rest of the relatives of the high priest who happened to be in the city.

Annas here is called the high priest. He was officially high priest from A.D. 6-15. Then his son Jonathan was appointed for about three years. Next Caiaphas, the son-in-law of Annas was made the official high priest (A.D. 18-36). But Annas remained the power behind the throne. The people did not accept his deposition by the Romans and still considered him to be the true high priest. In the Old Testament Aaron was made high priest for life. The Law made no provision for the secular governors to change this. Consequently, Jesus was taken to Annas' house first (John 18:13), then to Caiaphas (who probably occupied a portion of the same building around the same courtyard). Annas and Caiaphas, along with some of the rest of the relatives of Annas, actually formed a closed corporation that ran the Temple.

John here may have been Jonathan the son of Annas.[4] Alexander was probably one of the leading Sadducees.

They made Peter and John stand in the midst of the assembled court, which was basically the same one that convicted Jesus. (Their meeting place, according to Josephus, was just west of the Temple area.) Then they began their inquiry by asking them by what (what sort of) power (*dynamis,* mighty power) or by what name (that is, by what authority) "have you [plural] done this?"

"What" power is used here in a derogatory way. They were trying to awe the disciples or even scare them. Perhaps they remembered how the disciples fled in fear at the time of Jesus' arrest. Verse 13 shows they felt a contempt for them because they were not educated in their schools.

---

[3]The Sanhedrin was also called the Gerousia (Assembly, Senate, 5:21), and the Presbyterion (the Body of Elders, 22:5). The high priest was always its president and it consisted of 70 other members.

[4]Codex Bezae (D) has Jonathan instead of John here. Others take this John to be Johanan ben Azcchai who became the president of the Great Synagogue after A. D. 70, but this is not a likely identification.

Peter had indeed once cringed before a girl in the courtyard when this same group was gathered around Jesus. Now there was a difference. Peter, as he began to speak, was filled with the Holy Spirit. The form of the Greek verb here indicates a new fresh filling.[5] This does not mean he had lost any of the power and presence of the Spirit he received on the Day of Pentecost. In view of the pressures of this critical situation, the Lord simply enlarged his capacity and gave him this fresh filling to meet this new need for power to witness.

We can see here also a practical application of Jesus' instructions and promise given in Matthew 10:19, 20 and Luke 21:12-15. They were to take no advance thought of what they should speak; the Spirit of their Heavenly Father would speak in (and by) them. Thus instead of trying to defend themselves, the Spirit would make their words a witness. We may be sure Peter and John slept well the night before and awoke refreshed.

Peter, filled anew with the Spirit, did not let the Jewish leaders frighten him. As Paul told Timothy (2 Timothy 1:7), God has not given us a spirit of cowardly fear, but of power, of love, and of a sound mind (a mind that shows self-discipline). Politely, Peter addressed the Council as rulers (official members of the Sanhedrin) and elders. Then, in a dignified way, he told them that if they were making a judicial examination concerning the good deed done for a weak human being, by what means the man had been (and still was) made whole (saved, restored)[6], then he had the answer.

Peter then proclaimed that in (by) the name of Jesus, whom they crucified ("you" is plural), whom God raised from the dead, by (in) Him this man stood before them whole (restored to sound health). What a contrast Peter makes between what these leaders did to Jesus and what God did to Him!

Then Peter quoted a passage that these same chief priests and elders had heard from Jesus himself. On one occasion they challenged Jesus' authority to teach. He gave them parables and then quoted Psalm 118:22. (See Matthew 21:23, 42, 45; 1 Peter

---

[5]Greek aorist. See Alexander, *op. cit.*, p. 137; Hackett, *op. cit.*, p. 67; Earle, *op. cit.*, p. 300.

[6]The Greek word is the one usually translated "saved," but it also includes the ideas of saving from danger, disease, illness, sin, and sin's effects.

2:7). Peter, however, makes it personal. This one (emphatic) is the stone which was set at nought (ignored, despised) by you (plural) the builders, who has become the head of the corner. (That is, because He is exalted to the Father's right hand.) Then Peter explains what this means: There is no salvation in any other (the salvation which they hoped to be brought by the Messiah is not in any other), for there is no other name under heaven given among men (human beings) by which we must be saved.[7] "Must" is an emphatic word. If we do not find salvation through the name (Person) of Jesus, we shall never find it.

The healing of the lame man thus witnessed to Jesus as the only Saviour. The Jewish leaders could see no use in Jesus; yet God had made Him of unique and supreme value. In Him, as Isaiah chapter 53 also shows, is (the promised) salvation. There is only one salvation, only one way (Hebrews 10:12-22). There will never be another Messiah sent from God or another Saviour.

Many have claimed to be Messiahs or Saviours; many have presented other ways of salvation. But they are all put in opposition to our Lord Jesus Christ. We have only one choice when we face the claims of Christ: We can accept or reject. Other ways which may seem right can only lead to destruction (Proverbs 14:12; Matthew 7:13).

It is not popular to be so exclusive. Most unbelievers who are not atheists want to think that there are many ways to find God. Some cults even try to combine what they suppose is the good in various religions. But all this is in vain. God has rejected all other ways. In Christ alone is there hope. It is this that places the heavy responsibility of the Great Commission upon us. If there were any other way of salvation, we could afford to take it easy. But there is no hope for anyone apart from *the* salvation through Christ.[8]

Peter and John Speak Boldly (4:13-22)

[13]Now when they saw the boldness of Peter and John, and perceived that they were unlearned and ignorant men, they marveled; and they took knowledge of them, that they had been with Jesus. [14]And beholding

[7]A few ancient manuscripts have "you" instead of "we."

[8]Even in the Old Testament one of the things the prophets condemn most strongly is the worship of the Lord *plus* other gods.

the man which was healed standing with them, they could say nothing against it. [15]But when they had commanded them to go aside out of the council, they conferred among themselves, [16]saying, What shall we do to these men? for that indeed a notable miracle hath been done by them *is* manifest to all them that dwell in Jerusalem; and we cannot deny *it.* [17]But that it spread no further among the people, let us straitly threaten them, that they speak henceforth to no man in this name. [18]And they called them, and commanded them not to speak at all nor teach in the name of Jesus.

[19]But Peter and John answered and said unto them, Whether it be right in the sight of God to hearken unto you more than unto God, judge ye. [20]For we cannot but speak the things which we have seen and heard. [21]So when they had further threatened them, they let them go, finding nothing how they might punish them, because of the people: for all *men* glorified God for that which was done. [22]For the man was above forty years old, on whom this miracle of healing was showed (Acts 4:13-22).

The priests and elders marveled (wondered) when they saw the boldness (freedom in speech) of Peter and John, especially since they perceived they were unlearned (uneducated in the sense of not having attended a rabbinical school or having sat under a great rabbi like Gamaliel)[9] and ignorant men (unprofessional men, laymen). This does not mean they were totally unschooled. They had gone to the synagogue schools in their home towns, but they were not professional teachers or trained speakers like the scribes and lawyers. Ordinary laymen did not speak with authority like this.

It must have been hard for Peter and John to face such snobbishness. But the key to their boldness and freedom in speaking was, of course, the new fresh filling with the Spirit. *He* gave them the words to say.

Then something else struck these Jewish leaders. The phrase "took knowledge of them" does not mean they inquired further of them. Rather, the Greek simply means they gradually recognized that they had been with Jesus. Perhaps the words of Peter jogged their memory of what Jesus had said. As they thought about their confrontation with Jesus, they remembered there were disciples with Him. Now they recognized Peter and John as having been among that number.

Jesus also spoke with authority. They must have been shocked,

[9]The word sometimes means illiterate, but scholars agree that this is not the meaning here. Cf. Bruce, *op. cit.*, p. 122.

for they believed they would be rid of Jesus by crucifying Him. But now the disciples, trained by Him, spoke in the same way. Jesus had done miracles as signs. Now the apostles were doing the same.

Now the elders were confronted with something else. The man who was healed was standing there with Peter and John.[10] Suddenly, the priests and elders had nothing else to say. What could they say against such a miracle?

The leaders then commanded Peter and John to go outside the council (the Sanhedrin), that is, out of the room where they were meeting. The Sanhedrin then engaged in a discussion among themselves.[11] They did not know what to do with Peter and John. They could not deny that a notable miracle (a known supernatural sign) had been done by (through) them, visible to all the inhabitants of Jerusalem.

This could imply that they did not deny the resurrection of Jesus. The thing that bothered them was the fact that the apostles were using it to teach a future resurrection for all believers. In order to avoid this problem earlier, they had bribed the soldiers to say the body of Jesus had been stolen (Matthew 28:12, 13). Some, even today, contend that the women and the disciples looked in the wrong tomb. But the women paid special attention to where Jesus was laid (Luke 23:55). Actually, these Jewish leaders were neither stupid nor unsophisticated. They knew how difficult it is to get rid of a body and, so, would have made an intensive search for the body if they had not known He was risen from the dead. But it takes more than a head belief or a mental acceptance of the truth of Christ's resurrection to be saved (Romans 10:9, 10).

Since they had no logical reply to Peter and John, they decided the best course was to suppress their teaching about Jesus and the resurrection. They knew they could not bribe the disciples. They would therefore threaten them to speak no longer in (on the ground of) this Name to any of mankind.

When they called Peter and John back into the room, they

[10]Some believe this man was arrested also and brought in with Peter and John. Others believe he was let go and came back in the morning to observe the questioning. The man himself was not questioned, nor does he speak. Thus, the latter is probable. The man himself was not on trial.

[11]Emil Schuerer, cited by Earle, *op. cit.*, p. 303, suggests that Saul (Paul) was in this session of the Sanhedrin and later told Luke what was said behind the scenes here.

commanded them not to speak (open their mouth, utter a word) at all or teach at all in the name of Jesus. But these threats did not intimidate the two apostles. Courteously, but very firmly, they put the responsibility back on the Jewish leaders to judge (or decide) whether it was right before God to listen to them rather than to Him. Then they boldly declared that they were not able to stop talking about what they had seen and heard.

The Sanhedrin members wanted to find some way to punish Peter and John. In fact, the implication is that they did try to find some way. But they could not because of the people. Everyone was glorifying God for what was done, especially since this man who was born lame was now over 40 years old. Therefore, they simply added more threats to their previous warning and let them go.

This was a big mistake on their part, for it let the people know God could deliver from the Sanhedrin. It illustrated that the Jewish leaders had no case against these apostles, nor did they have any way to refute their message.

Renewed Boldness (4:23-31)

[23]And being let go, they went to their own company, and reported all that the chief priests and elders had said unto them. [24]And when they heard that, they lifted up their voice to God with one accord, and said, Lord, thou *art* God, which hast made heaven, and earth, and the sea, and all that in them is; [25]who by the mouth of thy servant David hast said, Why did the heathen rage, and the people imagine vain things? [26]The kings of the earth stood up, and the rulers were gathered together against the Lord, and against his Christ.

[27]For of a truth against thy holy child Jesus, whom thou hast anointed, both Herod, and Pontius Pilate, with the Gentiles, and the people of Israel, were gathered together, [28]for to do whatsoever thy hand and thy counsel determined before to be done. [29]And now, Lord, behold their threatenings: and grant unto thy servants, that with all boldness they may speak thy word, [30]by stretching forth thine hand to heal; and that signs and wonders may be done by the name of the holy child Jesus. [31]And when they had prayed, the place was shaken where they were assembled together; and they were all filled with the Holy Ghost, and they spake the word of God with boldness (Acts 4:23-31).

As soon as they were released Peter and John went back to their own people (the assembled believers who were most certainly gathered to pray for them). There they reported all the high priest and elders had said to them, holding nothing back.

The people responded by raising their voice (voice is singular, indicating they prayed in unison) in one accord, with one purpose, praying to God. Probably the prayer which the Bible records here was given, however, by one of them who became the spokesman for them all.

We can learn much from this prayer. First, as in the case of most prayers in the Bible, they recognized who God is. They addressed Him as Lord (a different word from that used elsewhere in the Bible, this one meaning Master, Owner, Sovereign). Then they recognized that He alone is God, the Creator of the universe and all that is in it.

Second, they based their petition on the inspired Word of God spoken by the Spirit, through the mouth of David. Again, most of the prayers of the Bible are based on the Word of God already given. In Psalm 2:1, 2 they saw a Word from the Lord that was fulfilled in the opposition of these Jewish leaders. The Psalm speaks of the heathen (the nations, the Gentiles) raging, and the peoples (plural) imagining (planning, devising) a vain (empty, foolish, ineffective) thing. The kings of the earth and their rulers who gather together against the Lord and His Christ (His Messiah, His Anointed One) are also Gentiles. Thus, this prayer, inspired by the Spirit, recognized that the Jewish leaders were in the same class as the outside nations who were always raging, always conspiring against God and against Jesus. There is precedent for this in the Old Testament prophets who sometimes used the word *goi* for Israel because they had turned from God.

Herod (Herod Antipas), Pilate, the Gentiles, and the people (peoples) of Israel truly were gathered together (in a hostile way) against God's Holy Child Jesus. As before, Holy Child means the dedicated, consecrated Servant of the Lord (as in Isaiah 52:13 to 53:12). Yet they could do only what God's hand (that is, God's power) and God's will had determined before (limited beforehand) to be done. They were, however, responsible for their deeds, for they chose freely to do them.

Third, the believers based their petition on what God did through Jesus. God's hand was in control when He permitted the death of Jesus; Jesus was indeed God's Servant who accomplished God's will in their behalf. They could come to God on the basis of what was fully accomplished through His death and resurrection (1 Corinthians 1:23, 24; 3:11; 2 Corinthians 1:20).

Their petition was that the Lord would now look on the threatenings of the Sanhedrin and give His servants (slaves) opportunities to keep on speaking His Word with all boldness (and freedom of speech). They probably felt less confident now, after they left the courtroom, than while they were in it and felt they needed renewed boldness. Even after a spiritual victory, Satan may suggest to us that we were fools; we must pray for continued boldness. Abraham, too, became afraid during the night after boldly testifying before the king of Sodom; God came to reassure and comfort him (Genesis 15:1).

What opportunities would they have? The healing of the lame man was just a beginning. There would be more such opportunities provided by God's stretching out His hand for healing and for signs and wonders to be done through the name of His holy Child (servant) Jesus.[12]

Thus, they prayed for boldness to keep on doing the same thing that had brought their arrest and the threats of the Sanhedrin. They did not want miracles for miracles' sake, however, but as opportunities to preach the gospel and as signs so that the people would recognize that Jesus was indeed risen from the dead.

After they prayed the place where they were gathered was shaken (by the Spirit, not by an earthquake), indicating a mighty move of God. At the same time they were all filled with the Holy Spirit, and in His power they all continued speaking the Word of God with boldness (and freedom of speech). This was as great a work of the Spirit as the miracles.

The Greek indicates again a new, fresh filling of the Spirit. Some writers contend that only the new people (the 5,000 mentioned in 4:4) were filled at this time. But the Greek does not uphold this. All the believers, including the apostles, received this fresh filling to meet the continued need and the pressures upon them. New, fresh fillings of the Holy Spirit are part of God's wonderful provision for all believers.

Great Grace (4:32-37)

[32]And the multitude of them that believed were of one heart and of one soul: neither said any *of them* that aught of the things which he

[12]"Holy" (separated to God and His service) emphasizes His consecration and dedication to the work His Father gave Him to do. See John 10:36; 17:4, 18, 19.

possessed was his own; but they had all things common. [33]And with great power gave the apostles witness of the resurrection of the Lord Jesus: and great grace was upon them all. [34]Neither was there any among them that lacked: for as many as were possessors of lands or houses sold them, and brought the prices of the things that were sold, [35]and laid *them* down at the apostles' feet: and distribution was made unto every man according as he had need. [36]And Joses, who by the apostles was surnamed Barnabas, (which is, being interpreted, The son of consolation,) a Levite, *and* of the country of Cyprus, [37]having land, sold *it*, and brought the money, and laid *it* at the apostles' feet (Acts 4:32-37).

The increasing number of believers continued in one heart and one soul. That is, they formed a community of believers who were in one accord with a unity of mind, purpose, and desire. None of them said, "What I have is mine and I am afraid I might need it myself." Instead, they felt a love and responsibility for each other, and all things were shared. God was supplying their needs and they believed He would continue to provide. The same attitude that sprang up after they were first filled with the Spirit on the Day of Pentecost still prevailed (Acts 2:44, 45). Again, there was no compulsion. Their sharing was simply an expression of their love and their unity of mind and heart in the one Body of Christ. (Compare Galatians 6:10.)[13]

At the same time the apostles kept on giving witness to the resurrection of the Lord Jesus. But the work of the Spirit was not limited to the apostles, for great grace was upon all the believers.

Verse 34 shows how this grace was expressed. No one lacked (was in need, was needy) for as many as were owners of fields or houses were selling them and kept bringing the price of the things that were sold. The Greek here does not mean that everyone sold their property at once. Rather, from time to time this was done as the Lord brought needs to their attention.[14] Then the money was laid at the apostles' feet (and put under their authority); they distributed to each one in proportion to his need.

After this general statement Luke gives a specific example, chosen because it gives background for the events at the beginning of the next chapter.

Joses (Joseph) who was surnamed (given the additional name

[13]This is not mere repetition of chapter 2. It gives background for what Barnabas did and for what Ananias and Sapphira did.

[14]Cf. Lenski, *op. cit.*, pp. 189, 190.

of) Barnabas by the apostles, sold a field, brought the money and laid it at the apostles' feet.

It is not clear whether he was given this name because of what he did at this time or his previous actions. From what we see of Barnabas later, he had a character which fitted the meaning of the name Barnabas, son of consolation (or, of exhortation, encouragement). "Son of" was often used in Hebrew and Aramaic to indicate a person's character or nature. The name Barnabas is probably derived from an Aramaic phrase meaning "son of prophecy or exhortation." The name stuck. He is never called Joses (Joseph) again.

Barnabas was a Levite from the country of Cyprus, a large island off the south coast of Asia Minor. He was a good example of those who were concerned about the needy believers and also of Christian stewardship.[15]

---

[15]Cf. Earle, *op. cit.*, p. 307.

ACTS

CHAPTER 5

With the example of Barnabas before them, two members of the believing community conspired to get the same kind of attention given to him. It is clearly implied that they were believers enjoying the blessings of God. They knew what it was to be filled with the Spirit. They listened to the teaching of the apostles, saw the miracles, and shared the fellowship.[1]

Apparently they were a little jealous of Barnabas, especially since he was from out of town. So they, like he, sold a field, a piece of farm property. But in every other way what they did was in strong contrast to him.

SWIFT JUDGMENT (5:1-10)

[1]But a certain man named Ananias, with Sapphira his wife, sold a possession, [2]and kept back *part* of the price, his wife also being privy *to it*, and brought a certain part, and laid *it* at the apostles' feet. [3]But Peter said, Ananias, why hath Satan filled thine heart to lie to the Holy Ghost, and to keep back *part* of the price of the land? [4]While it remained, was it not thine own? and after it was sold, was it not in thine own power? why hast thou conceived this thing in thine heart? thou hast not lied unto men, but unto God. [5]And Ananias hearing these words fell down, and gave up the ghost: and great fear came on all them that heard these things. [6]And the young men arose, wound him up, and carried *him* out, and buried *him*.

[7]And it was about the space of three hours after, when his wife, not knowing what was done, came in. [8]And Peter answered unto her, Tell me whether ye sold the land for so much? And she said, Yea, for so much. [9]Then Peter said unto her, How is it that ye have agreed together to tempt the Spirit of the Lord? behold, the feet of them which have buried thy husband *are* at the door, and shall carry thee out. [10]Then fell she down straightway at his feet, and yielded up the ghost: and the young

[1]Cf. Harrison, *op. cit.*, p. 93.

men came in, and found her dead, and, carrying *her* forth, buried *her* by her husband (Acts 5:1-10).

Ananias[2] kept back part[3] of the price for himself. Sapphira shared the knowledge of this and was therefore in accord with him and equally guilty. Then he brought a certain part of it and laid it at the apostles' feet, giving the impression he had done just as Barnabas had done.

Peter, acting as representative and spokesman for the 12 apostles, knew immediately what was done. He did not have spies out to report to him; but he had the Holy Spirit. Perhaps this was revealed to him through one of the gifts of revelation such as the Word of Wisdom or the Word of Knowledge.

Peter asked Ananias why Satan (the Satan, the Adversary)[4] had filled his heart to lie to the Holy Spirit and keep back for himself part of the price of the field. The question "why?" draws attention to the fact that their action was voluntary; there was no excuse for what they did. Before they sold it, it remained theirs, and they were under no compulsion to sell it. After it was sold, it was still in their power (authority). There was nothing compelling them to give it all. What he had conceived in his heart was a lie, not to men, but to God.

Satan was behind what Ananias and Sapphira did. It seems that because of their jealousy, unbelief, and love of money, the Spirit of the Lord was grieved, and they lost out with God. These things did not happen overnight. But by the time they conspired together Satan had filled their hearts (their whole inner beings) and there was no room for the Holy Spirit to remain there.

They could have resisted Satan (James 4:7). But they let pride, self, and the love of money possess them. The love of money is the root of all (kinds of) evil (1 Timothy 6:10). That is, once the love of money takes possession of a person, there is no evil that he cannot

---

[2]Ananias is used in the Greek Septuagint version for both Hananiah ("the Lord is gracious") and Ananiah ("the Lord protects"). Sapphira may mean a sapphire stone or may be an Aramaic word meaning fair or beautiful. Someone has said both names were too good for them.

[3]The same verb is translated "purloining" in Titus 2:10 (in the sense of stealing or embezzling). The Septuagint version of Joshua 7:1 uses it of Achan's sin. Unfortunately, it is not impossible for believers to become liars and deceivers.

[4]Compare Revelation 12:9, 10.

or will not do. With the love of money in control a person will do things he never would do otherwise, including murder and every other sin. It is clear also that if a person is filled with the love of money he cannot love God (Matthew 6:24).

Keeping back part of the land was also a sign of unbelief and failure to trust God fully. Perhaps they feared the Church might collapse and thought they had better save back a good portion in case that happened.

It is clear also that in lying to the Holy Spirit who was guiding the Church, the believers, and the apostles, they were lying to God. This comparison in verses 3 and 4 makes it clear that the Holy Spirit is a divine Person.

While Ananias was still listening to Peter, "falling down, he gave up the ghost." That is, he breathed out his last breath. This may seem severe punishment. It was indeed. But God brought this judgment near the beginning of the Church's history to let the Church know what He thinks of unbelief, greed, and self-seeking hypocrisy that lies to God. (See 1 Peter 4:17.) In times of beginnings God is often more severe.[5] When the sons of Aaron offered strange (foreign, heathen) fire before the Lord, fire came out from the Holy of Holies and struck them down (Leviticus 10:1, 2). After that the people were more careful to seek God for His way to do things.

When Israel first went into the promised land, Achan was made an example (Joshua, chapter 7). David first attempted to bring back the ark on a cart, just as the Philistines had sent it. A death resulted. The second time, he was careful to bring it on the shoulders of the Levites as God had commanded.

It should be emphasized also that Ananias' lie was premeditated. When he died great fear (including terror and awe) came on all who heard. They knew now that the Holy Spirit is a mighty power. He is indeed holy, and it does not pay to lie to Him. This undoubtedly kept others from the same kind of sin.

They did not wait long to bury people in those days. According to custom, the young men[6] quickly wrapped him up in a linen winding sheet, took him out of the city, and buried him.

---

[5]Cf. Hackett, *op. cit.,* pp. 76, 77.

[6]Younger men. Some consider these a class of younger men who assisted the elders of the Church. They were probably just some of the younger believers who were present.

About three hours later, Sapphira came in, not knowing what had happened to her husband. She obviously was looking for commendation and praise. Peter answered her inquiring look by asking her if she and her husband had sold the land for the amount he brought in. Peter thus gave her an opportunity to confess the truth. But she too lied.

Peter was just as severe with her. His question clearly indicated he knew she and her husband had agreed together to tempt the Holy Spirit (put Him to the test). They were deliberately trying to see how far they could go in disobedience without provoking God's wrath. (Compare Exodus 17:2; Numbers 15:30, 31; Deuteronomy 6:16; Luke 4:12.)

Then Peter directed her attention to the feet of the young men at the door who had now returned from burying her husband. They would carry her out too. Thus, by the same kind of miracle of divine judgment, Sapphira fell down immediately at Peter's feet and breathed out her last breath. The young men then came in, found her dead, carried her out, and buried her by Ananias. (They were probably laid in a niche in a tomb, either in a cave or in one hewed out of the hillside.)

Purified and Growing (5:11-16)

[11]And great fear came upon all the church, and upon as many as heard these things. [12]And by the hands of the apostles were many signs and wonders wrought among the people; (and they were all with one accord in Solomon's porch. [13]And of the rest durst no man join himself to them: but the people magnified them. [14]And believers were the more added to the Lord, multitudes both of men and women;) [15]insomuch that they brought forth the sick into the streets, and laid *them* on beds and couches, that at the least the shadow of Peter passing by might overshadow some of them. [16]There came also a multitude *out* of the cities round about unto Jerusalem, bringing sick folks, and them which were vexed with unclean spirits: and they were healed every one (Acts 5:11-16).

Once more it is emphasized that great fear came on the whole Church[7] and on all who heard these things. But the fear was a

[7]Congregation, assembly. The Greek word *(ekklesia)* was normally used in New Testament times for an assembly of free citizens. (See Acts 19:39; Ephesians 2:19.) Here it is used of all the believers in Jerusalem and the surrounding area. It shows that the believers now considered themselves a distinct body, though they still thought of themselves as Jews. It should be noted, however, that Greek-speaking Jews used the same word *(ekklesia)* for the congregation of Israel.

holy fear and did not split up the Church or hinder the work of God. Some people imagine we must lower God's standards for the Church to make progress in today's world. But this has never been true. The Church has always been strengthened when it catches a vision of the holiness of God.

The apostles continued to be full of the Spirit and power and kept right on doing many miraculous signs and supernatural wonders. These miracles were never done for display. Instead, they all pointed to the truth of the gospel and to the fact that Jesus cared about His people and their needs.

The Church also remained in one accord, meeting daily at the hours of prayer in Solomon's portico of the Temple (and probably overflowing into the Temple court beside it). The fear that resulted from the death of Ananias and Sapphira also affected the unbelievers, so that no one dared to join them.[8] That is, no unbelievers dared to mix in with the crowd of believers pretending to be one of them (perhaps out of curiosity or perhaps hoping to get an overflow of the blessings).

This did not mean, however, that the Church's growth was slowed down. When the people saw how God dealt with sin among the believers, they realized that the Church as a whole was pleasing God and held high standards of honesty and righteousness. Therefore they magnified them. The actual result was that more and more believers were added to the Lord (to the Lord Jesus, not just to the Church as an external body), multitudes (crowds) both of men and of women. It has been suggested that the number of believers was over 10,000 by this time.[9]

Because the believers had confidence in the Lord they brought the sick (including the lame, the crippled, and the infirm) out into the streets (into wide streets or into public squares) and laid them on beds (couches, litters) and couches (mattresses, mats), so that when Peter passed by even his shadow might overshadow some of them. That is, they believed the Lord would honor Peter's faith and theirs even if Peter was not able to stop and lay hands on each one of them.

---

[8]Harrison, *op. cit.,* p. 96, suggests it was the believers who did not dare join the apostles lest they be judged as Ananias and Sapphira were. But there is no evidence that there was any less fellowship with the apostles, thus this interpretation seems unlikely.

[9]Cf. Earle, *op. cit.,* p. 312.

The word of what God was doing spread into the surrounding towns of Judea. Soon, because of their newfound faith, a crowd came from these towns bringing the sick (including the diseased, the weak, the lame, and the crippled) and those who were vexed (tormented, troubled) by unclean spirits.[10] All of them, probably including those in verse 15, were healed. This was a critical point in the history of the Church, and God did special things.

Twelve Apostles Arrested (5:17-26)

[17]Then the high priest rose up, and all they that were with him, (which is the sect of the Sadducees,) and were filled with indignation, [18]and laid their hands on the apostles, and put them in the common prison. [19]But the angel of the Lord by night opened the prison doors, and brought them forth, and said, [20]Go, stand and speak in the temple to the people all the words of this life. [21]And when they heard *that,* they entered into the temple early in the morning, and taught.

But the high priest came, and they that were with him, and called the council together, and all the senate of the children of Israel, and sent to the prison to have them brought. [22]But when the officers came, and found them not in the prison, they returned, and told, [23]saying, The prison truly found we shut with all safety, and the keepers standing without before the doors: but when we had opened, we found no man within. [24]Now when the high priest and the captain of the temple and the chief priests heard these things, they doubted of them whereunto this would grow. [25]Then came one and told them, saying, Behold, the men whom ye put in prison are standing in the temple, and teaching the people. [26]Then went the captain with the officers, and brought them without violence: for they feared the people, lest they should have been stoned (Acts 5:17-26).

Once again the local Sadducees, including the high priest and his close friends, were upset. This time they were filled with indignation. The Greek word *(zeloo)* can mean zeal or enthusiasm in a good sense or it can mean the worst kind of jealousy. It is not hard to see how the word is used here. It also implies a party spirit and a zeal for their Sadducean teachings against the resurrection. We can be sure they hated to see the crowds gathering around the apostles.

Jealous indignation, then, caused these Sadducees to rise up

[10]As in the Gospels, the Bible makes a clear distinction between the sick and the demon possessed. Obviously, the majority of the sick were not demon possessed.

(go into action), arrest the apostles, and throw them into the common prison. "Common" here is actually an adverb meaning publicly. That is, this was done with a crowd looking on. Apparently the priests and Sadducees had become desperate. This time they dared to risk the disapproval of the crowds.

During the night an angel (the Greek does not have the article "the") of the Lord opened the prison doors and told the apostles to go and take their stand and keep on speaking in the Temple to the people all the words of this life, that is, the words that are life-giving to those who believe. (See John 6:68.) The gospel is more than a philosophy or a set of precepts. It, through the work of the Holy Spirit, gives life.

Because of this angel's command, they went early in the morning (at dawn) into the Temple and proceeded to teach publicly. This must have astonished the people who had seen them arrested and thrown into prison the night before. It must also have helped them to see that God was still with the apostles and behind their message.

Some time later that morning the high priest and his associates called the council (the Sanhedrin) together. This council is further identified as the whole Senate of the people of Israel.[11] This seems to mean that all 70 members were present.

It also implies that on the previous occasion when Peter and John were arrested (and on some other occasions such as the trial of Jesus) only those who were Sadducees under the domination of the high priest were called. This included the major portion of the Sanhedrin and constituted a quorum. But this time, because they knew they were going against most of the people in Jerusalem, they brought in the full body, expecting them to concur in their decision and uphold punishment of the apostles.

When they sent the officers (servants, attendants) to the prison to bring in the apostles, they were not there. Returning, the officers reported that they found the prison still shut with all safety (security), that is, with the doors still locked, and with the keepers (guards) standing by the doors. But, when they opened the doors they didn't find anyone inside.

These words caused the high priest and his associates to be in

[11]"And" in Greek sometimes means "even." This is the meaning in verse 21. The council and the senate are the same body.

doubt (and troubled) concerning them, wondering what would come of this. ("Grow" here translates a form of the Greek word for become, happen.) This also implies they wondered and were worried about what would happen next.

About this time someone arrived and reported that the men who were supposed to be in the prison were in the Temple, standing there openly and publicly teaching the people. Then the captain (commander of the Temple guard) went with the officers (servants, attendants of the Temple) and brought the Twelve without violence (without the use of force). They were careful because they were afraid the people would turn on them and stone them. They had dealt with mobs before and knew what a mob spirit and mob violence could do.

Actually, of course, they did not need to use force. The apostles went willingly even though they also knew they had but to say the word and the mob would have stoned these officers as blasphemers of God's servants and enemies of God. The apostles, however, undoubtedly hoped this arrest would become another opportunity to witness for their Messiah and Saviour.

The Verdict: Kill Them! (5:27-33)

[27]And when they had brought them, they set *them* before the council: and the high priest asked them, [28]saying, Did not we straitly command you that ye should not teach in this name? and, behold, ye have filled Jerusalem with your doctrine, and intend to bring this man's blood upon us. [29]Then Peter and the *other* apostles answered and said, We ought to obey God rather than men. [30]The God of our fathers raised up Jesus, whom ye slew and hanged on a tree. [31]Him hath God exalted with his right hand *to be* a Prince and a Saviour, for to give repentance to Israel, and forgiveness of sins. [32]And we are his witnesses of these things; and *so is* also the Holy Ghost, whom God hath given to them that obey him. [33]When they heard *that,* they were cut *to the heart,* and took counsel to slay them (Acts 5:27-33).

The high priest avoided asking the disciples how they got out of the prison. It was obviously something supernatural, and it may be he did not want to hear about angels he did not believe in. So, he began by asking the apostles if the Sanhedrin hadn't given them strict orders not to teach in this name (a derogatory reference to the Name of Jesus). Then he accused them of filling

Jerusalem with their doctrine (teaching), desiring to bring on the Jewish leaders "this man's blood."[12]

The statement that they had filled Jerusalem with their teaching was a great admission of the effectiveness of the apostles' witness. Yet the high priest totally misunderstood their purpose, probably because, in spite of himself, he felt guilty for what had been done to Jesus. Thus, the statement that the apostles wanted to bring vengeance on them for the death of Jesus was nothing but pure slander and was completely false.

Peter and the apostles (with Peter as the spokesman for all) did not apologize. Without hesitation they answered, "It is necessary to obey God rather than men (human beings). "Obey" here is a word used of obedience to one in authority as in Titus 3:1. With a consciousness of Christ's authority, they said the equivalent of: "We must obey." Before, in Acts 4:19, they said "you judge." But the Sanhedrin did not judge that the apostles were under divinely appointed necessity to spread the gospel. Therefore, the apostles had to declare themselves very strongly here.

Peter didn't hesitate to remind them how the God of their fathers (the covenant-keeping God, the God who gave the Promise to Abraham) raised up Jesus. Then, once again, he contrasted the way God treated Jesus with the way the Jewish leaders treated Him, hanging him on a tree.[13]

Contrary to their fears, it was not the apostles' desire nor was it God's purpose to punish them for this. Rather, God had exalted Jesus, the very One they crucified, with (to) His right hand to be a Prince (author, founder) and a Saviour, in order to give repentance (that is, the opportunity for repentance) to Israel and forgiveness of sins.

Peter, of course, does not mean to restrict this offer of forgiveness to Israel but simply to apply it to those to whom he was speaking. God's purpose was to give forgiveness and salvation to all sinners. Their guilt would be cancelled if they would repent. By exalting Jesus, God put Him in a position where it should be easy to repent or change their attitude toward Him.

---

[12]i.e., make us answerable for this man's death (murder). "This man" is another derogatory reference to Jesus. It also shows they wanted to avoid mentioning the name of Jesus if possible.

[13]The Greek word for "tree" also means wood or anything made of wood, and so includes the cross. The cross was made of rough-hewn wood.

As before, the apostles emphasized that they were Christ's witnesses to these things (these words; Greek *rhematon,* used of the "words" of this life in verse 20). Then Peter adds that so also is the Holy Spirit whom God has given (and still gives just as on the Day of Pentecost) to those who obey Him (recognizing His authority). He is the Giver (John 15:26, 27). It is quite clear that the giving of the Spirit was not to be limited to the apostles or to their time.

Apparently the majority of the Sanhedrin took Peter's words to mean that the apostles not only considered them guilty of Christ's death, but also guilty of a refusal to accept God's authority and obey Him. (The apostles did link their witness to the Spirit's witness.)[14] Thus, instead of accepting the offer of repentance,[15] they were cut to the heart (sawn through, cut through, cut to the quick with anger, indignation, and jealousy). Immediately they started proceedings to kill the apostles. (The same word for kill is used of killing Jesus in Acts 2:23.)

Gamaliel's Advice (5:34-42)

[34]Then stood there up one in the council, a Pharisee, named Gamaliel, a doctor of the law, had in reputation among all the people, and commanded to put the apostles forth a little space; [35]and said unto them, Ye men of Israel, take heed to yourselves what ye intend to do as touching these men. [36]For before these days rose up Theu'das, boasting himself to be somebody; to whom a number of men, about four hundred, joined themselves: who was slain; and all, as many as obeyed him were scattered, and brought to nought. [37]After this man rose up Judas of Galilee in the days of the taxing, and drew away much people after him: he also perished; and all, *even* as many as obeyed him, were dispersed. [38]And now I say unto you, Refrain from these men, and let them alone: for if this counsel or this work be of men, it will come to nought: [39]but if it be of God, ye cannot overthrow it; lest haply ye be found even to fight against God.

[40]And to him they agreed: and when they had called the apostles, and beaten *them,* they commanded that they should not speak in the name of Jesus, and let them go. [41]And they departed from the presence of the council, rejoicing that they were counted worthy to suffer shame for his name. [42]And daily in the temple, and in every house, they ceased not to teach and preach Jesus Christ (Acts 5:34-42).

---

[14]Cf. Guthrie, *op. cit.,* pp. 52, 53.

[15]See Matthew 3:7, 8. These leaders did not believe they needed repentance.

The ones who took the lead against the apostles were the Sadducees. But this time they had the entire Sanhedrin together; and it included some prominent Pharisees.[16] Among them was Gamaliel, a doctor (authoritative teacher) of the Law, valued highly by all the people. In the Jewish Talmud he is said to be the grandson of Hillel (the most influential teacher of the Pharisees, held in high esteem by all later orthodox Jews). Paul was trained by Gamaliel and became one of his most prominent students.[17]

Standing up, Gamaliel took charge of the situation and ordered that the apostles be taken outside for a little while. Then he proceeded to warn the Sanhedrin to be cautious about (and give careful attention to) what they were intending to do (or, were about to do) to these men.

By two examples he reminded them that individuals in the past had gathered a following, but came to nothing. The first example was Theudas who said of himself that he was something.[18] Theudas was a common name, and he was probably one of the rebels who arose after Herod the Great died in 4 B.C. (Josephus speaks of another Theudas who came later.) To this Theudas about 400 men attached themselves. He was murdered, and all who obeyed him (and believed in him) were dispersed and came to nothing.

After Theudas, Judas the Galilean rose up in the days of the taxing (the census for the purpose of taxing).[19] He drew away a considerable number of people after him. But he also perished, and all who obeyed him were scattered.

Gamaliel's conclusion was that they should refrain (withdraw) from these men and leave them alone (let them go), for if this counsel or this work was from (out from) men it would come to

---

[16]"Pharisees" probably means "separated ones," possibly referring to their emphasis on washings and ceremonial purity.

[17]Sadducees dominated the Temple and priesthood at this time. But Pharisees had the most influence in the synagogues and among the majority of the Jews. Pharisees were generally careful not to exceed the demands of justice in administering the Law. Cf. Harrison, *op. cit.*, p. 101.

[18]Codex Bezae (D) has "something great."

[19]The Romans ordered the first census of the people and their property in 10-9 B.C.; it reached Palestine about 6 B.C. (Luke 2:2). There was another census every 14 years after that. The second census reached Palestine, however, in A.D. 6 when this Judas arose and, according to Josephus, taught the people not to pay tribute to Caesar.

naught (be overthrown, be destroyed). But if it was from God they would not be able to overthrow it (or them), "lest also you be found (be proved unexpectedly to be) fighting against God."[20]

We must keep in mind that this was a Pharisee saying. That is, the inspired record makes it clear that Gamaliel said this; his recorded words were the conclusions of his own thinking, human reasoning, not God's truth. It is true, of course, that what is from God cannot be overthrown. It is true also that it is foolish to try to use physical means to overthrow spiritual forces. But it is not true that everything from men is soon overthrown and its followers scattered. There are many heathen religions, false doctrines, and modern cults that maintain a following after many years. The judgments at the end of this age will bring them all to an end, and the things of God will continue.

We must be careful not to press the words of Gamaliel too far, however. His words did have their effect on the Sanhedrin and the rulers were persuaded (convinced) by him.

Then they called in the apostles and severely flogged them (with whips that took skin off their backs). The Greek word can actually mean "skinned." Thus the council still took out their spite and indignation on the apostles, probably by the usual 39 stripes. (See 2 Corinthians 11:24; Deuteronomy 25:3). (Jesus had warned them this would happen, Mark 13:9.) Then the council commanded (ordered) them not to speak in the name of Jesus and let them go (set them free).

They went away from the presence of the Sanhedrin rejoicing because they were counted worthy to suffer disgrace for the sake of the Name. That is, they suffered for the sake of all that the Name of Jesus, and therefore His character and nature, includes, especially His Messiahship, deity, saviourhood, and Lordship. (See Philippians 2:9, 10.)

The opposition of the Jewish leaders subsided for a time and the apostles were free to continue their ministry. Every day in the Temple and from house to house they never ceased teaching and preaching the good news (the gospel) of Jesus Christ (the Messiah Jesus). They boldly defied the orders of the Sanhedrin and paid no attention to their threats.

[20]One word in the Greek, "God-fighting," or "God-fighters."

ACTS

CHAPTER 6

Acts 4 tells of the first attack on the Church from the outside. Acts 5 describes an attack from the inside. In both cases the Church kept growing. Now we see in Acts 6 that the number of the disciples (learners, those believers desiring to learn more about Jesus and the gospel) was still multiplying.

The Seven Chosen (6:1-7)

> [1]And in those days, when the number of the disciples were multiplied, there arose a murmuring of the Grecians against the Hebrews, because their widows were neglected in the daily ministration. [2]Then the twelve called the multitude of the disciples *unto them,* and said, It is not reason that we should leave the word of God, and serve tables. [3]Wherefore, brethren, look ye out among you seven men of honest report, full of the Holy Ghost and wisdom, whom we may appoint over this business. [4]But we will give ourselves continually to prayer, and to the ministry of the word.
>
> [5]And the saying pleased the whole multitude: and they chose Stephen, a man full of faith and of the Holy Ghost, and Philip, and Prochorus, and Nicanor, and Timon, and Parmenas, and Nicolas a proselyte of Antioch; [6]whom they set before the apostles: and when they had prayed, they laid *their* hands on them. [7]And the word of God increased; and the number of the disciples multiplied in Jerusalem greatly; and a great company of the priests were obedient to the faith (Acts 6:1-7).

What happens when a community of people grows? All those newcomers crowding in cause problems. In this case the growing Church was a cross section of society as it was in Jerusalem and Judea. Some of them were born there and spoke Hebrew[1] in their

---

[1]Most take this to mean Aramaic, though there is evidence that Jerusalem Jews kept alive the Biblical Hebrew.

homes; they knew Greek as a second language, for Greek had been the language of trade, commerce, and the government since the days of Alexander the Great. However, the Jews born outside of Palestine did not know Hebrew well and normally spoke in Greek. Since they represented many countries, Greek was the one language they all understood.

In previous chapters we saw that believers contributed to a common fund for the benefit of the needy. As time went on, most people found jobs and no longer needed this help. Widows, however, could not go out and get a job. It was not uncommon in those days, especially among the Gentiles, for widows to starve to death.[2] Thus, by the time this chapter begins, the widows were the only ones left who needed help from this fund. Apparently, those believers who could still brought money to the apostles for the fund; the apostles were responsible to see that the widows' needs were supplied.

Tension probably built up for some time between the Greek-speaking and Hebrew-speaking believers before it began to surface. Language is always a serious barrier between peoples. It is easy for a minority group to feel neglected, especially if they do not understand the language. In fact, their inability to understand could have caused the Greek-speaking widows to hold back and so be easily overlooked.

Finally, a murmuring (a grumbling half under their breath) arose among the Greek-speaking believers against the Hebrew-speaking believers because their widows were being neglected (overlooked) in the daily ministration.[3]

Then the Twelve (the apostles, including Matthias) called the multitude (the whole mass) of the disciples to themselves and told them it was not reason (pleasing, satisfactory, acceptable) for them to leave (abandon) (teaching and preaching of) the Word of God to serve[4] tables (money tables).

---

[2]The Law of Moses shows God's special concern for widows and others who had no one to help them. (See Exodus 22:22-24; Deuteronomy 10:18. See also 1 Timothy 5:3-16.)

[3]Greek, *diakonia,* "service." Codex Bezae (D) adds that it was administered by the Hebrew speakers.

[4]Greek, *diakonein*; a verb used in early Greek of keeping wine glasses full by a special waiter called a *diakonos* (deacon). In New Testament times the verb was used of any type of serving.

They told the believers to look out from among themselves seven men full of the Holy Spirit and practical wisdom. These the apostles would appoint (set) over this business (need). In other words, the apostles laid down the qualifications and the people looked over the congregation to see who had these qualifications in a high degree. Then the people chose the seven through some kind of an election. "Appoint" means simply "put in charge." This was not arbitrary appointment. The congregation did the choosing, not the apostles.

The seven are not called deacons here, though the verb is a form of *diakoneo,* from which deacon is derived. Most probably, this election gave precedent for what we find as an office in the church later. (See 1 Timothy 3:8-12; Romans 16:1, where Phoebe is a deacon, not deaconess.)

Some see a special significance in the number seven here. It may signify a "complete" number. More likely the only reason for having seven was because seven were needed to keep the accounts and give out the money to the widows. (The Greek word for tables in this passage means money tables.)

Choosing the seven enabled the apostles to give themselves to prayer and the ministry (ministration)[5] of the Word. That is, the apostles served the Word, dished out the Word, while the seven dished out the money.

There was no dissent to this for the saying (word, *logos*) pleased the multitude (of the believers). They proceeded to choose out Stephen (Greek for "victor's crown or wreath"), a man full of faith and the Holy Spirit; Philip (Greek for "lover of horses"); Prochorus; Nicanor; Timon; Parmenas; and Nicolas, a proselyte (Gentile convert to Judaism) from Antioch (of Syria).[6]

All of these have Greek names and were undoubtedly from among the Greek-speaking believers. Surely this shows the grace of God and the work of the Holy Spirit in the hearts of the Hebrew-speaking believers. They were in the majority, but they chose all the "deacons" out of the minority group. These seven would have charge of the administration of the fund for the needy for both groups. Thus, no possible complaint could be lodged by the Greek-speaking believers any more.

---

[5]Greek, *diakonia,* the same word used in verse 1.

[6]Later traditions tried to connect this Nicolas with the Nicolaitans of Revelation 2:6, 15; but there is no real evidence for this.

This was wisdom. It also shows how the Holy Spirit broke down this first barrier that rose up in the Church. The people stood the seven before the apostles, who laid their hands on them. This laying on of hands was probably like the public recognition of Joshua in Numbers 27:18, 19. It did not confer anything spiritual on him for he was already a man "in whom is the Spirit." But it inaugurated a new level of service. Stephen and the others were all full of the Spirit before this. The laying on of hands also symbolized prayer for God's blessing on them. They probably prayed also that the Spirit would give them whatever gifts and graces would be necessary to carry out this ministry.

Luke concludes this incident with another summary statement saying that the Word of God increased (kept on growing). That is, the proclaiming of the Word increased, implying that not only the apostles were involved in spreading it. The number of disciples kept on multiplying (increasing) in Jerusalem and a large crowd of priests were obedient to the faith also.[7] Their acceptance of the gospel and obedience to the teaching of the apostles was a major breakthrough, since most of the priests were Sadducees who did not believe in the resurrection.[8] These priests probably continued in their priestly office, since the Jewish Christians were all faithful to the worship in the Temple.

Stephen Accused (6:8-15)

[8]And Stephen, full of faith and power, did great wonders and miracles among the people. [9]Then there arose certain of the synagogue, which is called *the synagogue* of the Libertines, and Cyrenians, and Alexandrians, and of them of Cili'cia and of Asia, disputing with Stephen. [10]And they were not able to resist the wisdom and the spirit by which he spake. [11]Then they suborned men, which said, We have heard him speak blasphemous words against Moses, and *against* God. [12]And they stirred up the people, and the elders, and the scribes, and came upon *him,* and caught him, and brought *him* to the council, [13]and set up false witnesses, which said, This man ceaseth not to speak blasphemous words against this holy place, and the law: [14]for we have heard him say, that this Jesus of Nazareth shall destroy this place, and shall change the customs which

[7]Josephus said there were 20,000 priests in that time.

[8]Some say that those priests who were converted did not include any of the Sadducees but were humble priests like the father of John the Baptist. Cf. Harrison, *op. cit.,* p. 107.

Moses delivered us. [15]And all that sat in the council, looking steadfastly on him, saw his face as it had been the face of an angel (Acts 6:8-15).

The fact that the seven (deacons) were chosen to carry out a rather routine service did not limit their ministry. Stephen, full of faith (or grace)[9] and mighty power, began to do (and kept on doing) wonders and great signs among the people. The people were not merely spectators but experienced the miracles as God's gifts to meet their needs.[10]

This is the first time we read of miracles being done by those who were not apostles. The important thing, however, is that the Holy Spirit was working through Stephen. The supernatural power of the Spirit was doing the work.

Soon opposition arose. This time it came from Greek-speaking Jews, who, like Stephen, had returned to live in Jerusalem. They had their own synagogue (or synagogues),[11] and included Jews who were Libertines (freedmen, probably taken as slaves to Rome and later set free by their Roman masters). Some were Cyrenians (from Cyrene, west of Egypt on the Mediterranean coast) and Alexandrians (from Alexandria in Egypt). Others were from Cilicia (Paul's home province in southeastern Asia Minor) and from the province of Asia (in western Asia Minor).

Most of these Jews in the dispersion had to face many threats to their teaching, living as they did, surrounded by Gentiles. Thus, they were quicker to defend themselves against anything different from what their rabbis taught them. But, though they kept trying to dispute (or debate with) Stephen, they did not have the strength or power to stand against the wisdom and the Spirit by which he was speaking. In other words, Stephen was not depending on his own wisdom, but on the anointing and gifts of the Holy Spirit. No wonder all their arguments fell flat!

In spite of this, they still refused to believe and were determined to stop Stephen. So they suborned men (obtained them in

[9]Grace rather than faith seems to be the correct reading here. Stephen was both the recipient and the channel of God's grace (unmerited favor).

[10]Codex Bezae (D) and some other ancient manuscripts and versions add that he did these miracles through the name of the Lord Jesus Christ.

[11]The word is singular, but many take it as distributive and apply it to each group, for Jewish tradition says there were a great many synagogues in Jerusalem at this time. Cf. Bruce, *op. cit.*, p. 153; Harrison, *op. cit.*, p. 109; Earle, *op. cit.*, p. 328.

some unfair way) who said they had heard him speaking blasphemous (abusive, scurrilous) words against Moses and against God. Probably what they did was twist and misinterpret the teachings of Jesus which Stephen repeated. Jesus was also accused of blasphemy.[12]

Then they stirred up the people (violently) and also the elders and scribes (experts in the law). With all these supporting them, they came upon Stephen (suddenly and unexpectedly), caught him (took hold of him violently and kept a firm grip on him), and brought him to the council (the Sanhedrin, or the place where the Sanhedrin was meeting).

Then they set up false witnesses, witnesses who misrepresented the words of Stephen in a false and misleading way, putting them in as bad a light as possible. These took the stand and said that this man did not cease to speak words against this holy place (the Temple) and against the Law (of Moses). They also claimed they heard Stephen say that Jesus the Nazarene[13] will destroy (break up) this place and will change the customs (including the rites and institutions) which Moses delivered (handed down) to us. This, of course, refers to Matthew 26:61, Mark 14:58, and John 2:19-21 where Jesus was really speaking of the temple of His body and of His death and resurrection. (See also Mathew 12:42 where Jesus said, "A greater than Solomon is here.")

At this point all those who were seated in the Sanhedrin fixed their eyes on him and saw his face as if it were the face of an angel. This probably means there was a glow or brightness that was more than human and came from heaven. Possibly this was similar to Moses when he came down from the presence of God in the mountain, or perhaps like Jesus when he was transfigured and the inner glory showed through.

---

[12]Cf. Bruce, *op. cit.,* pp. 134, 135.

[13]Or, "this 'Jesus the Nazarene.' " "This" is used in a contemptuous way here.

ACTS

CHAPTER 7

The high priest (probably Caiaphas) gave Stephen opportunity to respond to the charges by asking if these things were so.

JOSEPH REJECTED (7:1-16)

[1]Then said the high priest, Are these things so? [2]And he said, Men, brethren, and fathers, hearken; The God of glory appeared unto our father Abraham, when he was in Mesopotamia, before he dwelt in Haran, [3]and said unto him, Get thee out of thy country, and from thy kindred, and come into the land which I shall show thee. [4]Then came he out of the land of the Chaldeans, and dwelt in Haran: and from thence, when his father was dead, he removed him into this land, wherein ye now dwell. [5]And he gave him none inheritance in it, no, not *so much as* to set his foot on: yet he promised that he would give it to him for a possession, and to his seed after him, when *as yet* he had no child. [6]And God spake on this wise, That his seed should sojourn in a strange land; and that they should bring them into bondage, and entreat *them* evil four hundred years. [7]And the nation to whom they shall be in bondage will I judge, said God: and after that shall they come forth, and serve me in this place. [8]And he gave him the covenant of circumcision: and so *Abraham* begat Isaac, and circumcised him the eighth day; and Isaac *begat* Jacob; and Jacob *begat* the twelve patriarchs.

[9]And the patriarchs, moved with envy, sold Joseph into Egypt: but God was with him, [10]and delivered him out of all his afflictions, and gave him favor and wisdom in the sight of Pharaoh king of Egypt; and he made him governor over Egypt and all his house. [11]Now there came a dearth over all the land of Egypt and Canaan, and great affliction: and our fathers found no sustenance. [12]But when Jacob heard that there was corn in Egypt, he sent out our fathers first. [13]And at the second *time* Joseph was made known to his brethren; and Joseph's kindred was made known unto Pharaoh. [14]Then sent Joseph, and called his father Jacob to *him,* and all his kindred, threescore and fifteen souls. [15]So Jacob went down into Egypt, and died, he, and our fathers, [16]and were carried over

into Shechem, and laid in the sepulchre that Abraham bought for a sum of money of the sons of Hamor, *the father* of Shechem (Acts 7:1-16).

After politely addressing the Sanhedrin, Stephen began a review of the history of Israel, a history they all knew well. His purpose was to defend the gospel against false charges and to show a parallel between the way Old Testament Jews treated their prophets and the way the Jewish leaders treated Jesus.

He reminds them how the God of glory (the God who revealed himself in glory) appeared to Abraham while he was in Mesopotamia (in Ur of the Chaldees)[1] before he lived in Charran (a spelling of Haran that is closer to the Hebrew pronunciation). The Book of Genesis does not mention this word to Abraham in Ur, but Nehemiah 9:7 confirms that he received it.

God commanded him to go out of his country and from his kinsmen (relatives, countrymen) and come into the land (whatever land) God would show him.[2] After stopping in Haran until his father died,[3] he transported himself into the land which later became Israel's. But God gave him no inheritance in it, not even the space covered by a footstep. Yet God, while Abraham still had no child, promised to give it to him and to his descendants for a (permanent) possession. He accepted the promise and put his life in God's hand.

God also spoke of Abraham's descendants living temporarily as resident aliens in a land belonging to others who would make them slaves and treat them badly 400 years.[4] But He also promised to judge the nation that made them slaves. After that they would come out and serve (worship) God in this place (the promised land).

---

[1]Some archaeologists, such as Cyrus Gordon, believe this was a northern Ur rather than the Ur east of Babylon. There is some evidence that the Chaldeans did come from the north and did not come into Babylonia until after Abraham's time.

[2]Stephen is using the language of the Greek Septuagint version.

[3]Terah's age given in Genesis 11:26 is his age at the birth of his eldest son. Abraham was actually born years later but is mentioned first because he was the most important.

[4]See Genesis 15:13, 14 in the Greek Septuagint version. Four hundred is a round number here and is given exactly as 430 in Exodus 12:40, 41. Paul seems to understand the 430 years as including all the time from Abraham to Moses (Galatians 3:17).

Another thing God gave Abraham was the covenant of circumcision, so that Isaac was circumcised the eighth day after his birth. Then came Jacob and the 12 patriarchs (tribal heads or tribal rulers).[5] These, moved with envy, sold Joseph into Egypt. But God was with him. God delivered him out of all his afflictions (distressing circumstances) and gave him favor and wisdom before Pharaoh and made him governor (leader, leading man) over Egypt and all Pharaoh's household (including all his business affairs). (Stephen here is making a strong contrast between the way Joseph's brothers treated him and the way God treated him.)

When the famine came and great affliction (distress), the patriarchs (now identified as "our fathers") found no food. Jacob, hearing there was wheat[6] (or, bread) in Egypt sent them there. The second time they came, Joseph made himself known and revealed his race to Pharaoh. Then Joseph sent for Jacob and all his relatives, 75 souls (persons).[7] So Jacob went down and died, as did the fathers (Jacob's sons) and they were transferred to Shechem and placed in the tomb bought for a price of silver from the sons of Emmor (Hamor), the father of Shechem (Genesis 33:19).[8]

In all this there is a subtle emphasis on the way Joseph was sold by his jealous brothers yet was used by God to save their lives. There is also emphasis on the faith of Abraham who believed God's promise even when he saw absolutely no evidence that it would be fulfilled.

These members of the Sanhedrin were refusing to believe God even though He had provided evidence of the fulfillment of His promise through the resurrection of Jesus. The treatment of Joseph by the brothers and the contrast to the way God treated him also parallels the way the Jewish leaders had treated Jesus.

---

[5]The emphasis here is that they were all born under the covenant of circumcision. This was a change from the situation before Abraham.

[6]"Corn" is old English for grain. The Hebrew means both wheat and bread.

[7]The Greek Septuagint gives 75 in Genesis 46:27; Exodus 1:5; and in some copies of Deuteronomy 10:22. The Hebrew has the round number 70.

[8]The reference here is to the burial of the 12 patriarchs. Jacob was buried in Machpelah near Hebron (Genesis 23:17, 19; 50:13). Joseph was buried in Shechem (Joshua 24:32). Stephen believed the other brothers were also buried there. Genesis 33:19 and Joshua 24:32 indicate Jacob did the actual buying. However, Abraham was still alive and it was undoubtedly done in the name of the head of the clan.

MOSES REJECTED (7:17-37)

[17]But when the time of the promise drew nigh, which God had sworn to Abraham, the people grew and multiplied in Egypt, [18]till another king arose, which knew not Joseph. [19]The same dealt subtilely with our kindred, and evil entreated our fathers, so that they cast out their young children, to the end they might not live. [20]In which time Moses was born, and was exceeding fair, and nourished up in his father's house three months: [21]and when he was cast out, Pharaoh's daughter took him up, and nourished him for her own son. [22]And Moses was learned in all the wisdom of the Egyptians, and was mighty in words and in deeds.

[23]And when he was full forty years old, it came into his heart to visit his brethren the children of Israel. [24]And seeing one *of them* suffer wrong, he defended *him,* and avenged him that was oppressed, and smote the Egyptian: [25]for he supposed his brethren would have understood how that God by his hand would deliver them; but they understood not. [26]And the next day he showed himself unto them as they strove, and would have set them at one again, saying, Sirs, ye are brethren; why do ye wrong one to another? [27]But he that did his neighbor wrong thrust him away, saying, Who made thee a ruler and a judge over us? [28]Wilt thou kill me, as thou didst the Egyptian yesterday? [29]Then fled Moses at this saying, and was a stranger in the land of Midian, where he begat two sons.

[30]And when forty years were expired, there appeared to him in the wilderness of mount Sinai an angel of the Lord in a flame of fire in a bush. [31]When Moses saw *it,* he wondered at the sight: and as he drew near to behold *it,* the voice of the Lord came unto him, [32]*saying,* I *am* the God of thy fathers, the God of Abraham and the God of Isaac, and the God of Jacob. Then Moses trembled, and durst not behold. [33]Then said the Lord to him, Put off thy shoes from thy feet: for the place where thou standest is holy ground. [34]I have seen, I have seen the affliction of my people which is in Egypt, and I have heard their groaning, and am come down to deliver them. And now come, I will send thee into Egypt.

[35]This Moses whom they refused, saying, Who made thee a ruler and a judge? the same did God send *to be* a ruler and a deliverer by the hand of the angel which appeared to him in the bush. [36]He brought them out, after that he had showed wonders and signs in the land of Egypt, and in the Red sea, and in the wilderness forty years. [37]This is that Moses, which said unto the children of Israel, A Prophet shall the Lord your God raise up into you of your brethren, like unto me; him shall ye hear (Acts 7:17-37).

Stephen next recounts the way the Israelites grew and multiplied in Egypt as the time came for the fulfillment of the promise God had sworn to Abraham (the promise that his descendants would possess the land of Canaan).

This increase continued until a king arose (belonging to a new dynasty) who did not know Joseph. He victimized Israel by trickery and treated the Israelites badly. He even cast out (exposed) their infants so they would not live. ("Cast out" is a term used for exposing babies in some place where the elements or wild animals would cause them to die.)

At this time Moses was born and was exceeding fair, literally, fair (lovely, fine) to God. This may mean he was made so by God or considered so by God. But we know God was with Moses from his birth. God's care was shown when Moses was exposed after three months in his father's house. Pharaoh's daughter took him up and reared him as a son for herself. Thus Moses was learned (trained, educated) in all the wisdom of Egypt and was mighty (powerful) in his words and deeds. This was significant, for Egyptians had already made great advances in science, engineering, mathematics, astronomy, and medicine.

At the age of 40 Moses desired to visit (look after, take care of, relieve, protect) his Israelite brothers. Seeing one being injured unjustly, he defended him, avenged (did justice to) the ill-treated one, and struck the Egyptian.

This was Stephen's point in this part of the history. Moses did this because he supposed his Israelite brothers would understand that God, by his hand, would give them deliverance,[9] but they did not. Stephen saw a clear parallel here to the way the Jewish leaders failed to understand what God had done through Jesus in providing salvation. Their rejection of Jesus was nothing against Him, either, since their fathers for a time rejected Moses.

Continuing the history, Stephen reminded them how Moses wanted to reconcile fighting Israelites and have them at peace and said, "Men, you are brothers, why do you harm (injure unfairly) each other?" But the one harming his neighbor repelled Moses saying, "Who made you a ruler and a judge over us? Do you want to kill me the way you killed the Egyptian yesterday?"

At this, Moses fled and was a resident alien in Midian where his two sons were born. When 40 years had passed an angel of the Lord[10] appeared to him in the desert of Mount Sinai in the flame

[9]Greek, *soterian,* salvation, a word that is used of deliverance, health, well-being, as well as salvation.

[10]That is, the Angel of the Lord, a manifestation of God himself, or rather of the preincarnate Son. Note that He is distinguished as a separate person, and yet is identified with God. Jesus is and has always been the one Mediator between God the Father and man. Cf. Lenski, *op. cit.,* pp. 280, 281.

of fire in a thorn bush. Moses was amazed at the sight. As he drew near (out of curiosity) to look at it, God spoke, declaring himself to be the God of Abraham, Isaac, and Jacob. Then Moses trembled and did not dare look (take notice). The Lord told him to take off his shoes for the place where he was standing was holy ground (even though it was far from the promised land). God had definitely seen[11] the ill treatment of His people in Egypt and heard their groaning. He had come down now to deliver them; He would send Moses to Egypt.

Stephen then emphasizes his main point in this part of the history. This Moses whom they refused (denied, rejected), God sent with the hand (power) of the Angel who appeared to him in the thorn bush, to be a ruler and a deliverer (ransomer, liberator; originally used of those who paid a ransom to liberate slaves or prisoners).

After showing wonders and signs in Egypt and in the wilderness, he brought them out. Then, as a climax to this section, Stephen reminds them that this was the same Moses (the Moses whom they rejected and God used to save them out of Egypt) who told the Israelites God would raise up a prophet for them like himself. Him they should hear (listen to and obey.)

The Jewish leaders knew how the apostles applied this passage about the prophet like unto Moses: All the believing Jews applied it to Jesus. Stephen was saying that by not listening to Jesus they were disobeying God and treating Moses with contempt.[12]

Rejecting God (7:38-43)

[38]This is he, that was in the church in the wilderness with the angel which spake to him in the mount Sinai, and *with* our fathers: who received the lively oracles to give unto us: [39]to whom our fathers would not obey, but thrust *him* from them, and in their hearts turned back again into Egypt, [40]saying unto Aaron, Make us gods to go before us: for *as for* this Moses, which brought us out of the land of Egypt, we wot not what is become of him. [41]And they made a calf in those days, and offered sacrifice unto the idol, and rejoiced in the works of their own hands.

[42]Then God turned, and gave them up to worship the host of heaven; as it is written in the book of the prophets, O ye house of Israel, have ye

[11]"I have seen, I have seen"; a Hebrew way of giving emphasis. Here it draws attention to the faithfulness of God.

[12]Cf. Hackett, *op. cit.,* p. 100.

offered to me slain beasts and sacrifices *by the space of* forty years in the wilderness? [43]Yea, ye took up the tabernacle of Moloch, and the star of your god Remphan, figures which ye made to worship them: and I will carry you away beyond Babylon (Acts 7:38-43).

Stephen in this section goes on to an even worse rejection, a rejection of God. Again he speaks of Moses. Moses was in the church (congregation, assembly, Greek, *ekklesia*) in the wilderness with the angel that spoke to him on Mount Sinai and with all the fathers.[13] He received (and welcomed) the living oracles (divine utterances) given to Israel. But the fathers, refusing to become obedient to him, rejected him and in their hearts turned back to Egypt. They showed this by asking Aaron to make gods to go before them. They despised Moses by saying in a derogatory way, as for *this* Moses who brought us out of Egypt, we don't know what has become of him (Exodus 32:1). Then they made (an image of) a calf[14] and sacrificed to the idol (image) and rejoiced (made merry, revelled) in the works of their own hands.

Because this was a rejection, not merely of Moses, but of God, God turned and gave them up (handed them over) to the worship of (to serve) the host of heaven. They received the consequences due to them because of their action. Stephen saw this confirmed in Amos 5:25-27. His quotation shows that the Israelites in the wilderness did not really offer their sacrifices to the Lord during the remainder of the 40 years in the wilderness. They apparently did go through the forms, but the idolatry that began there continued to tempt Israel (and did so until they went into exile in Babylonia). Thus, even in the wilderness after seeing God's glory, they took up the tabernacle (tent) of Moloch (a Venus god worshiped by the Ammonites and several other Semitic peoples). What a contrast to the tabernacle of witness mentioned in verse 44! They also worshiped the star of the god Remphan (probably the Assyrian name for the planet Saturn, called Chiun in Amos 5:26). Both were figures (images) they made for themselves to worship. (These images were probably small images carried se-

[13]The repeated mention of the fathers of Israel (in this case, the tribes in the wilderness) prepares for the conclusion in verse 51.

[14]Many believe that this calf was a small golden bull but was called a calf because of its small size.

cretly by these Israelites.) As a result, God told Israel He would transport them beyond Babylon.[15]

From this also we see that Stephen is saying that it was their fathers who rejected Moses and the Law, thereby rebelling against the God who gave the Law. Though Stephen does not say so, they knew Jesus was not like that. The Fathers of Israel, not Jesus, had been the ones who wanted to change the laws, customs, and teachings given by Moses.

THE TEMPLE INSUFFICIENT (7:44-50)

[44]Our fathers had the tabernacle of witness in the wilderness, as he had appointed, speaking unto Moses, that he should make it according to the fashion that he had seen. [45]Which also our fathers that came after brought in with Joshua into the possession of the Gentiles, whom God drave out before the face of our fathers, unto the days of David; [46]who found favor before God, and desired to find a tabernacle for the God of Jacob. [47]But Solomon built him a house. [48]Howbeit the Most High dwelleth not in temples made with hands; as saith the prophet, [49]Heaven *is* my throne, and earth *is* my footstool: what house will ye build me? saith the Lord: or what *is* the place of my rest? [50]Hath not my hand made all these things? (Acts 7:44-50).

Now Stephen goes on to answer their accusation concerning what he said about the Temple. He does not try to explain what Jesus really meant by "destroy this temple." Instead, he reminds them that the Fathers had the tabernacle (tent) of witness (of the testimony), so called because it contained the ark of the covenant with the two tables (tablets) of stone which were a testimony (or witness) to the covenant between God and His people. This tent God had appointed (commanded), telling Moses to make it according to the fashion (pattern) he had seen (Exodus 25:9, 40; 26:30; 27:8).

The next generation of the Fathers received it in their turn and brought it in with Joshua (Jesus is the Greek form of Joshua, as in Hebrews 4:8) into what was previously the possession of the nations whom God drove out before the fathers until the days of David. That is, the tabernacle lasted until the days of David.

David found favor before God and personally desired to find a

[15]Stephen here is condensing the account. Amos said beyond Damascus. Stephen is thinking of the later deportation to the east of Babylon which was also prophesied.

tabernacle (a permanent dwelling) for the God of Jacob.[16] But it was Solomon who built Him a house. Then Stephen declared that the Most High does not dwell (permanently) in what is made by hands.

To prove this Stephen quoted Isaiah 66:1 and part of verse 2. There, God told Isaiah that heaven is His throne and the earth His footstool. What house could they build Him, or what was the place of His rest? Or, in what place could God settle down and make it His permanent abode?[17] Had He not made all these things?

Stephen was not denying that God had manifested His presence in the Temple. But, like the prophets, he saw that the God who created the heavens and the earth cannot be limited to any earthly building or Temple. Actually, Solomon agreed with this. (See 1 Kings 8:27; 2 Chronicles 6:1, 2, 18. See also Isaiah 57:15.)

The Holy Spirit Rejected (7:51-60)

[51]Ye stiffnecked and uncircumcised in heart and ears, ye do always resist the Holy Ghost: as your fathers *did,* so *do* ye. [52]Which of the prophets have not your fathers persecuted? and they have slain them which showed before of the coming of the Just One; of whom ye have been now the betrayers and murderers: [53]who have received the law by the disposition of angels, and have not kept *it.*

[54]When they heard these things, they were cut to the heart, and they gnashed on him with *their* teeth. [55]But he, being full of the Holy Ghost, looked up steadfastly into heaven, and saw the glory of God, and Jesus standing on the right hand of God, [56]and said, Behold, I see the heavens opened, and the Son of man standing on the right hand of God. [57]Then they cried out with a loud voice, and stopped their ears and ran upon him with one accord, [58]and cast *him* out of the city, and stoned *him:* and the witnesses laid down their clothes at a young man's feet, whose name was Saul. [59]And they stoned Stephen, calling upon *God,* and saying, Lord Jesus, receive my spirit. [60]And he kneeled down, and cried with a loud voice, Lord, lay not this sin to their charge. And when he had said this, he fell asleep (Acts 7:51-60).

Stephen apparently saw that his message was not being accepted. Possibly there was angry whispering among his hearers. He therefore rebuked them. They were stiffnecked (stubborn)

---

[16]Several ancient manuscripts have "the house of Jacob."

[17]Rest also suggests the ceasing of activity. Where would God do this? As Isaiah 40:28 shows, God is never weary.

and uncircumcised in heart and ears. (See Leviticus 26:41; Deuteronomy 10:16; 30:6; Jeremiah 6:10; 9:26; Ezekiel 44:7.) That is, their attitude and their refusal to listen to the gospel put them in the same class as the Gentiles who were outside God's covenant and were rejecting Him. They were hearing, thinking, and planning in the way unbelieving Gentiles did.

In fact, these Jewish leaders were actively resisting the Holy Spirit just as their fathers had. None of the prophets escaped persecution by the Fathers. (See Matthew 5:11, 12; 23:30, 31.) They killed those who announced beforehand the coming of the Just One (the righteous One). It was He they had now betrayed and murdered. In fact, their guilt was greater than those who killed the prophets. These Jewish leaders who rejected Jesus had received the Law which was given by the disposition (ordaining, ordinance) of angels.[18] But they did not keep (observe) it. That is, the Jewish leaders, not Jesus, nor the Christians, had disregarded the Law in killing Jesus.

This rebuke cut (sawed through) to the heart, and these dignified Sanhedrin members gnashed (crunched) their teeth over Stephen. By this expression of rage and exasperation they only proved they were truly resisting the Holy Spirit. In contrast to them, Stephen, being still full of the Holy Spirit, fixed his gaze into heaven and saw the glory of God and Jesus standing at the right hand of God (in the place of authority). Other passages speak of Jesus seated at the right hand of God (Mark 14:62; Luke 22:69). This seems to indicate that Jesus rose to welcome the first martyr who gave a witness at the cost of his life. Note, too, that Stephen used the term the Sanhedrin had heard Jesus use so often of himself, "the Son of man."

Hearing this, the Sanhedrin cried out (shrieked) with a loud voice, put their hands over their ears to shut out Stephen's words, and with one accord (with one spontaneous impulse and purpose) rushed[19] upon him, threw him out of the city (Numbers 15:35), and proceeded to stone him. Roman law did not allow the Jews to carry out the death penalty (John 18:31). However, this

[18]Jewish traditions and the Septuagint translation interpreted Deuteronomy 33:2, 3 to mean that angels were active in the giving or expounding of the Law. See Galatians 3:19; Hebrews 2:2.

[19]The same word is used of the swine rushing down into the sea.

was probably near the close of Pilate's governorship when he had fallen into disfavor with the Roman government, and these Jews took advantage of his weakness. There is also evidence that the imperial legate Vitellus (A.D. 35-37) was at this time trying to win Jewish favor and would have been inclined to overlook whatever they did.

The Sanhedrin did follow legal procedure, however, with the witnesses casting the first stone (Deuteronomy 17:7). They, in fact, took off their outer garments in order to be more free to throw the stones and laid the garments at the feet of a young man[20] named Saul. By this we see that Saul was an eyewitness to Stephen's death and probably to his preaching. This is the first mention of Saul and prepares us for what is said later.

While they were stoning Stephen he was calling on God saying, "Lord Jesus, receive (welcome) my spirit." Then he knelt and cried out with a loud voice, "Lord, do not let this sin stand against them." ("Lay not this sin to their charge" is a paraphrase which does give the meaning.) How like Jesus this was! (See Luke 23:34.)

Having said this, Stephen fell asleep. That is, he died. (Compare 1 Thessalonians 4:15; 2 Corinthians 5:8; Philippians 1:23.)There was something peaceful about his death in spite of its violent nature. Thus Stephen went to be with Jesus and became the first martyr of the Early Church, the first of a long line of believers who gave their lives for Jesus and the gospel.

[20]A man in his prime, up to the age of 40. Saul (Paul) was old enough to be a member of the Sanhedrin. Acts 26:10: "gave my voice," is literally "cast my pebble," that is my vote. To vote, he had to be a member of the Sanhedrin. It is important to note that Saul was present at the death of Stephen and probably heard Stephen in the synagogue.

ACTS

CHAPTER 8

Verses 1 and 3 of this chapter mention Saul. Then he is not mentioned again until chapter 9.[1] It says here that Saul was consenting to Stephen's death. The Greek is a little stronger: Saul wholly and completely approved of Stephen's death (murder), and continued to act accordingly. He did not share the feelings of his former teacher, Gamaliel (Acts 5:38). Instead, he considered Stephen's ideas dangerous and felt that they should be rooted out. But neither he nor the rest of the Sanhedrin could root out the work of the Spirit.

Persecution Spreads the Gospel (8:1-4)

[1]And Saul was consenting unto his death. And at that time there was a great persecution against the church which was at Jerusalem; and they were all scattered abroad throughout the regions of Judea and Samaria, except the apostles. [2]And devout men carried Stephen *to his burial,* and made great lamentation over him. [3]As for Saul, he made havoc of the church, entering into every house, and haling men and women committed *them* to prison. [4]Therefore they that were scattered abroad went every where preaching the word (Acts 8:1-4).

Saul was undoubtedly one of the chief instigators of the persecution that arose against the Church in Jerusalem at that time (in the very day Stephen was murdered). So intense was this persecution that the Christians were all scattered throughout Judea and Samaria.[2]

---

[1]The first sentence of Acts 8:1 really belongs with the end of chapter 7.

[2]Some commentators believe the persecution was primarily, or even entirely, against the Hellenistic or Greek-speaking Jewish Christians and that only these fled. But the Bible says they all fled except the apostles. Some modern writers also suppose that the Jerusalem church contained no Hellenists after this. But the presence of Barnabas, a Hellenist, in Acts 11:22 and his being sent as a representative of the Jerusalem Church refutes this idea. Cf. Harrison, *op. cit.,* p. 130.

Only the apostles remained in Jerusalem. Verse 2 may indicate why. Devout men carried Stephen out, buried him, and made a great lamentation (beating their breasts) over him. This was unusual for Jewish tradition was against showing this kind of respect or sorrow for an executed person. "Devout men" refers to men like those of Acts 2:5 where the same word is used. They were sincere, godly Jews who had not yet accepted Christ as their Messiah and Saviour, but who respected Stephen and rejected the decision of the Sanhedrin as wrong and unjust.[3] Through them the Church in Jerusalem would grow again. In fact, by the time Paul returned to Jerusalem after his conversion there was a strong church there.

In contrast to the devout men who lamented over Stephen, Saul became more and more furious, more energetic in his persecution. In fact, he made havoc of the Church. Literally, he ravaged and devastated it.[4] Entering into house after house, he dragged out men and women and handed them over to be put into prison. Then, as we see later, when they were brought to trial he cast his vote to have them killed (Acts 26:10).

The persecution did not stop the spread of the gospel, however. It had exactly the opposite effect. Prior to this persecution they were receiving teaching and training from the apostles; now they were ready to move out. It took the persecution to make them do it, but move out they did.

Those who were scattered did not settle down. Instead, they kept traveling from place to place, spreading the good news, the gospel. Acts 11:19 says some traveled as far as Cyprus, Phoenicia, and Antioch. We can be sure they traveled equally as far in other directions as well.

This does not mean they were all preachers in the modern sense. They simply were joyous and free in their witness to Jesus. Though they were just ordinary people, they knew the Word and became channels for the love and power of Jesus. Apparently, none complained because of the persecution. They seized it as another opportunity to see what God would do.

---

[3]Cf. Hackett, *op. cit.*, p. 107; Earle, *op. cit.*, p. 349.

[4]The Greek Septuagint version uses this word of a wild boar tearing up vineyards (Psalm 80:13).

Philip Goes to Samaria (8:5-13)

[5]Then Philip went down to the city of Samaria, and preached Christ unto them. [6]And the people with one accord gave heed unto those things which Philip spake, hearing and seeing the miracles which he did. [7]For unclean spirits, crying with loud voice, came out of many that were possessed *with them:* and many taken with palsies, and that were lame, were healed. [8]And there was great joy in that city.

[9]But there was a certain man, called Simon, which beforetime in the same city used sorcery, and bewitched the people of Samaria, giving out that himself was some great one: [10]to whom they all gave heed, from the least to the greatest, saying, This man is the great power of God. [11]And to him they had regard, because that of long time he had bewitched them with sorceries. [12]But when they believed Philip preaching the things concerning the kingdom of God, and the name of Jesus Christ, they were baptized, both men and women. [13]Then Simon himself believed also: and when he was baptized, he continued with Philip, and wondered, beholding the miracles and signs which were done (Acts 8:5-13).

Many did preach or proclaim the gospel publicly, however. After the general statement in verse 4, Luke gives us an example of what must have happened all over. Philip the deacon is chosen as this example, not because what happened in Samaria was greater than what happened elsewhere, but because of the lessons learned there and because Samaria was next in line in the commission given in Acts 1:8.

Samaria was important, too, because another barrier was broken down there by the Spirit. Samaritans were descended from those of the ten northern tribes who intermarried with the people the Assyrians brought in after Samaria was captured. At first, they worshipped the Lord plus other gods (2 Kings 17:24-41). Later they also built a temple on Mount Gerizim. But about 100 years before Christ the Jews went up and destroyed that temple and forced the Samaritans to give up their idolatry. In New Testament times the Samaritans followed the Law of Moses much as the Jews did, but said sacrifices must be made on Mount Gerizim instead of at the Jerusalem Temple.

Jews avoided going through Samaria if at all possible. So it took courage for Philip to go to Samaria. But, like the others, he was led by the Spirit. When he came to the city of Samaria,[5] about ten

[5]A few ancient manuscripts have a city of Samaria rather than the city. The city of Samaria was rebuilt by Herod the Great and renamed Sebaste (The Greek for Augustus, thus honoring the Emperor, Caesar Augustus). But the Jews still called it Samaria.

miles north of where Jesus talked to the woman at the well, he began to preach Christ (proclaim the truth about Him as the Messiah and Saviour). We can be sure the ministry of Jesus in Samaria (John 4) was not forgotten. These things were not done in a corner. The Samaritans, like the Jews, looked for a Messiah in fulfillment of Deuteronomy 18:15, 18, 19.

The people (the crowds, including all classes of people) with one accord paid attention to Philip's message, listening to him, both hearing and seeing the miracles (signs) he kept doing. Here we see that the Lord's promise to confirm the Word with signs following was not limited to the apostles (Mark 16:20). The people heard those having unclean spirits shouting with a loud voice as they came out. They saw those who were paralyzed[6] and who were deaf healed. The result was great joy in that city, the joy of health and salvation.

This success of the gospel was an even greater miracle than it first appeared. For these people previously had been bewitched (were astonished and amazed)[7] by a man named Simon who practiced sorcery (magic), saying he was someone great (or some great being). To Simon all, from the least to the greatest in Samaria, gave attention and said, "This man is the power of God which is called great."[8] They had paid attention to him for a considerable time because he amazed them with his magic tricks.

The people saw something far more wonderful in the miracles of Philip, and they believed the good news of the kingdom (rule, power and authority) of God and the name of Jesus Christ. The gospel Philip preached emphasized this rule and power of God manifest through Christ in His character and nature as Messiah and Saviour. Certainly he told them all that Peter told the people on the Day of Pentecost and later.

The people believed, not just Philip, but also the truth he preached. They believed what he said about the kingdom (rule) of God; they believed the name (power and authority) of Jesus;

[6]Palsy here is the old English word for a paralytic. It does not refer to "shaking" palsy. These were in a helpless condition.

[7]The same verb is translated *wondered* in verse 13. It does not imply any supernatural powers on the part of Simon. He tricked them.

[8]Or, as many ancient manuscripts have it, "This man is the great power of God." Like some modern cult leaders, he did not exactly say he was a manifestation of God or that he was the Messiah, but he tried to leave that impression.

they accepted what Philip told them about Christ's work as the crucified and risen Saviour and Lord. Then they were baptized, both men and women.

Finally, even Simon himself believed and was baptized. Then he attached himself persistently and constantly to Philip. Simon was used to deceiving people by his magic tricks and knew astonishing things can be done by trickery. He had watched Philip with the professional eye of a magician and had to come to the conclusion that these miracles were real. Clearly, these signs and great deeds of power were supernatural. So he too wondered (was filled with wonder and amazement). These miracles were quite unlike the magic tricks he performed.

Some have questioned whether Simon truly believed. But the Bible says he did and does not qualify the statement in any way. Moreover, Philip, a man led by the Spirit, surely would not have baptized him if he did not give evidence of being a true believer.

PETER AND JOHN IN SAMARIA (8:14-25)

[14]Now when the apostles which were at Jerusalem heard that Samaria had received the word of God, they sent unto them Peter and John: [15]who, when they were come down, prayed for them, that they might receive the Holy Ghost: [16](for as yet he was fallen upon none of them: only they were baptized in the name of the Lord Jesus.) [17]Then laid they *their* hands on them, and they received the Holy Ghost. [18]And when Simon saw that through laying on of the apostles' hands the Holy Ghost was given, he offered them money, [19]saying, Give me also this power, that on whomsoever I lay hands, he may receive the Holy Ghost.

[20]But Peter said unto him, Thy money perish with thee, because thou hast thought that the gift of God may be purchased with money. [21]Thou hast neither part nor lot in this matter: for thy heart is not right in the sight of God. [22]Repent therefore of this thy wickedness, and pray God, if perhaps the thought of thine heart may be forgiven thee. [23]For I perceive that thou art in the gall of bitterness, and *in* the bond of iniquity. [24]Then answered Simon, and said, Pray ye to the Lord for me, that none of these things which ye have spoken come upon me. [25]And they, when they had testified and preached the word of the Lord, returned to Jerusalem, and preached the gospel in many villages of the Samaritans (Acts 8:14-25).

The news that Samaria had received (welcomed) the Word of God soon reached the apostles in Jerusalem. They sent Peter and John to them (with a message and a purpose) to encourage the new believers. There is no indication in this, however, that they thought Philip's ministry was in any way inferior or lacking. They just wanted to help.

When the two apostles arrived, the first thing they did was to pray for the Samaritan believers to receive the Holy Spirit. Clearly, the apostles believed the baptism in the Holy Spirit is important for everyone. Though the Samaritans had been baptized in water and in the name (into the worship and service) of the Lord Jesus, none had received the gift of the Spirit with the evidence of speaking in other tongues. That is, the Spirit had not fallen on any in the way He fell on the believers on the Day of Pentecost.[9]

Some suppose the faith of the Samaritans was not truly in Jesus until Peter and John came and prayed. But Philip was a man full of the Spirit and wisdom. He would not have baptized any of them if their faith was not real.

Others suppose Philip did not teach the Samaritans about the baptism in the Holy Spirit. But the very fact that Philip came and preached Christ to them shows he believed the promise was for them. It is clear also that the believers were not able to withhold any part of the message. (See Acts 4:20.)

As we have seen, the Samaritans believed what Philip preached concerning the kingdom (rule) of God and the name (authority) of Jesus. The preaching in Acts associates these things with the promise of the Holy Spirit. Philip, we can be sure, like the other preachers in the Book of Acts, included the message of the exaltation of Jesus to the right hand of the Father and the giving of the promise of the Father, the baptism in the Holy Spirit.

"The problem seems to be on the side of the Samaritans. Now they realized they had been wrong, not only about the deceptions of Simon the sorcerer, but also about their Samaritan doctrines. Perhaps, humbled, they found it difficult to express the next step of faith necessary to receive the baptism in the Spirit. When Jesus found faith expressed in a simple way based solely on His Word, He called it great faith, and things happened (Matthew 8:10, 13). When faith rose above hindrances and testing, Jesus called it great faith, and things happened (Matthew 15:28). But when faith was weak, He did not destroy what there was. He helped it, sometimes by laying on His hands."[10]

---

[9]Cf. Packer, *op. cit.,* p. 65.

[10]Horton, *op. cit.,* p. 154.

Whether Peter and John gave further teaching first or not, we are not told. But when we compare what was done at other times, it seems very probable that they did.

Then, after they prayed for them, the two apostles laid their hands on them. God confirmed the faith of the believers, and they received the Spirit (were receiving the Spirit publicly, probably one after the other as the apostles laid their hands on them).

Something that happened caught Simon's attention. Luke does not tell what it was, but as we have seen, Luke often does not explain everything when it is clear elsewhere. For example, he does not mention water baptism every time he tells about people believing or being added to the Church, but it is clear that the failure to mention this is not significant. Other places show that all believers were baptized in water. For this reason we can say that the fact Luke does not mention speaking in tongues here is not significant.

It is clear, however, that Simon had already seen Philip's miracles. Prophecy would not have attracted his attention, because it would have been in a known language and not obviously supernatural. There is actually only one thing that fits. On the Day of Pentecost, they spoke in tongues as the Spirit gave utterance; this attracted the attention of the crowd. Speaking in tongues by the Samaritan believers obviously did the same for Simon. But tongues is not the point at issue in this passage. Nor did it have the same effect as on the Day of Pentecost, for there were no others present who knew foreign languages. Luke says nothing about the tongues, therefore, in order to focus attention on Simon's wrong attitude.

Simon, when he saw that through the laying on of hands by the apostles the Holy Spirit was given, did not come himself to receive. Instead, he fell back into his old greed and offered them money (brought to them riches as an offering) if they would give him the power (the authority) to lay his hands on people with the same result.

Verses 17 and 18 do not mean, however, that the apostles had any such authority. They prayed first that the believers might receive the Spirit. They certainly recognized that it was the promise of the Father and that it must come from heaven. The word "through" in verse 18 indicates secondary agency. That is, Jesus is the baptizer in the Holy Spirit (Acts 2:33). The apostles were just

His agents to pray for and encourage the faith of these believers to receive.

Nor is there any implication here that the laying on of hands was necessary to receive the Spirit, though Simon jumped to that conclusion, just as many modern teachers have.[11] Many other passages show Simon was wrong. There was no laying on of hands on the Day of Pentecost or at the house of Cornelius. Nor was the laying on of hands limited to the apostles, since Ananias, a layman of Damascus, laid his hands on Paul for both healing and the receiving of the Holy Spirit. The laying on of hands here was a means of welcoming them as fellow believers as well as a means of encouraging their faith to receive the Gift of the Spirit in answer to their prayers.[12]

Peter rebuked Simon severely. Literally, he said, "Let your money (silver) together with you go into destruction (probably the destruction of the lake of fire) because you thought the gift of God (that is, God's gift of the Holy Spirit, as in 2:38; 10:45) could be purchased with money (earthly riches). You have neither part (portion, share) nor lot (portion) in this matter,[13] for your heart is not right (upright, straight) before God." He had a crooked heart and a twisted view of things.

Some suppose that Simon's desire to purchase God's gift (free and freely given) for money means that he wanted to offer it for sale. But this would have been impossible. The apostles were offering it freely, as the free Gift of God. Anyone could receive it. More probably, Simon saw an opportunity to restore his prestige and leadership among the people by becoming an authoritative giver of the Gift of the Spirit, as he jumped to the conclusion that the apostles were.

Actually, Peter's rebuke for thinking that the gift of God could be bought with money suggests also that Simon could have had part or lot in this matter if he had come in faith and received the gift himself instead of coming and offering money. In other words, anyone receiving the free Gift of the Spirit can pray for others to receive the same gift.

Peter then showed that Simon's case was not entirely hopeless

---

[11]Rudolph Bultmann, *Theology of the New Testament* (New York: Charles Scribner's Sons, c1951), I, 139.

[12]Cf. Alexander, *op. cit.*, p. 332; Bruce, *op. cit.*, pp. 182, 183.

[13]Part and lot are synonyms here. The repetition is for emphasis.

by exhorting him to repent from this his wickedness and pray to God (request of the Lord) if perhaps the thought (including the purpose) of his heart might be forgiven. There is no question here about God's willingness to forgive. God always freely forgives those who come to Him confessing their sin (1 John 1:9). Peter added the "if perhaps" because of the heart condition. Simon's pride and greed had caused him to fall into this sin. Peter realized Simon had an embittered, resentful spirit (the gall of bitterness) because the people ceased to give him prominence. (Compare Deuteronomy 29:18 and Isaiah 58:6 for the Old Testament's use of these expressions.) Such a spirit often refuses reconciliation and certainly grieves the Holy Spirit (Ephesians 4:30, 31). Simon was also in the bond (that is, in the grip) of iniquity (injustice, unrighteousness); he was unjust in wanting to receive this power for himself, and also, his wrong attitude had such a grip on him that it would be difficult for him to break loose. It is possible, however, that the Greek means Simon was headed for the gall of bitterness and the bond of iniquity. This would mean he was not yet bound by them and there was greater hope for him if he would repent immediately.

Simon responded by begging Peter and John to pray in his behalf (emphatic, you add your prayers to mine) so that none of these things Peter had spoken would come upon him.[14]

There is considerable controversy about what happened to Simon. Some suggest that he only wanted prayer because he was afraid of judgment. But the Greek indicates he wanted the apostles to pray along with him. This does indicate a change of attitude and therefore repentance. The Bible says nothing more about him. The traditions that arose about him in later times have no Biblical basis.[15]

Peter and John continued in Samaria for a time giving strong witness (strong Biblical evidence) and speaking the Word of the Lord. Probably they included more of the life, ministry, and

---

[14]Codex Bezae (D) adds that Simon did not stop weeping much tears.

[15]Some say he introduced a gnostic sect. Others try to connect him with an Italian deity and say he went to Rome and made himself a god there. But there is not a shred of real evidence for any of this. Because of what he did "simony" has become a term for buying a place of authority or an office in the church. Actually, as Lenski points out, we should be thankful to God for his repentance. Cf. Lenski, *op. cit.*, pp. 332, 333.

teachings of Jesus. Then they preached the gospel (the good news) in many Samaritan villages on the way back to Jerusalem.

The Ethiopian Eunuch (8:26-40)

[26]And the angel of the Lord spake unto Philip, saying, Arise and go toward the south, unto the way that goeth down from Jerusalem unto Gaza, which is desert. [27]And he arose and went: and, behold, a man of Ethiopia, a eunuch of great authority under Candace queen of the Ethiopians, who had the charge of all her treasure, and had come to Jerusalem for to worship, [28]was returning, and sitting in his chariot read Isaiah the prophet. [29]Then the Spirit said unto Philip, Go near, and join thyself to this chariot. [30]And Philip ran thither to *him,* and heard him read the prophet Isaiah, and said, Understandest thou what thou readest?

[31]And he said, How can I, except some man should guide me? And he desired Philip that he would come up and sit with him. [32]The place of the Scripture which he read was this, He was led as a sheep to the slaughter; and like a lamb dumb before his shearer, so opened he not his mouth: [33]in his humiliation his judgment was taken away: and who shall declare his generation? for his life is taken from the earth.

[34]And the eunuch answered Philip, and said, I pray thee, of whom speaketh the prophet this? of himself, or of some other man? [35]Then Philip opened his mouth, and began at the same Scripture, and preached unto him Jesus. [36]And as they went on *their* way, they came unto a certain water: and the eunuch said, See, *here is* water; what doth hinder me to be baptized?[37]And Philip said, If thou believest with all thine heart, thou mayest. And he answered and said, I believe that Jesus Christ is the Son of God. [38]And he commanded the chariot to stand still: and they went down both into the water, both Philip and the eunuch; and he baptized him. [39]And when they were come up out of the water, the Spirit of the Lord caught away Philip, that the eunuch saw him no more: and he went on his way rejoicing. [40]But Philip was found at Azotus: and passing through he preached in all the cities, till he came to Caesarea (Acts 8:26-40).

At this point the angel (Greek, an angel) of the Lord spoke to Philip telling him to rise and go toward the south to the road going down from Jerusalem to Gaza, which is desert. "Desert" also means deserted, abandoned, desolate. Here, the emphasis is that the area was largely uninhabited. Gaza was the most southern of the five cities of the Philistines in Old Testament times. It was about 60 miles southwest of Jerusalem.

The Bible tells of angels appearing to people comparatively few times. Yet they are often present and function as "ministering spirits, sent forth to minister for them who shall be heirs of salvation" (Hebrews 1:14).[16] However, since they are spirits, God has to give them a physical form temporarily in order for them to appear and speak to men.

There may have been a special reason for sending an angel. Philip was in the midst of a great revival in Samaria. It probably took something unusual to get him to leave the crowds and go down to a deserted back road that was seldom used any more. Some take "which is desert" to refer to Old Testament Gaza, which was destroyed in 93 B.C. In 57 B.C. a new city was built nearer the Mediterranean Sea. The road to old Gaza might be called the road to desert (deserted) Gaza.

When the angel spoke, Philip did not hesitate. He arose and went in obedience, and, we can be sure, with faith and expectation.

At the very time he reached the Gaza road,[17] the chariot of an Ethiopian eunuch was approaching. Most officers in palaces were eunuchs in ancient times. He was a highly placed officer (a potentate), a member of the court of the Ethiopian queen Candace, in charge of all her treasure. We might say, he was a member of the cabinet and would compare to the secretary of the treasury, but with full responsibility for the care and disbursement of funds.

Candace was the hereditary title of the queens of Ethiopia, whose seat of government was on the island of Meroe in the Nile River. Ethiopia itself corresponds to what is today called the Sudan, though it may have included part of modern Ethiopia.

This eunuch had come a long distance to worship in Jerusalem. Though he was probably a proselyte to Judaism, because of his being a eunuch, he could only go as far as the court of the Gentiles.[18] Even so, he purchased scrolls of the Old Testament to take back with him. These were hand-copied and extremely ex-

[16]Hebrews chapter 1 shows Christ's superiority to angels; Jesus himself at the cross could have had ten legions of angels if He had desired them. Hebrews 12:22 speaks of an innumerable company of angels. Revelation 5:11 also speaks of great numbers.

[17]"Behold" indicates something unexpected or surprising. He was surprised, but God's timing was just right.

[18]See Deuteronomy 23:1; some writers believe that because of Isaiah 56:3-5, this rule was relaxed in New Testament times. On the other hand, the fact that he was a eunuch may have kept him from being a full proselyte, so that he would be classed as a God-fearing Gentile who worshiped the true God but could not go beyond the court of the Gentiles in the Temple.

pensive in those days. Usually a whole synagogue would join together to buy one set, which they would keep locked up except for use in the worship and in the synagogue school.

Now the eunuch was returning home, sitting in his chariot reading the book (roll, scroll) of Isaiah. At this point the Spirit spoke to Philip, possibly by an inner voice. (Guidance by the Spirit is prominent in Acts.) Philip did not need an angel to speak to him this time. He was undoubtedly looking to the Lord to know what to do. The Spirit's command was to go and join himself (closely; literally, glue himself) to this chariot.

In obedience Philip ran to the chariot. As he ran alongside the chariot he heard the eunuch reading aloud from the prophet Isaiah. (Reading in those days was almost always done aloud.) Philip interrupted him and asked if he understood what he was reading. His reply was, "How can I [how am I capable] except some man should guide me?" Then he desired (asked, invited) Philip to come up and sit with him.

Philip did not need a second invitation. In the providence of God the eunuch was reading Isaiah 53:7, 8 (from the Greek Septuagint version). This must have been exciting to Philip as he saw how wonderful and how exact God's timing was!

The eunuch then requested Philip to tell him about whom the prophet was speaking—of himself or of some other person. Isaiah 53 speaks of the One who suffers wholly for the sins of others and not for any of his own. The eunuch knew no one who could do that and he was puzzled.

This was Philip's great opportunity. Beginning at that very Scripture passage, he preached Jesus (preached the gospel, the good news about Jesus) to him. He alone never sinned and never did anything to deserve suffering or death. For those who will see it, no passage in the prophets more clearly pictures the vicarious suffering, death, resurrection, and triumph of Jesus.[19] But Philip

---

[19]Because this passage so clearly applies to Christ, this chapter is seldom read in Jewish synagogues and I have found that some of the Jews are not familiar with it. I have also heard Jewish rabbis (especially in one of the classes I took at Harvard) claim that Isaiah 53 applies to the nation of Israel and that since Jews have no temple now, and therefore cannot offer sacrifices, on the basis of Isaiah 53 they are made acceptable to God by their own sufferings. But who among them or among any of us can say we have never sinned or that we have never brought any of our sufferings on ourselves. Thus, the passage can only apply to Jesus. Jesus actually identified himself with the suffering Servant of this passage. Compare Mark 10:45 and Isaiah 53:11, 12.

only began at Isaiah 53. He went on to explain the gospel further with its commands, promises, and call to repentance as Peter did (Acts 2:38).

As Philip and the eunuch went down the road they came to some water. The eunuch called attention to it. "See" is the same word translated "behold" in verse 27 and indicates something unexpected. Most of southern Palestine is rather dry. The eunuch did not want to pass it by without being baptized. He put his request in the form of a question, "what doth hinder me to be baptized?" Probably, he was afraid that his being a Gentile and a eunuch might bar him from this, just as it barred him from most of the Jewish worship.

Philip then asked for and received a confession of faith.[20] Then, after commanding the driver of the chariot to stop, they both left the chariot and went down into the water. In fact, Luke draws attention to the fact that both went down into the water. Then Philip baptized him and they came up out of the water. The language here makes it clear that the word "baptize" has its usual meaning of immerse, submerge, dip under. Many other passages make it clear that immersion was the practice of the Early Church.[21]

After they came up out of the water the Spirit caught away Philip, and the eunuch saw him no more, and he went on his way rejoicing. A few ancient manuscripts and versions add that the Holy Spirit fell on the eunuch. We can be sure that he was indeed baptized in the Spirit and that this added to his rejoicing. Undoubtedly, he then spread the gospel in his own country.

Luke does not explain how the Spirit caught away Philip. The verb used usually means "to snatch away." In 1 Thessalonians 4:17 it is used of the rapture of the Church. Apparently, the Spirit gave him a supersonic ride over to the coast at Azotus (near the site of the ancient Ashdod, about 20 miles north of Gaza).

From there Philip proceeded northward along the Mediterra-

[20]Some ancient manuscripts omit verse 37, but it fits the context and reflects the practice of the Early Church. It also is quoted by Early Church fathers such as Cyprian and Irenaeus.

[21]Archaeologists have discovered baptistries for immersion in the ruins of second century church buildings, showing that baptism continued to be by immersion for a long time.

nean coast preaching the gospel (evangelizing) in all the cities until he came to Caesarea. This Caesarea, built by Herod the Great, was the capital of the province of Judea. Philip was still there years later. Evidently he made it his home and headquarters from this point on. But he still traveled around and became known as Philip the evangelist (Acts 21:8).

ACTS
CHAPTER 9

What happened at Samaria apparently did not concern Saul. But others who were scattered went north, probably through Galilee, and on to Damascus. Damascus was the oldest and most important city in Syria.[1] It seems to have had a large Jewish population at this time, for verse 2 speaks of the synagogues in the plural. Saul must have at least heard rumors that the scattered believers were having success in preaching the gospel there. This leads to a most important event, one so important that it is recorded three times in the Book of Acts.

Saul's (Paul's) Conversion (9:1-9)

[1]And Saul, yet breathing out threatenings and slaughter against the disciples of the Lord, went unto the high priest, [2]and desired of him letters to Damascus to the synagogues, that if he found any of this way, whether they were men or women, he might bring them bound unto Jerusalem. [3]And as he journeyed, he came near Damascus: and suddenly there shined round about him a light from heaven: [4]and he fell to the earth, and heard a voice saying unto him, Saul, Saul, why persecutest thou me?

[5]And he said, Who art thou, Lord? And the Lord said, I am Jesus whom thou persecutest: *it is* hard for thee to kick against the pricks. [6]And he trembling and astonished said, Lord, what wilt thou have me to do? And the Lord *said* unto him, Arise, and go into the city, and it shall be told thee what thou must do. [7]And the men which journeyed with him stood speechless, hearing a voice, but seeing no man. [8]And Saul arose from the earth; and when his eyes were opened, he saw no man: but they led him

[1]At this time Damascus was probably outside the Roman Empire and was under King Aretas who made it part of Arabia. Aretas was anti-Roman; so were the Jews. Thus, it seems Aretas allowed Jews freedom and gave the Jerusalem leaders authority over the Jews in Damascus. Cf. Harrison, *op. cit.*, p. 146.

by the hand, and brought *him* into Damascus. [9]And he was three days without sight, and neither did eat nor drink (Acts 9:1-9).

Some of the others who joined in the persecution of Acts 8:1 may have lost their zeal against the Christians, but not Saul. He was still breathing out threatening (the Greek is singular) and slaughter (murder) against those who were disciples (learners, students, and followers) of the Lord Jesus. Later (Acts 26:10) he told about how he voted for their death.

"Breathing out" here is literally "breathing in." It is a Greek participle *(empneon)* indicating this had become characteristic and continuous. In other words, Saul created an atmosphere around him of threat and murder so that he was constantly breathing it in. As oxygen enables an athlete to keep going, so this atmosphere kept Saul going.

Now, however, most of the believers had left Jerusalem. So Saul went of his own accord to the high priest and asked for official letters to the synagogues at Damascus giving him authority to arrest any of this Way (the Way), men or women, and to bring them bound to Jerusalem (Acts 26:11, 12). This would mean a trial before the Sanhedrin and probably the death sentence. "The Way" was an interesting title for the believers, one they could accept. Christ is the way of salvation, the way of life. (See Acts 19:9, 23; 22:4; 24:14, 22.)

Damascus was about 140 miles northeast of Jerusalem, but probably nearly 200 miles by road in those days. Near the end of the journey a light from heaven suddenly shined (flashed like lightning) around Saul. As Acts 26:13 shows, it continued to shine around him with a light brighter than the noonday sun.

Light in the Bible is often associated with manifestations of the presence of the Lord. In John 17:5, Jesus prayed to His Father, saying, "glorify thou me with thine own self with the glory I had with thee before the world was." When Jesus rose from the dead, His resurrection body was transformed—it was immortal and incorruptible, as ours will be (1 Corinthians 15:52, 53). But the glory was not restored until after He ascended. Probably the disciples could not have stood the glory during the 40 days He remained on earth with them. But now He appeared to Saul as the risen and glorified Christ. Later on, Saul referred to this: "Last of all [after the other resurrection appearances] he was seen of me also, as of one born out of due time" (1 Corinthians 15:8).[2]

Saul, who was probably walking, fell to the ground, overwhelmed. Then he heard a voice, "Saul, Saul why do you keep persecuting me?" Luke in referring to Saul, always uses the Greek form of his name (as in verse 1, "Saulos"). Jesus used the Hebrew form *(Saoul),* which the Book of Acts is careful to preserve here. Saul later confirms that Jesus was speaking in Hebrew[3] (Acts 26:14).

Saul knew the Hebrew Bible very well and recognized this had to be a divine manifestation. But the question confused him. Who was he persecuting other than the Christians? So he asked, "Who are you, Lord?" Some take this to mean, "Who are you, sir?" using the word lord merely as a term of polite address. But in response to this obviously supernatural manifestation, the word can only mean divine Lord.

The answer came at once, "I (emphatic) am Jesus whom you (emphatic) keep persecuting." In persecuting the Church, Saul was persecuting the Body of Christ whose individual members are in Christ. (See Matthew 25:40, 45; Ephesians 1:23; 2:6.) Then Jesus added, "It is hard [rough, dangerous] for you to kick against the pricks [against the ox goads]."[4]

By this Jesus recognized that much of Saul's persecution of the Christians was because he knew he had no answer for their arguments. It was a reaction by which he was trying to resist the conviction of the Holy Spirit. Like a man driving an ox, the Holy Spirit had been driving Saul toward the truth of the gospel, but he was resisting violently, kicking against the goads. The arguments of Stephen were just such a goad; his final speech and the way he died were goads; the spread of the gospel and the response of the believers were goads; the miracles that confirmed the Word were all goads. In all this, he was dangerously hurting himself.

---

[2]Born out of due time usually means a birth before the time, but it is used by Saul to mean that this appearance of the risen Christ was something special, something extraordinary, beyond the normal. Jesus made no other such appearances on earth after His ascension.

[3]Some take this to mean Aramaic, a related language spoken by the Jews after their return from Babylon.

[4]See Acts 26:14. Some ancient manuscripts leave out this phrase here in chapter 9.

This does not mean Saul was conscious that these were goads, or that he even realized he had no good arguments against the believers. He was so full of fury that he could think of nothing but how He could stop them. But now that he was faced with it and with Christ, not just as the man Jesus, but as the divine Lord, he answered simply, "What shall I do Lord?"[5] This shows a complete change in Saul's attitude, which is the evidence of genuine repentance on his part.

The Lord then told him to rise and go into the city of Damascus. There he would be told what it would be necessary for him to do. Jesus actually told Saul more here, but Luke leaves the rest for Saul to tell in his defense before Agrippa (Acts 26:16-18). In Galatians 1:1, 11, 12, 16 Saul also makes it clear that he was comissioned directly by Jesus, not by man. In other words, he was a genuine apostle or "sent one," sent by Jesus himself.

Meanwhile, the men who were traveling with Saul stood speechless, hearing the voice (the sound) but seeing no one.[6] They, as Acts 26:14 says, all fell to the ground but were able to get up before Saul did.

Saul, it seems, shut his eyes because of the continuing brightness, but He did see Jesus. Then, when he got up off the ground, he could see nothing. His traveling companions took him by the hand and led him into Damascus. He was there three days unable to see, and he neither ate nor drank anything.[7]

Ananias Sent to Saul (9:10-19)

[10]And there was a certain disciple at Damascus, named Ananias; and to him said the Lord in a vision, Ananias. And he said, Behold, *I am here,* Lord. [11]And the Lord *said* unto him, Arise, and go into the street which is

[5]Saul's response in the first part of verse 6 for some reason was omitted (probably in copying) and is not found in any of the Greek manuscripts we now have. It is in Acts 22:10, and in the Latin Vulgate version it is found in Acts 9:6.

[6]Some see a contradiction here between Acts 9:7 and 22:9 which reads, "They heard not the voice." The Greek construction is different in 22:9, however. Here in 9:7 it simply says they heard the sound. Bruce, *op. cit.,* p. 197, suggests it was the sound of Saul's voice they heard here, and that they did not hear the voice of Jesus at all. One old Latin manuscript (h) confirms this.

[7]The Jewish way of counting made the first day the day he entered Damascus and the third day the day Ananias came. This gave Saul a day in between to think things over and to pray. Some relate these three days to Jesus' three days in the tomb. Cf. Harrison, *op. cit.,* p. 150.

called Straight, and inquire in the house of Judas for *one* called Saul, of Tarsus: for, behold, he prayeth, [12]and hath seen in a vision a man named Ananias coming in, and putting *his* hand on him, that he might receive his sight. [13]Then Ananias answered, Lord, I have heard by many of this man, how much evil he hath done to thy saints at Jerusalem: [14]and here he hath authority from the chief priests to bind all that call on thy name. [15]But the Lord said unto him, Go thy way: for he is a chosen vessel unto me, to bear my name before the Gentiles, and kings, and the children of Israel: [16]for I will show him how great things he must suffer for my name's sake.

[17]And Ananias went his way, and entered into the house; and putting his hands on him said, Brother Saul, the Lord, *even* Jesus, that appeared unto thee in the way as thou camest, hath sent me, that thou mightest receive thy sight, and be filled with the Holy Ghost. [18]And immediately there fell from his eyes as it had been scales: and he received sight forthwith, and arose, and was baptized. [19]And when he had received meat, he was strengthened. Then was Saul certain days with the disciples which were at Damascus (Acts 9:10-19).

On the third day the Lord (Jesus) appeared to a disciple named Ananias, a devout Jew converted to the Lord (Acts 22:12). The appearance was in a vision in which Jesus told him to go to the street (narrow street) called Straight. In ancient times it went straight from one end of the city to the other, and it is still an important street in Damascus today. There he was to inquire (seek, search) in the house of Judas for Saul of Tarsus: for behold, surprisingly and unexpectedly, while Saul was praying he had seen (in a vision) a man named Ananias coming in and laying hands on him, so that he recovered his sight.

Ananias objected at first. He had heard from many about the many bad things Saul had done to the Lord's saints[8] in Jerusalem. Ananias was apparently a Jew who was born in Damascus or who had lived there for a long time. Obviously, many of the believers who fled from the persecution had come there and brought news of Saul's fury. The news had already come also that Saul had authority from the chief priests to bind all who called on the name of Jesus. Thus, the church in Damascus may have been getting

[8]Holy (separated) dedicated ones, consecrated to the Lord and to His service. All believers were so named because they turned their backs on the world to follow Jesus. The word "saint" does not imply ultimate perfection. Rather, it simply means they were headed in the right direction. Saul later calls believers saints about 40 times in his preaching and writings. Cf. Earle, *op. cit.,* p. 365.

ready to face the same sort of scattering that occurred because of the persecutions in Jerusalem.[9]

The Lord again commanded Ananias to go and reassured him that Saul was His own chosen vessel to carry His name before the Gentiles (the nations) and also before both kings and the children (sons, people) of Israel. Moreover, Jesus himself would show Saul (warn him, point out to him) how much it would be necessary for him to suffer for the sake of His name.

Then Ananias obeyed, entered the house, and laid his hands on Saul, calling him brother. By this he recognized that Saul was now a believer. Then he explained that the Lord sent him, and identified the Lord as Jesus who appeared to Saul on the road as he was coming (to Damascus). This explanation probably seemed necessary to Ananias, for the Jews normally used the term Lord to mean Jehovah (Yahweh), the one true God. But it really was not necessary, as Saul had already recognized Jesus as Lord.

Ananias added that the Lord sent him for two reasons. First, that Saul might recover his sight; second, that he might be filled with the Holy Spirit.[10]

Immediately something like scales fell from Saul's eyes; he could see again; and he rose up and was baptized. Then he ended his fast, took food, and was filled with strength. After that he stayed some days with the disciples in Damascus.

Verse 12 does not tell the command of Jesus to lay hands on Saul that he might be filled with the Spirit. Neither does verse 18 tell how Saul did receive the Spirit. Once again, we see that Luke does not repeat everything in every place. Thus, he really indicates that Saul's experience in being filled with the Holy Spirit was no different from that experienced on the Day of Pentecost. We can be sure he spoke in other tongues at that time as they did in Acts 2:4.

Titus 3:5-7 confirms this by showing that the Holy Spirit was poured out on both Saul and Titus abundantly. Each had his own

[9]Cf. Guthrie, *op. cit.,* p. 73.

[10]Again we see that, since Ananias was a "layman," God did not limit this ministry to the apostles or to officers of the Church. Also, since Ananias was a native of Damascus and the apostles had not left Jerusalem, no apostle had laid his hands on him. He was simply being obedient to the command of Jesus.

personal Pentecost.[11] Actually, there is really no question about whether Saul spoke in tongues or not. He told the Corinthians years later that he spoke in tongues more than them all (1 Corinthians 14:18).[12]

Nothing more is said of Ananias. He undoubtedly continued living in humble obedience to the Lord and to His Word. But Saul never forgot this godly man who was the first believer to call him brother.

Saul Preaches in Damascus (9:20-25)

[20]And straightway he preached Christ in the synagogues, that he is the Son of God. [21]But all that heard *him* were amazed, and said; Is not this he that destroyed them which called on this name in Jerusalem, and came hither for that intent, that he might bring them bound unto the chief priests? [22]But Saul increased the more in strength, and confounded the Jews which dwelt at Damascus, proving that this is very Christ.

[23]And after that many days were fulfilled, the Jews took counsel to kill him: [24]but their laying wait was known of Saul. And they watched the gates day and night to kill him. [25]Then the disciples took him by night, and let *him* down by the wall in a basket (Acts 9:20-25).

Saul at once became part of the body of disciples in Damascus. Because he accepted the Lord's commission, he did not wait to start preaching Christ. Immediately he went to the synagogues where he had intended to search out the believers and send them bound to Jerusalem. But to everyone's amazement (total astonishment that almost knocked them out of their senses), he proclaimed Christ (Jesus) as the Son of God.[13] The people could hardly believe that this was really the same person who destroyed (laid waste, brought destruction on) those in Jerusalem who called on this Name.

Saul, however, was more and more filled with mighty power and confounded the Jews living in Damascus, proving (that is,

---

[11]Bruce, *op. cit.,* p. 201 suggests that Saul may have been filled with the Spirit immediately before he was baptized in water, as was the case with Cornelius (Acts 10:44-47). Certainly there are parallels between the way God sent Ananias to Saul and the way He sent Peter to Cornelius. Cf. Earle, *op. cit.,* p. 366.

[12]The fact he preferred to limit his speaking in tongues in the public meeting shows he spoke in tongues primarily in his private devotions, "speaking unto God" (1 Corinthians 14:2, 19).

[13]This is the first time in Acts that the title "Son of God" is used of Jesus.

deducing from the Scriptures) that this One (Jesus) is the Christ, the Messiah (God's anointed Prophet, Priest, and King). In other words, he used Old Testament prophecies and showed how they were fulfilled in Jesus.

After a considerable time, the Jews (that is, the unbelieving Jews) counseled with one another to kill him. But their plot became known to Saul. They were watching the gates very carefully day and night intending to kill him. Second Corinthians 11:32 indicates that the governor (ethnarch) under King Aretus IV of Arabia (who reigned 9 B.C. to A.D. 40) cooperated in this plot, or perhaps was paid by the Jews to help them seize Saul.

Saul's disciples (converts) foiled their plot, however, by letting him down by the wall in a large flexible basket made of rushes, or something similar, woven together. In 2 Corinthians 11:33 Saul adds that he was let down through a window. (Houses with a section built over the city wall can still be seen in Damascus.)[14]

Galatians adds here that Saul received the gospel he preached (including the sayings of Jesus) by revelation directly from Jesus himself (Galatians 1:12, 16). He also says he left Damascus for a time during this period and went into Arabia, returning again to Damascus. Since, as most scholars believe, the kingdom of the Nabatean Arabs included Damascus at this time, Saul did not need to go very far out of the city. (He probably went east.)

Galatians also indicates that it was not until 3 years later (or the third year) that the many days were fulfilled and he went to Jerusalem. Jesus may have given Saul some of this revelation during the time he was blind, but probably most of it was given during that time he was in Arabia.

Barnabas Befriends Saul (9:26-31)

[26]And when Saul was come to Jerusalem, he assayed to join himself to the disciples: but they were all afraid of him, and believed not that he was a disciple. [27]But Barnabas took him, and brought *him* to the apostles, and declared unto them how he had seen the Lord in the way, and that he had spoken to him, and how he had preached boldly at Damascus in the name of Jesus. [28]And he was with them coming in and going out at Jerusalem. [29]And he spake boldly in the name of the Lord Jesus, and disputed against the Grecians: but they went about to slay him. [30]*Which* when the

[14]Probably took place in A.D. 38. Cf. Packer, *op. cit.*, p. 74.

brethren knew, they brought him down to Caesarea, and sent him forth to Tarsus.

[31]Then had the churches rest throughout all Judea and Galilee and Samaria, and were edified; and walking in the fear of the Lord, and in the comfort of the Holy Ghost, were multiplied (Acts 9:26-31).

Arriving at Jerusalem, Saul tried to join the disciples (in the worship and service of the Church). But they were all afraid of him. They knew what he had done to the Church; their first thought was that surely this was some sort of trick or deception to find out who they were and to destroy them.

Barnabas, however, was sympathetic, living up to his name as the "son of encouragement." Apparently he did some investigation, then took hold of Saul, brought him to the apostles,[15] and explained how he saw the Lord and that he spoke boldly in Damascus. This implies Barnabas gave them all the details.

For a time Saul was associated with the believers coming in and going out of Jerusalem. He continued to speak boldly and freely in the name of the Lord, but he spent most of his time talking to and disputing (discussing, debating) with the "Grecians," that is, with the Hellenistic or Greek-speaking Jews. He went to the Hellenistic synagogues, including the same ones that debated with Stephen (Acts 6:9). He did not visit the churches of Judea (outside Jerusalem), however, for he says later that he was "unknown by face" to them at this time (Galatians 1:22).

As with Stephen's, Saul's message of the gospel roused the anger of these Hellenistic Jews, and they attempted to kill him. Probably they considered him a traitor who did not need a trial.

As soon as the Jerusalem believers heard about this, they brought Saul down to Caesarea and sent him away to Tarsus. Jesus also appeared to him and told him to leave Jerusalem (Acts 22:17-21). The believers did not send him away simply to save him from being a martyr, however. He was sent out as their representative and as a person qualified to take the gospel to Tarsus, his birthplace. Tarsus, about 300 miles to the north, was the capital and most important city of Cilicia. It was located on the coastal plain, ten miles from the Mediterranean Sea. It was a free

[15]Some of the apostles. Galatians 1:18-24 shows that Saul (Paul) met only Peter and James the brother of Jesus at this time. James was considered an apostle because of Jesus' special appearance to him (1 Corinthians 15:7).

city and a well-known university city, exceeded in educational opportunities only by Athens and Alexandria. Saul was needed there.

With Saul gone, everything quieted down again. Luke, in another brief summary, shows that the Church throughout the whole of Judea, Galilee, and Samaria had rest (peace), was edified (built up spiritually and in numbers), walked in the fear of the Lord and the encouragement of the Holy Spirit, and was multiplied.

We see from this that both Galilee and Samaria had been well evangelized by this time, even though Luke gives no details about how it was done. Notice also that the word Church is singular. The various assemblies in these regions were in fellowship with each other and constituted one body under the headship of Christ (Ephesians 1:22, 23).

Peter in Lydda (9:32-35)

> [32]And it came to pass, as Peter passed throughout all *quarters,* he came down also to the saints which dwelt at Lydda. [33]And there he found a certain man named Aeneas, which had kept his bed eight years, and was sick of the palsy. [34]And Peter said unto him, Aeneas, Jesus Christ maketh thee whole: arise, and make thy bed. And he arose immediately. [35]And all that dwelt at Lydda and Sharon saw him, and turned to the Lord (Acts 9:32-35).

After the summary statement in verse 31, Luke begins a sequence that leads to Peter's bringing the gospel to the Gentiles in Caesarea. Since the conditions in Jerusalem were now peaceful, he could leave the city. So he began to go through all the region mentioned in verse 31. As he journeyed he came down to visit the saints (dedicated believers) living at Lydda (on the road to Joppa).

Finding a paralytic there named Aeneas who lay paralyzed on his bed (mattress) for eight years, he said, "Aeneas, Jesus Christ is healing you. Rise and make your bed" (now, at this moment, while Peter was speaking).[16] His healing was instantaneous. All the inhabitants of Lydda and the Sharon plain west and northwest of Lydda saw him and turned to the Lord (Jesus).

---

[16]"Make your bed" is a phrase that in Greek can be used of making a bed but is also used of preparing a meal (as in Mark 14:15 and Luke 22:12). Thus, another possible meaning is that Aeneas should take food.

PETER BROUGHT TO JOPPA (9:36-43)

[36]Now there was at Joppa a certain disciple named Tabitha, which by interpretation is called Dorcas: this woman was full of good works and almsdeeds which she did. [37]And it came to pass in those days, that she was sick, and died: whom when they had washed, they laid *her* in an upper chamber. [38]And forasmuch as Lydda was nigh to Joppa, and the disciples had heard that Peter was there, they sent unto him two men, desiring *him* that he would not delay to come to them. [39]Then Peter arose and went with them. When he was come, they brought him into the upper chamber: and all the widows stood by him weeping, and showing the coats and garments which Dorcas made, while she was with them. [40]But Peter put them all forth, and kneeled down, and prayed; and turning *him* to the body said, Tabitha, arise. And she opened her eyes: and when she saw Peter, she sat up. [41]And he gave her *his* hand, and lifted her up; and when he had called the saints and widows, he presented her alive. [42]And it was known throughout all Joppa; and many believed in the Lord. [43]And it came to pass, that he tarried many days in Joppa with one Simon a tanner (Acts 9:36-43).

At Joppa, a seaport on the Mediterranean coast about ten miles northwest of Lydda and 39 miles from Jerusalem, lived Tabitha (her Aramaic name). She was also known by the corresponding Greek name, Dorcas ("gazelle"; an antelope that was considered a symbol of gracefulness). She was full of good deeds, especially deeds for the poor which she kept doing. Some believe her ministry is an example of the gift of helps (1 Corinthians 12:28).

While Peter was at Lydda, Dorcas became sick and died. They washed her, put her in an upper room, and sent two men to ask Peter not to hesitate to come. When Peter arrived in the upper room, all the widows were standing around weeping and showing the tunics (undergarments) and the long, flowing outer garments Dorcas was (always) making while she was with them.

Because of their hopeless attitude, Peter put them all out of the room, went on his knees, prayed, and then turned to the body and in faith said, "Tabitha, arise!" (Many see a parallel here between "Tabitha cumi" and Talitha cumi" in Mark 5:41.) Putting the mourners out paralleled what Jesus did when He raised the daughter of Jairus (Luke 8:54). Peter was with Him then and learned that an atmosphere of unbelief is not conducive to the faith that sees miracles. Peter did something Jesus did not do at that time, however. He spent time in prayer.

In answer to his prayer, Dorcas opened her eyes, looked at Peter, then sat up. Giving her his hand, he raised her up. Then, calling the saints (all the believers), he presented her alive.

This became known throughout the whole of Joppa and became a means of spreading the gospel. Many believed on the Lord (Jesus), but Peter took no credit for this. However, he stayed in Joppa for a considerable time with a certain Simon, a tanner (considered an unclean occupation by many).

ACTS
CHAPTER
10

Chapters 10 and 11 bring us to an important turning point in the Book of Acts. Though Jesus commissioned the apostles to teach (make disciples of) all nations (Matthew 28:19), they were not anxious to do this. Those who were scattered by the persecution after Stephen's death at first preached the gospel to Jews only (Acts 11:19). Apparently they interpreted all nations to mean the Jews scattered among all nations.

It was obvious from the beginning of the Church that being converted to Christ and even being baptized in the Holy Spirit did not automatically remove the prejudices people grew up with. Peter had made some progress: He accepted the Lord's work in saving the Samaritans. But they were circumcised and kept the Law about as well as many of the Jews did. He was also willing to stay in the home of an "unclean" tanner who was a believer. He had not faced the biggest barrier, however. Many laws and customs separated Jews from Gentiles, especially the dietary laws.[1] Nor would any Jew eat food prepared by a Gentile, for he believed this too would make him unclean.

Cornelius Sends for Peter (10:1-8)

[1]There was a certain man in Caesarea called Cornelius, a centurion of the band called the Italian *band,* [2]*a* devout *man,* and one that feared God with all his house, which gave much alms to the people, and prayed to God always. [3]He saw in a vision evidently, about the ninth hour of the day, an angel of God coming in to him, and saying unto him, Cornelius. [4]And when he looked on him, he was afraid, and said, What is it, Lord?

[1]The laws against unclean food had good reason behind them. Much of the ceremonially unclean food was likely to spread diseases such as trichinosis and tapeworm.

And he said unto him, Thy prayers and thine alms are come up for a memorial before God. [5]And now send men to Joppa, and call for *one* Simon, whose surname is Peter: [6]he lodgeth with one Simon a tanner, whose house is by the sea side: he shall tell thee what thou oughtest to do. [7]And when the angel which spake unto Cornelius was departed, he called two of his household servants, and a devout soldier of them that waited on him continually; [8]and when he had declared all *these* things unto them, he sent them to Joppa (Acts 10:1-8).

In Caesarea (about 30 miles north of Joppa), the capital of Judea under the Roman procurators, Rome stationed a special band (cohort)[2] of soldiers known as the Italian cohort. One of them, Cornelius, was a centurion commanding 100 infantry. He would compare to a modern army captain in authority and responsibility. Like all the centurions mentioned in the New Testament, he was a good man, and, like the one Jesus commended in Matthew 8:10,11, he was also a man of faith.

Some Gentiles in those days were tired of the foolishness, idolatry, and immorality of the religions of Rome and Greece. Many, including Cornelius, found something better in the teaching of the synagogues and accepted the truth of the one true God. Luke calls Cornelius devout. In other words, he was right in his attitudes toward both God and man and by grace was living a godly life. He also feared (reverenced) God, as did his entire household (including both family and servants). Through his influence they all attended the synagogue, sat in the back, listened to the teaching, and believed God. However, they had not become full proselytes or converts to Judaism. Consequently, they had not accepted circumcision and did not keep the dietary laws. Cornelius, however, was generous in charitable giving to the people (the Jews) and prayed to God always ("through all"; that is, daily, and in every circumstance). In other words, he really looked to the Lord to guide him in all things.

From verse 37 it is also evident that Cornelius knew the gospel. Many Bible scholars believe that Cornelius wanted to accept Christ and be filled with the Holy Spirit, but was told that he would have to become a Jew first. It is very possible that at this very time he was considering taking that step.

---

[2]An ordinary cohort had 600 foot soldiers under a tribune. But evidence has been found that this was an auxiliary cohort of 1,000 men. See Bruce, *op. cit.*, p. 215.

We can be sure, however, that God saw his heart's desire. About 3 o'clock in the afternoon, the Jewish hour of evening prayer, he was fasting and praying. (See verse 30.) Suddenly an angel appeared to him in a vision ("something seen"), that is, in an actual appearance or revelation, openly in full daylight. This was no dream or dream-type vision; it was very real. Notice verse 7 where we read that the angel went away. This confirms that this was an actual occurrence, not merely a dream-type vision.

As Cornelius directed his gaze on the angel, he became afraid (full of awe, fear, even terror). This was a natural reaction to the supernatural by a man who had never experienced anything supernatural before. But, in spite of his fear, he asked, "What is it Lord?" thus taking the angel to be a divine manifestation. The angel, however, directed his attention to God. His prayers and charitable giving had gone up (ascended) as a memorial (reminder, or, better, a remembrance offering)[3] before God. Then the angel directed him to send men (of his own choice) to Joppa for Simon Peter who was being entertained by Simon the tanner. Peter would then tell him what it would be necessary for him to do.[4]

As soon as the angel left, Cornelius called two of his household slaves. As verse 2 indicates, these were God-fearers. He also called a devout (godly, God-fearing) soldier who was closely attached to him. After explaining to them in detail what the angel had said, he sent the three of them to Joppa to get Peter.

PETER'S VISIONS (10:9-22)

[9]On the morrow, as they went on their journey, and drew nigh unto the city, Peter went up upon the housetop to pray about the sixth hour: [10]and he became very hungry, and would have eaten: but while they made ready, he fell into a trance, [11]and saw heaven opened, and a certain vessel descending unto him, as it had been a great sheet knit at the four corners, and let down to the earth: [12]wherein were all manner of four-footed beasts of the earth, and wild beasts, and creeping things, and fowls of the air. [13]And there came a voice to him, Rise, Peter; kill, and eat. [14]But Peter said, Not so, Lord; for I have never eaten any thing that is common or unclean. [15]And the voice *spake* unto him again the second time, What

[3]The Old Testament offerings included memorials. See Leviticus 2:2; Numbers 5:26.

[4]Some ancient manuscripts omit the last part of verse 6, but it fits the context.

God hath cleansed, *that* call not thou common. [16]This was done thrice: and the vessel was received up again into heaven.

[17]Now while Peter doubted in himself what this vision which he had seen should mean, behold, the men which were sent from Cornelius had made inquiry for Simon's house, and stood before the gate, [18]and called, and asked whether Simon, which was surnamed Peter, were lodged there. [19]While Peter thought on the vision, the Spirit said unto him, Behold, three men seek thee. [20]Arise therefore, and get thee down, and go with them, doubting nothing: for I have sent them. [21]Then Peter went down to the men which were sent unto him from Cornelius; and said, Behold, I am he whom ye seek: what *is* the cause wherefore ye are come? [22]And they said, Cornelius the centurion, a just man, and one that feareth God, and of good report among all the nation of the Jews, was warned from God by a holy angel to send for thee into his house, and to hear words of thee (Acts 10:9-22).

The next day about noon the three men sent by Cornelius were nearing Joppa. God is always faithful to work on both ends of the line, and it was time to prepare Peter.

Peter went up to the flat roof of the house by an outside stairway. Most Jews considered noon one of the hours of prayer (Psalm 55:17; Daniel 6:10). But, even though he intended to pray, he became very hungry and wanted to eat. He let his hosts know this; while he remained on the roof waiting for them to prepare the food, he "fell into a trance." This does not mean a trance in the modern sense of the word, however, nor does it imply a hypnotic state. It simply means his mind was distracted from whatever he was thinking about as he sensed something important was about to happen.

Then he saw heaven opened and a vessel (container) descending. It was something like an enormous sheet[5] tied at the corners and filled with all kinds of quadrupeds, wild animals, reptiles of the earth, and birds of the air. A voice commanded, "Rise, Peter; kill and eat." Peter was spiritually sensitive enough to know that this was the voice of the Lord (that is, the Lord Jesus). But his prejudices overcame his normal desire to obey the Lord. So he replied, "Not so (not at all, never), Lord." For he had never at any time eaten anything common (profane, dirty) or unclean (that is, nonkosher).[6]

---

[5]or sailcloth. Cf. Packer, *op. cit.*, p. 82.

[6]See Leviticus 11:3. Clean animals were those that both chewed the cud and had split hooves. Jesus had already prepared His disciples for the abolishing of these food laws (Mark 7:15-19), but so far they failed to understand.

The voice replied, "What God has cleansed don't you regard as common (unclean)." The negative here is very emphatic. From now on he must not ever treat anything as unclean when God has cleansed it. Then, for further emphasis, this was repeated three times. Peter's prejudice was so strong it took this extreme emphasis to fix this truth in his mind.

Peter had enough spiritual discernment to know that this vision had a meaning beyond that of eating nonkosher food. The fact that he doubted what this meant does not mean he had any doubts that it had a meaning. "Doubted" means, rather, that he was having difficulty trying to figure out what it meant. He was perplexed, at a loss to explain it.

God did not let him speculate for long, however. The men sent by Cornelius were already at the gate, shouting to get attention and inquiring for Peter. So the Holy Spirit interrupted his thoughts (his ponderings, his weighing of this and that possibility) about the vision and told him three men were looking for him. He must arise, go down (the outside stairway)[7] from the rooftop, and go with them, doubting nothing, that is, without any hesitation. (*Doubt* in verse 20 translates a different Greek word [*diakrinomenos*] than the one used in verse 17 [*dieporei*]). The Holy Spirit had sent them by prompting the obedience by which Cornelius sent them.

Peter obeyed, told the men he was the one they were looking for, and politely asked the reason they had come. They explained, adding that Cornelius was a man of good report among the whole of the Jewish people.

PETER MEETS CORNELIUS (10:23-33)

[23]Then called he them in, and lodged *them.* And on the morrow Peter went away with them, and certain brethren from Joppa accompanied him. [24]And the morrow after they entered into Caesarea. And Cornelius waited for them, and had called together his kinsmen and near friends. [25]And as Peter was coming in, Cornelius met him, and fell down at his feet, and worshipped *him.* [26]But Peter took him up, saying, Stand up; I myself also am a man. [27]And as he talked with him, he went in, and found many that were come together. [28]And he said unto them, Ye know how that it is an unlawful thing for a man that is a Jew to keep company, or come unto one of another nation; but God hath showed me that I should

[7]The author has seen such outside stairways made of stone in the ruins of Biblical cities excavated in Palestine.

not call any man common or unclean. [29]Therefore came I *unto you* without gainsaying, as soon as I was sent for: I ask therefore for what intent ye have sent for me?

[30]And Cornelius said, Four days ago I was fasting until this hour; and at the ninth hour I prayed in my house, and, behold, a man stood before me in bright clothing, [31]and said, Cornelius, thy prayer is heard, and thine alms are had in remembrance in the sight of God. [32]Send therefore to Joppa, and call hither Simon, whose surname is Peter; he is lodged in the house of *one* Simon a tanner by the sea side: who, when he cometh, shall speak unto thee. [33]Immediately therefore I sent to thee; and thou hast well done that thou art come. Now therefore are we all here present before God, to hear all things that are commanded thee of God (Acts 10:23-33).

In the morning, after providing them with hospitality for the night, Peter went with the three men. But he was careful to take six good, believing Jewish brothers with him. (See Acts 11:12.) He knew he would be called into question by other believers for going into a Gentile house, so he wanted some witnesses he could depend on. Just to be sure, he took double the two or three required by the Law. (See Matthew 18:16; Deuteronomy 19:15.)

The next day when they arrived at Caesarea, they found Cornelius waiting for them with a house full of people. He believed the Lord's promise. Therefore, he expected Peter to come at once, judged the time of his arrival, and took it upon himself to call together all his relatives and close friends.

When Peter arrived, Cornelius was so conscious that God had sent him that as soon as he met him he fell down at Peter's feet and worshiped (bowed on his knees before him). Peter probably was shocked by this. Quickly he took hold of him and raised him up, telling him to stand and saying emphatically that he also was a man, a human being. Peter did not want anyone to give any human personality preeminence in the Church.

The text implies that when Peter came in he was surprised to see so many people. He began his sermon by reminding the assembled crowd that it was unlawful (illegal and abominable) for a Jew to keep company (join closely to)[8] or to come to (implying agreement with) a foreigner. But he was there because God had showed him not to say any man (any human being) is common or

[8]The same word is used of Paul attempting to join the disciples in Jerusalem (Acts 9:26).

unclean. Therefore, he came without saying anything against the request to come. Now, however, he inquired about their reason.

In answer, Cornelius recounted how four days before (counting that day as the fourth day) a man in bright (shining) clothing told him to send for Peter, which he did. Now Peter had done well to come. That is, they were pleased that he had come.[9] All of them were there before God (in the presence of God) to hear from Peter all that God commanded (instructed) him to tell them.

Good News for Gentiles (10:34-43)

[34]Then Peter opened *his* mouth, and said, Of a truth I perceive that God is no respecter of persons: [35]but in every nation he that feareth him, and worketh righteousness, is accepted with him. [36]The word which *God* sent unto the children of Israel, preaching peace by Jesus Christ: (he is Lord of all:) [37]that word, *I say,* ye know, which was published throughout all Judea, and began from Galilee, after the baptism which John preached; [38]how God anointed Jesus of Nazareth with the Holy Ghost and with power: who went about doing good, and healing all that were oppressed of the devil; for God was with him.

[39]And we are witnesses of all things which he did both in the land of the Jews, and in Jerusalem: whom they slew and hanged on a tree: [40]him God raised up the third day, and showed him openly; [41]not to all the people, but unto witnesses chosen before of God, *even* to us, who did eat and drink with him after he rose from the dead. [42]And he commanded us to preach unto the people, and to testify that it is he which was ordained of God *to be* the Judge of quick and dead. [43]To him give all the prophets witness, that through his name whosoever believeth in him shall receive remission of sins (Acts 10:34-43).

Peter's sermon at the house of Cornelius is a landmark in the history of the Early Church.[10] From the start, he shows that now he understood fully the meaning of his repeated vision given on the rooftop. He saw that God truly is no respecter of persons. That is, He does not show favoritism or partiality. In every nation, the one who fears (worships and reverences) God and works (gives operation to) righteousness (as evidence of the divine grace they have received by faith) is acceptable to Him.

---

[9]This is an idiomatic phrase that does not mean Peter had done a good thing, but rather, they were pleased.

[10]The phrase "opened his mouth" was used to introduce an important discourse. C. H. Dodd (cited by Harrison, *op. cit.,* p. 173) draws attention to the similarity between Peter's preaching here and the Gospel of Mark. Ancient tradition says Mark reported Peter's preaching in his Gospel.

God's impartiality is not a new idea here. It was taught in such Old Testament passages as Deuteronomy 10:17; 2 Samuel 14:14; 2 Chronicles 19:7. (See also Amos 9:7; Romans 2:11; 1 Peter 1:17). This does not mean that God cannot make a choice, but that He does not base His choice on, or limit it to, national or external differences. So, these Gentiles, if they fulfilled these qualifications of worship, faith, and faithfulness, were just as acceptable to God as any Jew.

Peter then reminds Cornelius and his friends of the Word (the message) God sent to Israel preaching (telling the good news, the gospel of) peace by (through) Jesus Christ.

At this point, Peter cannot help interjecting "He is Lord of all." Then he goes on, reminding them of the message[11] which they knew. "You know" is emphatic in the Greek here. This means they knew the facts about Jesus, including the promise of the Holy Spirit. Possibly they had heard Philip preach. In any case, Peter recognized that someone had given them the message for it was preached through all Judea beginning from Galilee after the baptism John preached. No one who attended the synagogues could have escaped hearing about it.

The message was Jesus himself, Jesus from Nazareth whom God anointed with the Holy Spirit and mighty power. (See Isaiah 11:2; 61:1, 2; Luke 4:18, 19.) This Jesus went about doing good (kind) deeds and healing all who were oppressed (overpowered or treated harshly) by the devil ("the slanderer"; the chief slanderer of all), for God was with Him.

Peter then adds, "We (meaning the apostles rather than the believers from Joppa) are witnesses of everything He did in Judea and in Jerusalem." Then Peter goes on with the message. This One who did nothing but good, they killed and hung on a tree (something made of wood, that is, the cross). In contrast to what men did to Jesus, God raised (resurrected) Him on the third day. (See Hosea 6:2; 1 Corinthians 15:4, 20, 23.) Then God permitted Him to be manifest (visible), not to all the people, but to witnesses chosen by God beforehand, namely, to Peter and the others who ate and drank with Him after He rose from (out from among) the dead. This was concrete proof of the reality of Christ's resurrec-

[11]Word or message is *logon* in verse 36 and *rhema* in verse 37. Clearly *logos* and *rhema* are used interchangeably.

tion body. He was not a spirit, not a figment of their imagination, but a very real person with whom they had fellowship.

Because of Christ's command these witnesses were proclaiming this good news to the people and solemnly testifying that Jesus was ordained (designated, appointed) as Judge of the living and the dead. By this Peter did not mean the spiritually living and the spiritually dead. Rather, Jesus is and will be Judge of all who have ever or will ever live on earth.[12] This bears out what Jesus said in John 5:22, "The Father judgeth no man, but hath committed all judgment unto the Son." Therefore, just as Jesus is the Mediator between God and man in redemption, so He will be in judgment.

Then, as he usually did, Peter brought in the witness of the prophets. Their witness as a whole gives further proof that whoever believes in Him receives remission (forgiveness) of sins through His name—by His authority and because of who He is (the crucified and risen Saviour).

The Holy Spirit Poured Out (10:44-48)

[44]While Peter yet spake these words, the Holy Ghost fell on all them which heard the word. [45]And they of the circumcision which believed were astonished, as many as came with Peter, because that on the Gentiles also was poured out the gift of the Holy Ghost. [46]For they heard them speak with tongues, and magnify God. Then answered Peter, [47]Can any man forbid water, that these should not be baptized, which have received the Holy Ghost as well as we? [48]And he commanded them to be baptized in the name of the Lord. Then prayed they him to tarry certain days (Acts 10:44-48).

While Peter was still speaking these words (Greek, *rhemata*), there came a sudden, unexpected interruption from heaven. The Holy Spirit fell on all who heard the Word.[13] This totally amazed the Jewish believers who had come with Peter. In fact, it almost knocked them out of their senses to see the Holy Spirit poured out on the Gentiles.

"Poured out" relates this occurence to what happened on the Day of Pentecost (Acts 2:17, 33). So does the fact they spoke with tongues (languages) and magnified God. This evidence clearly

---

[12]Alexander, *op. cit.*, I, 414.

[13]Greek, *logon*. What Peter spoke was *rhema*, but what they heard was *logos*. Again, the two words are used interchangeably.

convinced these Jewish believers. It also shows that the Pentecostal experience can be repeated.

Peter recognized that this was further confirmation that they were not only accepted by God but were made part of the Church. The Holy Spirit at Pentecost was poured out on believers who were already identified as the Church and as the Temple of the Holy Spirit.[14] With this kind of evidence, who could forbid baptism in water. Their experience in receiving the Spirit was exactly the same as that of the Jewish believers.

From this we can see that these Gentiles, whose hearts were prepared by the angel's message, believed and were saved while Peter was preaching. They then were ready for the outpouring of the Holy Spirit. Later, in Acts 15:8, Peter says, "God, which knoweth the hearts, bare them witness, giving them the Holy Ghost, even as He did unto us." This surely means that the baptism in the Holy Spirit bore witness to the faith they already had before they were filled with the Spirit.[15]

At Peter's instructions, they were baptized in the name (by the authority) of the Lord (Jesus Christ). This was a public declaration of their faith, a witness to the faith they already had, a witness to the faith that had already brought cleansing to their hearts (Acts 15:9).[16]

Then the people asked Peter to remain with them some (a few) days. Undoubtedly they wanted more instruction and desired to share spiritual fellowship with him.

---

[14]See Horton, *op. cit.*, pp. 141, 142.

[15]Compare Titus 3:5, 6, which shows that the pouring out of the Spirit in Pentecostal fullness is something that happens after regeneration. Cf. Horton, *op. cit.*, p. 250.

[16]See 1 Peter 3:21 noting it was the faith Noah had before the flood that was witnessed to by the fact he came through the flood. So water baptism testified to the faith which has already purified our hearts. The water is a symbol and had no power or grace in itself, nor does it convey any. Compare Romans 10:9, 10.

ACTS
CHAPTER 11

Peter was right in believing he would need witnesses with him when he went to the house of Cornelius. He found it necessary to explain everything that happened there. The fact that Luke records this, repeating much of what was said in chapter 10, shows how important these events in Caesarea were. From them they learned that God would accept the Gentiles without circumcision, that is, without their becoming Jews. The repetition thus gives emphasis to the fact that Christianity was not something just to add on or tack on to Judaism. Gentiles could come directly under the New Covenant without coming first under the Old Covenant. They could have the promise to Abraham without the outward sign of the Abrahamic covenant.

Peter's Explanation Accepted (11:1-18)

[1]And the apostles and brethren that were in Judea heard that the Gentiles had also received the word of God. [2]And when Peter was come up to Jerusalem, they that were of the circumcision contended with him, [3]saying, Thou wentest in to men uncircumcised, and didst eat with them. [4]But Peter rehearsed *the matter* from the beginning, and expounded *it* by order unto them, saying, [5]I was in the city of Joppa praying: and in a trance I saw a vision, a certain vessel descend, as it had been a great sheet, let down from heaven by four corners; and it came even to me: [6]upon the which when I had fastened mine eyes, I considered, and saw fourfooted beasts of the earth, and wild beasts, and creeping things, and fowls of the air. [7]And I heard a voice saying unto me, Arise, Peter; slay and eat.

[8]But I said, Not so, Lord: for nothing common or unclean hath at any time entered into my mouth. [9]But the voice answered me again from heaven, What God hath cleansed, *that* call not thou common. [10]And this was done three times: and all were drawn up again into heaven. [11]And, behold, immediately there were three men already come unto the house where I was, sent from Caesarea unto me. [12]And the Spirit bade me go

with them, nothing doubting. Moreover these six brethren accompanied me, and we entered into the man's house: [13]and he showed us how he had seen an angel in his house, which stood and said unto him, Send men to Joppa, and call for Simon, whose surname is Peter; [14]who shall tell thee words, whereby thou and all thy house shall be saved.

[15]And as I began to speak, the Holy Ghost fell on them, as on us at the beginning. [16]Then remembered I the word of the Lord, how that he said, John indeed baptized with water; but ye shall be baptized with the Holy Ghost. [17]Forasmuch then as God gave them the like gift as *he did* unto us, who believed on the Lord Jesus Christ, what was I, that I could withstand God? [18]When they heard these things, they held their peace, and glorified God, saying, Then hath God also to the Gentiles granted repentance unto life (Acts 11:1-18).

The Gentiles at the house of Cornelius received (welcomed) the Word of God. This means they received it willingly, acknowledged its truth, and accepted its message of repentance, forgiveness, and salvation. This was striking news, and to some of the Jews was probably not good news. Such news travels fast and reached the apostles and the rest of the brethren (the believers) in Jerusalem before Peter returned.

When he arrived "they of the circumcision" (which at this time would include all the believers in Jerusalem, for all were Jews or full proselytes) were ready for him.[1] Immediately they contended with him (criticized him, passed judgment on him) for entering the house of uncircumcised men (which they considered defiling), and, even worse, eating with them. The fact that these believers were upset is shown by the fact that they did not use the usual word for "uncircumcised." Instead, they used a slang word that was very derogatory toward the Gentiles. It is quite probable, also, that one reason they were upset was because they were afraid that Peter's action might bring to an end the period of peace they had been enjoying by turning the unconverted Jews against them.

Peter then proceeded to explain everything to them from the beginning, that is, from the time he saw the vision in Joppa. He does add that the sheet came down close to him so that he was able to look closely and inspect the contents without any possibility of being mistaken. He was also careful to point to the six witnesses who were with him at Caesarea and whom he had brought with

[1]This implies that all the Jewish believers up to this point believed Gentiles had to become Jews before becoming Christians. Cf. Hackett, *op. cit.*, p. 138. Harrison, *op. cit.*, p. 177 disagrees, but without sufficient reason.

him to Jerusalem (verse 12). As further proof of God's leading, he adds that the angel told Cornelius that Peter would speak words by which Cornelius and all his household would be saved.

Then, without repeating the sermon he gave at Caesarea, Peter told them that as he began to speak[2] the Holy Spirit fell on them "as on us." That is, just as really and as evidently as on the 120 and the 3,000 on the Day of Pentecost, "at the beginning." Some writers try to avoid mentioning the Day of Pentecost here. But this can only mean as on the Day of Pentecost (Acts 2:4), since there was no falling upon or pouring out of the Spirit in fulfillment of Joel's prophecy until then.

Peter next added something that had gone on in his own mind. He remembered the word of the Lord (Jesus) given in Acts 1:5, that John baptized in water but they would be baptized in the Holy Spirit. Thus, he clearly saw that this outpouring was also a baptism in the Spirit.

Peter then went on to say that God gave these Gentiles the like gift as He did to the Jewish believers. "Like" in the Greek means equal or identical.[3] This is significant because the convincing evidence was not wind or fire (which really only preceded the Pentecostal outpouring of the Spirit and were not actually part of it). They needed a convincing evidence, and the one convincing evidence given was the fact they spoke in other tongues and magnified God (gave glory to God).

The Gentiles did not have to ask if they had really received this mighty outpouring. They knew. Peter and the six witnesses did not say "I think" or "I suppose" or even "I trust" or "I believe" these Gentiles were baptized in the Spirit. They knew. Surely, in the midst of all the questioning and discussion about the Holy Spirit today, we need the same convincing evidence. We too can know that we have received the identical experience described in Acts 2:4.

Since God gave the Gentiles this gift of the Spirit, for Peter to refuse to accept them would be to withstand God—and who was he—and who is any man—to do that.

The Jewish believers in Jerusalem could not withstand God

[2]Evidently Peter considered what he said in Caesarea to be just the introduction to the sermon he could have preached.

[3]The masculine form of the same word is *isos,* and is found in the word *isosceles,* a triangle where two of the three sides are equal, that is, identical.

either. The facts of the case silenced all their previous objections; they were responsive enough to the Spirit and the Word to glorify God and to recognize that God had given even to the Gentiles repentance unto life. More specifically, God had accepted their repentance and given them spiritual life without their being circumcised; the baptism in the Holy Spirit bore witness to that.

GENTILES BELIEVE IN ANTIOCH (11:19-21)

[19]Now they which were scattered abroad upon the persecution that arose about Stephen traveled as far as Phoenicia, and Cyprus, and Antioch, preaching the word to none but unto the Jews only. [20]And some of them were men of Cyprus and Cyrene, which, when they were come to Antioch, spake unto the Grecians, preaching the Lord Jesus. [21]And the hand of the Lord was with them: and a great number believed and turned unto the Lord (Acts 11:19-21).

Though the Jerusalem apostles and believers accepted the fact that Gentiles in Caesarea were saved and had become part of the Church, this did not excite them very much. There was no rush to go out and win more Gentiles to the Lord. In fact, even Peter continued to consider his ministry as primarily to the Jews (Galatians 2:7-9). Thus Luke turns our attention to a new center for the spread of the gospel, Antioch of Syria, located on the Orantes River, over 300 miles north of Jerusalem. It was a great trade center, the largest city in Asia Minor, and the capital of the Roman province of Syria. Founded about 300 B.C. by Seleucus I Nicator, its importance was recognized by the Romans, who made it a free city in 64 B.C.

Verse 19 makes a connection with Acts 8:1, 4. (See also 9:31.) Up to this point the examples of what happened were taken from Judea and Samaria. Now we see that the wave of itinerant evangelism did not stop there. But, as always, Luke does not try to cover everything. Instead, following the inspiration of the Holy Spirit, he selects one direction this evangelism took and presents it as an example of what went on in many directions. There was a special reason for choosing the direction toward Antioch, however. It forms a link with the Apostle Paul and prepares for the account of his journeys that takes up the major portion of the rest of the Book of Acts.

Even outside of Palestine, however, those who spread the gospel preached the Word only to Jews. This may not have been entirely due to prejudice. The Jews had the Old Testament Scriptures and knew the prophecies. (See Romans 3:2.) These evangelists based their message on the fact that God, through Jesus had fulfilled prophecy. Most Gentiles had no background to understand this. But these evangelists were overlooking the fact that many Gentiles had lost their confidence in their idols and were looking for something better.

The evangelizers travelled up the coast of Asia Minor as far as Phenice (Phoenicia) where churches were established in Tyre and Sidon (Acts 21:3, 4; 27:3). From there some went to the island of Cyprus; others kept going north to Antioch. Some of these were men of Cyprus and Cyrene and may have been among the 3,000 who were saved and filled with the Spirit on the Day of Pentecost. They began (undoubtedly led and prompted by the Holy Spirit) at Antioch to speak to Greeks (Greek-speaking Gentiles),[4] telling the good news (the gospel) of the Lord Jesus.

The hand of the Lord was with them. This expression is often used in the Bible to mean the power of the Lord or even the Spirit of the Lord (as in Ezekiel 1:3; 3:14, 22, 24; 8:1; 11:1).[5] Certainly, the miracle-working power of the Lord was manifest, confirming the Word as in Samaria (Acts 8:5-8); a great number believed and turned to the Lord. This means they turned away from their heathen customs and worldly ways to follow Jesus. We can be sure also that they were all baptized in the Holy Spirit as was the household of Cornelius. As Peter said, God is not a respecter of persons.

Barnabas Sent to Antioch (11:22-26)

[22]Then tidings of these things came unto the ears of the church which was in Jerusalem: and they sent forth Barnabas, that he should go as far as Antioch. [23]Who, when he came, and had seen the grace of God, was glad, and exhorted them all, that with purpose of heart they would cleave unto the Lord. [24]For he was a good man, and full of the Holy Ghost and of faith: and much people was added unto the Lord. [25]Then departed Barnabas to Tarsus, for to seek Saul: [26]And when he had found him,

---

[4]Many ancient manuscripts have the word here for "Greek-speakers" which is sometimes used of Greek-speaking Jews, but in this context it clearly means Greek-speaking Gentiles.

[5]See Horton, *op. cit.*, p. 66.

he brought him unto Antioch. And it came to pass, that a whole year they assembled themselves with the church, and taught much people. And the disciples were called Christians first in Antioch (Acts 11:22-26).

When news of the conversion of these Gentiles in Antioch reached the Jerusalem Church, they recognized that this great spread of the gospel among Gentiles was an important new development. Antioch itself was significant, since it was the third most important city in the entire Roman Empire, exceeded only by Rome and Alexandria. So they sent out Barnabas to go as far as Antioch.

The choice of Barnabas is important. It shows that the Jerusalem Church (not just the apostles) was concerned about this new assembly in Antioch and sent out their best encourager to help them. That he was sent "as far as" Antioch implies also that he was to preach the gospel and encourage others all along the way.

Some writers have assumed that sending Barnabas meant the Church at Jerusalem wanted to maintain control over this new development. However, there is no evidence of this. It was just brotherly love and concern. The same loving Spirit that sent Peter and John to Samaria to help the people there moved the Church here also. Barnabas did not have to report back to Jerusalem, nor did he have to seek their advice about further steps in ministry that might be necessary.

At Antioch the sight of the manifest grace (unmerited favor) of God made him rejoice. He accepted these Gentiles just as Peter accepted the believers at the house of Cornelius. He then lived up to his name by exhorting (encouraging) them all to purpose openly from their hearts to abide in (or continue with) the Lord. Barnabas knew that difficulties, persecutions, and temptations lay ahead; persistence in a close walk with the Lord would be needed.

Because Barnabas was a good man and full of the Holy Spirit and faith, a considerable crowd of people were added to the Lord. His life, not simply his preaching and teaching, proved to be a most effective witness.

This growth in numbers made Barnabas see that he needed help. He did not, however, send back to Jerusalem to ask them to send someone. Led by the Spirit, we can be sure, he went to

Tarsus to search for Saul. Since he was the one who took the time and effort to find out about Saul and introduce him to the apostles in Jerusalem earlier (Acts 9:27), he obviously knew what God had said about sending Paul to the Gentiles (Acts 22:21). Now it was God's time for him to begin this ministry.[6]

This search for Saul probably took some time. When Barnabas found him, he brought him back to Antioch. The two of them then became the chief teachers of the Church, gathering the believers together and teaching a considerable crowd.

At Antioch, the disciples first received the name (and were publicly called by their fellow-citizens of Antioch) Christians. Up to this time the believers were practically all Jews. The Gentiles, and even the Jews, considered the believers simply as another sect of the Jews. In fact, they were hardly more different from the Pharisees than the Pharisees were from the Sadducees. But now there was an assembly of believers comprised largely of uncircumcised Gentiles.

Obviously, these Gentile believers could not be given a Jewish name, nor could they any longer be considered a sect of the Jews. They needed a new name. Soldiers under particular generals in the Roman army often took the name of their general and added "ian" (Latin *iani,* Greek *ianos)* to indicate they were a soldier and follower of that general. For example, Caesar's soldiers were called Caesariani, and Pompey's soldiers were called Pompeiani. Political parties were also designated by the same sort of suffix.

So the people of Antioch began to call the believers Christiani or Christians, soldiers, followers, partisans of Christ. Some believe the name was first given in derision, but there is no great evidence of this. The believers did not reject the name. They were indeed in the Lord's army, clothed with the full armor of God. (See Ephesians 6:11-18.) It should be noted, however, that the term "Christian" is used elsewhere in the New Testament only in Acts 26:28 and 1 Peter 4:16. For the most part the believers continued to refer to themselves as disciples, brethren, saints, those of the Way, or servants (slaves) of Jesus.

---

[6]Bruce, *op. cit.,* pp. 240, 241, suggests that Saul had been disinherited (see Philippians 3:8), and that he had begun his work evengelizing Gentiles in his native province of Cilicia. See Acts 22:21.

Agabus Prophesies a Famine (11:27-30)

[27]And in these days came prophets from Jerusalem unto Antioch. [28]And there stood up one of them named Agabus, and signified by the Spirit that there should be great dearth throughout all the world: which came to pass in the days of Claudius Caesar. [29]Then the disciples, every man according to his ability, determined to send relief unto the brethren which dwelt in Judea: [30]which also they did, and sent it to the elders by the hands of Barnabas and Saul (Acts 11:27-30).

The various assemblies of believers continued to keep in touch with each other. After Barnabas, others came from Jerusalem to encourage the believers at Antioch. In fact, about the time Saul's first year in Antioch was up, several prophets from Jerusalem came. These men were regularly used in the ministry of the gift of prophecy for edification (to build up spiritually and confirm faith), exhortation (to awaken, encourage, and challenge every believer to move ahead in faithfulness and love), and comfort (to cheer, revive, and encourage hope and expectation).[7] Their ministry thus dealt with the needs of the believers to whom they ministered.

Sometimes they reinforced their exhortations with a foretelling of the future. This was the exception rather than the rule, however. Prophecy in the Bible is always primarily "forthtelling" (speaking for God whatever His message may be) rather than foretelling the future. But on this occasion Agabus, one of the prophets, stood up and indicated by a word from the Spirit (a manifestation of the gift of prophecy given directly by the Spirit in their own language) that a great famine was about to come over the whole inhabited earth. This to them meant the Roman Empire.[8] The famine did take place in the days of Claudius Caesar (A.D. 41-54).

Because the disciples in Antioch felt gratitude for the blessings and teaching brought them from Judea, they decided that each one would contribute according to his ability (as he was pros-

[7]See 1 Corinthians 14:3; cf. Horton, *op. cit.*, p. 225.

[8]"World" is the Greek *oikoumenen*, "inhabited earth." But this word was used in those days to mean the Roman world, for the Romans did not think anything outside of the Empire was worth noticing.

pered) and send relief. This they did, sending it not to the apostles, but to the Jerusalem elders, by Barnabas and Saul. This was done probably about A.D. 46 when Judea especially was hard hit by famine.[9]

[9]Bruce, *op. cit.*, p. 244 also suggests that Saul's (Paul's) visit described in Galatians 2:1-10 fits here. The facts seem to favor this. Thus, at this time Peter, John, James, and other Jerusalem leaders recognized that the gospel Paul preached was the same one they preached.

ACTS
CHAPTER 12

The conversion of Cornelius and the spread of the gospel to Gentiles in Antioch gave a new direction to the Church. As we have seen in chapter 11, Jewish believers in Jerusalem lent their support and gave encouragement to this new development. Though the Jerusalem believers themselves were careful to observe the laws and customs of the Jews, the Jewish rulers and leaders must have been aware of what was happening outside of Jerusalem.

For some time there had been no persecutions of the believers in Jerusalem. In fact, persecution was never steady or continuous in the times of the Early Church, even under the later Romans. But the Jerusalem Jewish leaders always saw the Church as a threat. They were also aware of the ministry of the apostles and saw how many thousands were following them and turning to the Lord.

Herod Kills James (12:1, 2)

[1]Now about that time Herod the king stretched forth *his* hands to vex certain of the church. [2]And he killed James the brother of John with the sword (Acts 12:1, 2).

From A.D. 6 to 41 Judea was governed by procurators sent by the Roman emperor. These men were never popular. Pilate, especially, had angered the Jewish leaders in many ways. He had even taken money from the Temple treasury to build an aqueduct into Jerusalem.

In A.D. 41 the emperor added Judea to the realm of King Herod Agrippa I, who is the King Herod of this chapter. This

Herod was a grandson of the Idumaean (converted Edomite) Herod the Great and his wife Mariamne, a Jewish princess of the Hasmonean (Maccabean) family. Because Herod Agrippa I was a friend of the Roman emperors, Gaius made him king of part of Syria in A.D. 37. Then, in A.D. 39, he added Galilee and Perea after exiling Herod Antipas, the Herod who killed John the Baptist. (Herod Antipas was an uncle of Herod Agrippa I.)

When Herod Agrippa I became king over Judea and Jerusalem he did everything he could to gain and hold the favor of the Jews. Unlike most of the other Herods, he practiced the forms of the Jewish religion faithfully. Apparently, he also saw and heard enough from the Jewish leaders to know of their fears and frustration with respect to the apostles and the Church. He undoubtedly heard how the Sanhedrin had threatened the apostles and how they just kept right on preaching Jesus.

Somewhere in the early part of his reign over Jerusalem, then, he decided to take steps to show he was king and could do more than threaten. So he laid hands on (arrested) some from the Church with the intention of treating them badly. Among them was the Apostle James, John's brother the son of Zebedee. Together with Peter they constituted the inner circle of Jesus' disciples while He ministered on earth. Luke does not give any details, but there does not seem to have been a trial. James was given no opportunity even to witness to his faith. Herod simply had him killed (murdered) with a sword.[1]

Herod Arrests Peter (12:3-6)

[3]And because he saw it pleased the Jews, he proceeded further to take Peter also. (Then were the days of unleavened bread.) [4]And when he had apprehended him, he put *him* in prison, and delivered *him* to four quaternions of soldiers to keep him; intending after Easter to bring him forth to the people. [5]Peter therefore was kept in prison: but prayer was made without ceasing of the church unto God for him. [6]And when

[1]In the Roman style this would mean he was decapitated. Some modern critics suppose John was killed at this time too, since Jesus said they would both drink of the cup of suffering (Mark 10:39). But Jesus did not say they would die at the same time. John actually lived until about A.D. 100 and died in Ephesus, according to strong early tradition. (Papias, according to the Early Church historian Eusebius, supposedly spoke of another John in Ephesus, an elder John. But Papias has been shown to be wrong about other things.) John the Apostle did suffer much. See Revelation 1:9.

Herod would have brought him forth, the same night Peter was sleeping between two soldiers, bound with two chains: and the keepers before the door kept the prison (Acts 12:3-6).

The murder of James pleased (was pleasing, acceptable to) the Jewish leaders and their friends. They had never forgotten how the apostles defied them. Moreover, since most of these leaders were Sadducees, they did not like the teachings of the Christians. They wanted them stopped.

When Herod saw how pleased they were, he proceeded further to arrest Peter, who was the most outspoken of the apostles. But this arrest took place during the seven days of the Feast of Unleavened Bread. These were combined with the Passover feast at this time, and all eight days were called Passover (beginning on the 14th of Nisan, which in our calendar varies between March and April). The King James version in Acts 12:4 translates the word *Pascha,* which is the Aramaic name for the Passover, as "Easter." But the Passover and Unleavened Bread combined is what is meant.

Why Herod decided to wait until after the Passover season before bringing Peter out[2] to the people we are not told. The Jewish leaders did not hesitate to have Jesus killed during this period. Perhaps Herod wanted to show them how strict he was about keeping the Passover. Or, he may have wanted to wait until most of the crowd went home lest there be a riot he could not control. Others suggest he wanted the people's whole attention for the display he intended to put on. Whatever the reason, Herod put Peter in prison under a heavy guard of four squads of four soldiers each.

In the meantime, prayer was made to God continuously and very earnestly by the Church on his behalf. We can be sure they prayed that he would be sustained and be able to give a witness as well as be delivered.

The night before Herod intended to bring him out for trial, sentencing, and execution,[3] Peter was sleeping soundly. He must have committed his case to the Lord; even though he expected to

[2]"leading him up" out of the prison; that is, either for the people's amusement, or so they could witness his execution.

[3]The Greek here is like that used in Acts 25:26 of the apostle Paul being brought to trial before King Agrippa.

face execution on the morrow he could sleep peacefully. He had Christ with him. It would only be more of Christ if he died. (Compare Philippians 1:21.) The early believers were so full of the Lord they did not fear death.

Peter's situation did look hopeless in the natural. Two chains bound him to the two soldiers sleeping on each side of him; guards in front of the door were on watch over the prison. Herod surely had heard of how the apostles escaped from prison before, so he was taking no chances.

An Angel Rescues Peter (12:7-19)

[7]And, behold, the angel of the Lord came upon *him*, and a light shined in the prison: and he smote Peter on the side, and raised him up, saying, Arise up quickly. And his chains fell off from *his* hands. [8]And the angel said unto him, Gird thyself, and bind on thy sandals. And so he did. And he saith unto him, Cast thy garment about thee, and follow me. [9]And he went out, and followed him; and wist not that it was true which was done by the angel; but thought he saw a vision. [10]When they were past the first and the second ward, they came unto the iron gate that leadeth unto the city; which opened to them of his own accord: and they went out, and passed on through one street; and forthwith the angel departed from him. [11]And when Peter was come to himself, he said, Now I know of a surety, that the Lord hath sent his angel, and hath delivered me out of the hand of Herod, and *from* all the expectation of the people of the Jews. [12]And when he had considered *the thing*, he came to the house of Mary the mother of John, whose surname was Mark; where many were gathered together praying. [13]And as Peter knocked at the door of the gate, a damsel came to hearken, named Rhoda. [14]And when she knew Peter's voice, she opened not the gate for gladness, but ran in, and told how Peter stood before the gate. [15]And they said unto her, Thou art mad. But she constantly affirmed that it was even so. Then said they, It is his angel. [16]But Peter continued knocking: and when they had opened *the door*, and saw him, they were astonished. [17]But he, beckoning unto them with the hand to hold their peace, declared unto them how the Lord had brought him out of the prison. And he said, Go show these things unto James, and to the brethren. And he departed, and went into another place.

[18]Now as soon as it was day, there was no small stir among the soldiers, what was become of Peter. [19]And when Herod had sought for him, and found him not, he examined the keepers, and commanded that *they* should be put to death. And he went down from Judea to Caesarea, and *there* abode (Acts 12:7-19).

Suddenly an angel of the Lord came and stood by Peter. A light shined in the prison, possibly from the angel, or possibly as a

separate manifestation so Peter could see what to do. The angel then struck him sharply on the side, aroused him, and told him to get up quickly. (The Greek verb does not necessarily mean that the angel raised or lifted him, but simply that he woke him up.) At the same time, the chains fell off his hands.

After obeying the angelic command to put his belt around his tunic, to put on his sandals and his outer garment, and to follow him, he went out. But all this time he did not really know that what was happening was really true. He thought he was seeing a dream or vision. The guards also were not conscious of what was happening, nor did they see the angel.

After passing through two gates with their guards (which shows Peter was in the innermost prison), the great iron gate that opened into the city (street) opened of its own accord.[4] Then, after the angel led him through one of the narrow streets (probably the length of one),[5] the angel suddenly left him (and disappeared).

Not until the angel left and Peter found himself alone out in the street did he come to himself and realize the Lord had actually sent His angel to rescue him from Herod's power and from the expectation of the Jewish people. That is, from the expectation that Herod would do to him what he had done to the Apostle James.

Having realized this, Peter went to the house of Mary, John Mark's mother. (Mark or Marcus was an added Latin name.) There a considerable number of believers were assembled and were praying. Notice that after several days, people were still praying day and night for Peter. Faithful prayer marked the Early Church.

Mark's mother's house was a large one with a passageway from the street into the inner part of the house where the believers were gathered. The fact that a slave girl, Rhoda (Greek, *Rode,* "rose bush"), answered the door when Peter knocked shows that it was a wealthy home as well. It was obviously the regular meeting place for a large group of believers. Peter knew he would find people there. Undoubtedly, he also felt a special kinship with this

[4]Greek, *automata,* automatically. Codex Bezae (D) adds that they went down seven steps (to the street).

[5]Or, possibly to the next cross street.

group because Mark was his convert and one to whom he had given special training. (See 1 Peter 5:13 where Peter refers to Mark as "my son" in the sense of "my student.")

When Peter knocked at the heavy door of the gate (gateway, that is, the entrance passage that led to the inner court of the house), Rhoda answered. The sound of Peter's familiar voice so filled her with joy that in her excitement she did not open the gateway (door). Instead, she ran in and announced Peter's presence to the assembled believers.

They told her she was raving mad, absolutely crazy. But she kept asserting emphatically that it was so. Then they began to say it was his angel. Some of the Jews had a tradition that a guardian angel could take a person's form. There is absolutely no Biblical grounds for such a teaching, but Luke records what they said here to show they thought Peter was already dead. Though they were praying day and night for his deliverance, they could not believe it had really taken place.

It had been several years since the apostles were delivered from prison before. But it was not the passage of time alone that dulled their faith. The shock of James' death made them wonder if perhaps the Lord might let Peter be killed too. Jesus had indicated to Peter that he would die a martyr's death when he was old (John 21:18, 19). However, Jesus did not say how old, and Peter was older than the other apostles.

Actually, the Bible makes no explanation of why God let James be killed at this time and rescued Peter. We can be sure that in His divine wisdom he knew James' work was done and Peter was still needed on earth. God does all things well!

While all this discussion was going on in the prayer group, Peter was still standing out front knocking. Probably he did not knock too loudly lest he wake the neighborhood and someone sound an alarm. But finally they opened the door and the sight of him nearly made them all fall over with astonishment and amazement.

Apparently they started to cry out excitedly. But Peter waved his hand to silence them and told them how the Lord brought him out of prison. Then he asked them to take the report of this to

James (the brother of Jesus)[6] and to the brethren; that is, to the leading believers associated with James, possibly elders of other local house groups. There were undoubtedly other prayer meetings going on under the leadership of James and the other elders of the Church. James would get word to the rest about Peter's deliverance.

Then Peter, knowing that by dawn Herod's men would be searching for him, left and went to another place (other than Jerusalem). He did not tell anyone where he was going so that they could say honestly that they did not know where he was.[7]

From this also we can see the increasing place of leadership given to James. This may be partly due to the fact he was Jesus' brother. But Jesus had other brothers; there is no evidence that any of them drew attention to their relationship to Jesus or that they tried to capitalize on it in any way. Both James and Jude in their epistles simply refer to themselves as servants (slaves) of the Lord Jesus. James continued to be a leading elder in the Church at Jerusalem until he was stoned to death in A.D. 61 just after Festus died. This shocked the majority of the Jews in Jerusalem, as even those who did not accept Christ held James in high honor and appreciated his many prayers for the people.

It does seem that after Jesus appeared to James (1 Corinthians 15:7), James won his other brothers to the Lord and then they all received teaching from the apostles. From that point they gave themselves to prayer and the service of others. James especially seems to have grown spiritually at a very rapid pace. Later tradition says he had calluses like those of a camel on his knees and that he wore holes in a stone floor by kneeling repeatedly in the same place. All agree that prayer and the gifts of the Spirit made him a spiritual leader.

At dawn there was more than a little disturbance among the

---

[6]Some writers take this to mean James the son of Alphaeus. They also conjecture that he was the only apostle left in Jerusalem and was therefore in charge. Cf. Alexander, *op. cit.,* I, 454. But what is said later on in Acts and in Paul's epistles makes it clear that James the brother of Jesus is meant. See Galatians 1:19; 2:9.

[7]Some writers speculate that Peter went to Rome at this time. There is no evidence for this. In fact, there is no real evidence that Peter ever visited Rome before his martyrdom. Cf. Hackett, *op. cit.,* p. 146. Note that Peter was back in Jerusalem for the conference of Acts 15. He also visited Babylon later, for Babylon was the greatest center of orthodox Judaism outside Palestine (1 Peter 5:13, noting that there is every reason to take this as actual Babylon at the time Peter wrote). There was no reason to disguise Rome by calling it Babylon at that time.

soldiers as they tried to find out what became of Peter. Though Herod had a thorough search made for him, he was not to be found. Then Herod brought the guards in for a preliminary examination, but did not give them a formal trial. Instead, he had them led away and summarily executed. (Roman law punished a guard with the same punishment the escaped prisoner would have received.)

After that, probably in anger, disgust, and disappointment, Herod left Judea (that is, Jerusalem) and went to the other provincial capital on the seacoast (Caesarea) and stayed there. He felt he had been disgraced in Jerusalem, so he never returned.

Herod's Death (12:20-24)

[20]And Herod was highly displeased with them of Tyre and Sidon: but they came with one accord to him, and, having made Blastus the king's chamberlain their friend, desired peace; because their country was nourished by the king's *country.* [21]And upon a set day Herod, arrayed in royal apparel, sat upon his throne, and made an oration unto them. [22]And the people gave a shout, *saying, It is* the voice of a god, and not of a man. [23]And immediately the angel of the Lord smote him, because he gave not God the glory: and he was eaten of worms, and gave up the ghost. [24]But the word of God grew and multiplied (Acts 12:20-24).

At this time, and probably for some time previously, Herod was furiously angry with Tyre and Sidon, practically to the point of war, though war would not have been allowed between two Roman provinces or dependencies. To try to quiet him down, the leaders of Tyre and Sidon got together in one accord and came to Herod. But first they made a friend of Blastus, the king's chamberlain, who was one of Herod's confidential advisers. Using his influence, they asked for peace for themselves. They had good reason: Tyre and Sidon are on a narrow strip of land between the mountains and the sea and they had very little area suitable for agriculture; thus they depended on Palestine for their food supply. (See 1 Kings 5:11; Ezra 3:7; Ezekiel 27:17.) It is indicated also that Barnabas and Saul were in Jerusalem bringing an offering for famine relief at this time. This famine would have been affecting Tyre and Sidon too, so they must have been becoming desperate for a share of the food Palestine produced.

Herod responded, and the leaders along with, undoubtedly, many of the people of Tyre and Sidon gathered in Caesarea on an appointed day. The Greek-style open amphitheater beside the Mediterranean Sea at the ruins of ancient Caesarea is still a marvel of good acoustics. The crowd probably gathered there. Then Herod appeared on the stage in his royal robes. According to the Jewish historian Josephus, the outer robe was of silver (either adorned with silver or actually woven of silver threads). Josephus also adds that the sun's rays were reflected from Herod's silver robe.

After taking his seat on an elevated throne, Herod began an oration (a speech) to the multitude from Tyre and Sidon. These were Greek-speaking, and they had adopted Greek culture and Greek idolatry. In response to Herod's speech, they shouted out, "A god's voice, not a man's." Herod made no objection to this, nor did he give the true God any glory. Immediately an angel of the Lord struck him down. He was eaten by worms and died (expired). Josephus adds that Herod lingered five days with agonizing pains in his belly. This agrees with the text which only says he was struck down immediately, not that he died on the spot. This took place in A.D. 44. After that the Roman emperors again appointed procurators over Judea.

None of this hindered the continued growth of the Church or the spread of the gospel in Palestine. In spite of James' death, Peter's arrest, Herod's attitude, and Herod's death, "The Word of God grew and multiplied."

Barnabas and Saul Return to Antioch (12:25)

And Barnabas and Saul returned from Jerusalem, when they had fulfilled *their* ministry, and took with them John, whose surname was Mark (Acts 12:25).

It seems possible that Barnabas and Saul were in Jerusalem at least during the Passover season when these events took place. Others, because Josephus indicates the famine took place in A.D. 46, two years after Herod's death, suggest that the visit of Paul and Barnabas did not take place until then.[8]

Though the date is not certain, it is clear that Saul and Barnabas fulfilled their ministry and delivered the famine relief to

[8]See Bruce, *op. cit.*, pp. 257, 258; Rackham, *op. cit.*, p. 183.

the Jerusalem elders. Then they returned to Antioch, taking with them John Mark to assist them in the ministry of the church in Antioch. Colossians 4:10 tells us that Mark was the "nephew" (literally, the cousin) of Barnabas. The mention of Mark and the return to Antioch introduces the events of chapter 13.

ACTS

CHAPTER 13

This chapter moves us another important step in the progress of the gospel. Up to this point the gospel was carried to new places by those who were scattered abroad. But there were none who gave themselves specifically to the work of going to new places to start and organize new assemblies.

Barnabas and Saul Sent Out (13:1-3)

[1]Now there were in the church that was at Antioch certain prophets and teachers; as Barnabas, and Simeon that was called Niger, and Lucius of Cyrene, and Manaen, which had been brought up with Herod the tetrarch, and Saul. [2]As they ministered to the Lord, and fasted, the Holy Ghost said, Separate me Barnabas and Saul for the work whereunto I have called them. [3]And when they had fasted and prayed, and laid *their* hands on them, they sent *them* away (Acts 13:3).

By this time in the growing church at Antioch God had raised up others besides Barnabas and Saul to aid in ministering to the church. They are called prophets and teachers here. As prophets they were used by the Spirit to bring edification, exhortation, and comfort or encouragement. As teachers they received gifts from the Holy Spirit which would enable them to teach the Word of God effectively.[1]

These included Simeon (Simon) called Niger. Simeon (Simon) was a common Hebrew name; Niger means black. Some writers believe he was the child of a Jew who had married a Negro. Others speculate that he may have been Simon the Cyrenian who

[1]Some believe all were prophets and teachers, cf. Hackett, *op. cit.*, p. 148. However, Sir William Ramsay suggested that the first three were prophets and the last two teachers. This has some support from the Greek, but not all agree.

carried the cross (Mark 15:21; Luke 23:26). It is not said he was from Cyrene here, but since the first witnesses in Antioch included men from Cyrene, it is possible.

The next prophet or teacher, Lucius, is definitely said to be from Cyrene (in North Africa west of Egypt). Possibly he was one of those who first brought the gospel to Antioch (Acts 11:20).

Manaen (a Greek form of Menahem, "comforter"), the other prophet or teacher, was brought up with Herod the Tetrarch (Herod Antipas, who killed John the Baptist). He is literally called a foster-brother and was about the same age as Herod. He grew up in the palace, and some believe he also became a courtier or officer of this Herod. John the Baptist must have influenced him. Later he was saved. It is also possible that he was among those present on the Day of Pentecost when the Holy Spirit was first outpoured.

These, along with the congregation, were ministering to the Lord in a public service (as the Greek indicates here). They were also fasting. Fasting was not emphasized very much by Jesus. As long as He was with His disciples they were like friends or attendants of a bridegroom at a feast and could not be expected to fast (Luke 5:34). There are many passages, however, that show there is a place for fasting. Evidently the leaders, and probably the whole congregation, here had put other things aside for a time of worship, prayer, and praise.

During the service, the Holy Spirit spoke and commanded them (the whole church) to separate "to me" (set apart for me) Barnabas and Saul for the work to which He had (already) called them. The Greek is imperative here and includes a particle expressing a strong command or demand.

Just how the Holy Spirit gave this message we are not told. Perhaps it was by tongues and interpretation. More likely it was a message in prophecy for the Church, probably a message given by one of the three other prophets and teachers named in verse 1. This does not give grounds for so-called "directive prophecy," however. It was not meant to give direction for Barnabas and Saul. The Greek perfect tense used here means an action in the past with present results. This shows that the Holy Spirit had already dealt with both Barnabas and Saul personally. But they were serving not only the Lord, but the Church. They had responsibilities in the ministry to the Church at Antioch. Thus the

Church had to be made willing to let them go. The Spirit's message was therefore directed to the whole assembly, not to any individual.

They all fasted and prayed further then. Later (1 Corinthians 14:29) Paul says that prophecies should be judged by other members of the Body. It is always wise to hold steady until we are sure that the message is from the Lord.

The assembly also must have prayed for God's blessing on this new ministry. Then they sent them away (literally, set them free, released them; that is, from their obligations at Antioch, and thus they permitted them to depart). It is clear that the whole church was involved in this and concurred with their leaders.

Evangelizing Cyprus (13:4-13)

[4]So they, being sent forth by the Holy Ghost, departed unto Seleucia; and from thence they sailed to Cyprus. [5]And when they were at Salamis, they preached the word of God in the synagogues of the Jews: and they had also John to *their* minister. [6]And when they had gone through the isle unto Paphos, they found a certain sorcerer, a false prophet, a Jew, whose name *was* Bar-jesus: [7]which was with the deputy of the country, Sergius Paulus, a prudent man; who called for Barnabas and Saul, and desired to hear the word of God.

[8]But Elymas the sorcerer (for so is his name by interpretation) withstood them, seeking to turn away the deputy from the faith. [9]Then Saul, (who also *is called* Paul,) filled with the Holy Ghost, set his eyes on him, [10]and said, O full of all subtilty and all mischief, *thou* child of the devil, *thou* enemy of all righteousness, wilt thou not cease to pervert the right ways of the Lord? [11]And now, behold, the hand of the Lord *is* upon thee, and thou shalt be blind, not seeing the sun for a season. And immediately there fell on him a mist and a darkness; and he went about seeking some to lead him by the hand. [12]Then the deputy, when he saw what was done, believed, being astonished at the doctrine of the Lord. [13]Now when Paul and his company loosed from Paphos, they came to Perga in Pamphylia: and John departing from them returned to Jerusalem (Acts 13:4-13).

Verse 4 emphasizes that Barnabas and Saul were sent out by the Holy Spirit. The Church gave them their blessing and let them go. Thus, both the Holy Spirit and the Church were involved. This was a good example for us and ought to be the normal pattern for the sending out of missionaries.

Their first missionary journey took them to the Island of Cyprus over 100 miles to the southwest, then to the mainland cities in the southern part of the Roman province of Galatia, and finally back to Antioch where they reported to the home church (Acts 14:26, 27).

They began their journey, taking John (Mark) along as their minister (servant, attendant),[2] by going down from Antioch to its harbor, Seleucia, on the Mediterranean coast. There they took a sailing ship to the island of Cyprus. The Bible does not say why they took this direction. But since the Holy Spirit sent them out, we can be sure He continued to guide them. We can see wisdom also in the fact that the Holy Spirit took them first to Cyprus where Barnabas grew up (Acts 4:36) and where he knew the people and the customs.

At Salamis, on the eastern end of the island, they took advantage of the opportunities given by the synagogues for visiting rabbis to preach. It was always Saul's practice to go to the Jews first, for they had the Scriptures, the promises, and the background to understand the gospel (Romans 1:16; 3:2; 9:4, 5).

After proclaiming the Word of God (the gospel) there, they went all the way through the island, covering it rather thoroughly until they came to Paphos on the western end of Cyprus. Saul changed his method after they left Cyprus. After this, instead of trying to cover the whole territory, they went to key cities to establish churches. These assemblies then became centers where the local Body could spread the gospel into the surrounding area.

At Paphos they came in contact with a Jew named Bar-Jesus[3] who was a sorcerer and a false prophet. This means he falsely claimed to be a prophet. Like Simon the sorcerer at Samaria, he practiced magic to fool the people and gain power over them.

Saul and Barnabas found this man with the deputy (the proconsul, that is, the governor appointed by the Roman Senate).[4]

---

[2]Some believe that like Elisha who waited on Elijah, Mark helped them as a personal servant while he trained for the ministry. Luke 1:2 uses the same word as ministers of the Word, however. Other writers say they took Mark along because he was an eyewitness of the arrest, death, and resurrection of Jesus, probably being the young man mentioned in Mark 14:51, 52. However, Paul did not depend on others for the facts of the gospel. See Galatians 1:11, 12, 16.

[3]"Son of Joshua" or "son of Jesus." He may have claimed to be a new Joshua sent to lead people into a new promised land of spiritual power. Or he may have claimed to be a follower of Jesus, but only to try to get a following for himself by his trickery. The phrase "son of" often means a follower of, as in the case of the "sons of the prophets" in the times of Samuel and Elijah.

[4]Cyprus had been under the control of the Roman Senate since 22 B.C. Luke was careful to give the governor his correct title.

This man, Sergius Paulus was prudent (intelligent, sensible, and well-educated), and he called in Barnabas and Saul earnestly seeking to hear the Word of God. Then the sorcerer, now called by a Greek interpretation of his name, Elymas, took a stand against them, actively seeking to turn away (pervert, twist away) the proconsul from the faith. This implies that Barnabas and Saul presented the faith, the full content of the gospel, to the proconsul, and he was accepting it. Then Elymas tried to retain his influence over the proconsul by distorting and perverting what Barnabas and Saul were teaching. But Saul received a new, special filling of the Holy Spirit (just as Peter had when he faced the Sanhedrin in Acts 4:8).

Luke notes at this point also that Saul had another name, a Roman name, Paul. This is significant because in the rest of the Book of Acts he is always called Paul. In his Epistles also, he always calls himself Paul. The use of his Roman name, of course, fits in with his primary ministry to the Gentiles.

By this new special filling of the Spirit also, the Lord gave Paul the leadership in the missionary journey. In verse 13, instead of Barnabas and Saul, we read "Paul and his company." This is in line also with the prophecy given to Ananias after Paul was converted. (See Acts 9:15.)

What Paul did next was not his own idea but was a prompting given directly by the Spirit. Fixing his eyes on Elymas, he addressed him as one full of all kinds of subtlety (deceit, guile, treachery) and mischief (wickedness, unscrupulousness, reckless facility for doing evil, fraud), a son of the devil,[5] an enemy of all righteousness.

Then Paul asked a rhetorical question which was really an affirmation that Elymas was determined not to cease perverting (twisting, distorting) the right (upright, straight) ways of the Lord (including the way of salvation and God's purposes for the believer). Because of this, Paul declared, the hand (power) of the Lord would be (at last) upon him (that is, in judgment). He would be totally blind until a fitting season, that is, until God saw fit to let him see again. (Probably, this was intended as an opportunity for Elymas to repent.)

[5]See Genesis 3:15, the seed of the serpent and John 8:44. The devil means the slanderer and thus, the false accuser (as the plural form is translated in 2 Timothy 3:3).

Mist and darkness immediately fell on Elymas and he went around searching for someone to lead him by the hand. Apparently, the people all withdrew from him and he had a hard time finding anyone to lead him.

The proconsul, as soon as he saw what happened, believed. But he was not astonished (astounded, thunderstruck) so much by the judgment on Elymas as by the doctrine (teaching) of the Lord; this event drove home the truth about Jesus, the Cross, and the Resurrection, as well as the rest of the gospel that had been presented to him. As we have seen, Luke often condenses his account and does not tell us everything every time. But we can be sure that as a believer this man was baptized both in water and in the Holy Spirit with the evidence of speaking in other tongues.[6]

From Paphos Paul and his company set sail for Perga in Pamphylia (a district on the south coast of Asia Minor). Barnabas was still with Paul, of course. But "son of encouragement" that he was, he willingly dropped into the background and upheld Paul as the new leader of the group. He recognized, we can be sure, that this was the Holy Spirit's choice and that Paul was being led in a special way by the Spirit.

At Perga John Mark left (deserted) them and returned to Jerusalem. Later (Acts 15:38) it is implied that Mark left them in the lurch when they really needed him. It may be that the work became more difficult as they encountered unfamiliar territory on the mainland. Some have suggested that since Mark was from a wealthy home where there were servants, he decided to go home where life would be easier. Others suggest he left because he resented the fact that his cousin Barnabas was no longer the leader. In any case, Paul looked at this as an almost inexcusable failure on the part of Mark.

Preaching in Pisidian Antioch (13:14-41)

[14]But when they departed from Perga, they came to Antioch in Pisidia, and went into the synagogue on the sabbath day, and sat down.

---

[6]Sir William Ramsay disputed this and without any evidence did not believe it likely that the proconsul was baptized. However, Ramsay did find evidence that the proconsul's daughter and her son were Christians. Cf. Bruce, *op. cit.*, p. 265. This should have been taken as confirmation that the proconsul also was a true believer as Acts tells us he was. The gospel was reaching into every stratum of society.

[15]And after the reading of the law and the prophets, the rulers of the synagogue sent unto them, saying, *Ye* men *and* brethren, if ye have any word of exhortation for the people, say on.

[16]Then Paul stood up, and beckoning with *his* hand said, Men of Israel, and ye that fear God, give audience. [17]The God of this people of Israel chose our fathers, and exalted the people when they dwelt as strangers in the land of Egypt, and with a high arm brought he them out of it. [18]And about the time of forty years suffered he their manners in the wilderness. [19]And when he had destroyed seven nations in the land of Canaan, he divided their land to them by lot. [20]And after that he gave *unto them* judges about the space of four hundred and fifty years, until Samuel the prophet.

[21]And afterward they desired a king: and God gave unto them Saul the son of Kish, a man of the tribe of Benjamin, by the space of forty years. [22]And when he had removed him, he raised up unto them David to be their king; to whom also he gave testimony, and said, I have found David the *son* of Jesse, a man after mine own heart, which shall fulfil all my will. [23]Of this man's seed hath God, according to *his* promise, raised unto Israel a Saviour, Jesus: [24]when John had first preached before his coming the baptism of repentance to all the people of Israel. [25]And as John fulfilled his course, he said, Whom think ye that I am? I am not *he*. But, behold, there cometh one after me, whose shoes of *his* feet I am not worthy to loose.

[26]Men *and* brethren, children of the stock of Abraham, and whosoever among you feareth God, to you is the word of this salvation sent. [27]For they that dwell at Jerusalem, and their rulers, because they knew him not, nor yet the voices of the prophets which are read every sabbath day, they have fulfilled *them* in condemning *him*. [28]And though they found no cause of death *in him,* yet desired they Pilate that he should be slain. [29]And when they had fulfilled all that was written of him, they took *him* down from the tree, and laid *him* in a sepulchre. [30]But God raised him from the dead: [31]and he was seen many days of them which came up with him from Galilee to Jerusalem, who are his witnesses unto the people. [32]And we declare unto you glad tidings, how that the promise which was made unto the fathers, [33]God hath fulfilled the same unto us their children, in that he hath raised up Jesus again; as it is also written in the second psalm, Thou art my Son, this day have I begotten thee.

[34]And as concerning that he raised him up from the dead, *now* no more to return to corruption, he said on this wise, I will give you the sure mercies of David. [35]Wherefore he saith also in another *psalm,* Thou shalt not suffer thine Holy One to see corruption.

[36]For David, after he had served his own generation by the will of God, fell on sleep, and was laid unto his fathers, and saw corruption: [37]but he, whom God raised again, saw no corruption. [38]Be it known unto you therefore, men *and* brethren, that through this man is preached unto you the forgiveness of sins: [39]and by him all that believe are justified from all things, from which ye could not be justified by the law of Moses. [40]Beware therefore, lest that come upon you, which is spoken of in the

prophets. [41]Behold, ye despisers, and wonder, and perish: for I work a work in your days, a work which ye shall in no wise believe, though a man declare it unto you (Acts 13:14-41).

From Perga they went to Antioch in (of) Pisidia.[7] As usual, they went first to the synagogue. Someone else was appointed to read the selections from the Law (the Pentateuch) and from (one of) the Prophets. Then the rulers (leaders or elders) of the synagogue sent to them (for they were sitting in the back of the synagogue) and courteously asked them to give a word of exhortation (encouragement or challenge). Paul then stood, waved his hand for silence, and asked the Israelites and the God-fearers to listen. By this we see that there were interested Gentiles in the synagogue audience.

As mentioned previously, many Gentiles were tired of the immorality and idolatry of heathen religion. They were hungry for something better and were attracted to the synagogues and to the worship of the one true God, who, unlike their heathen gods, is holy. Yet many of them did not become full proselytes by accepting circumcision and by self-baptism and other rites. Some rabbis did not give them much encouragement to do so, for they would not promise them salvation if they did become a Jew. They would only say that their children would be counted as Jews and would be under the covenant blessings. But these Gentiles still came to hear the Word and to learn more about the God of Israel.

Paul's sermon at Pisidian Antioch is given in considerable detail. Luke records it here as an example of the kind of preaching Paul did in the Jewish synagogues. He does not, however, give such detail in the record of later sermons. As Paul began he courteously addressed both the Jews and Gentiles in the audience and recognized them both as "brethren," keeping both in mind throughout the sermon.[8]

The first part of the sermon (13:17-25) reviews the history of Israel, starting from God's choice of Israel and the deliverance

[7]Called "of Pisidia" to distinguish it from other cities named Antioch and also because it was near the border of Pisidia (not actually in Pisidia but in Phrygia) in the southern part of the Roman province of Galatia. Pisidia was the southwestern part of this province of Galatia.

[8]Cf. W. M. Ramsay, *The Cities of Saint Paul* (Grand Rapids: Baker Book House, 1979 reprint from 1907), pp. 300-303.

from Egypt and leading up to God's choice of David. All this was very familiar to his audience and showed them Paul knew the Scriptures.

Unlike Stephen, Paul did not emphasize Israel's failures. Rather, he spoke of God's choosing (for His own purpose and service) and God's exalting of the Israelites during their sojourn as foreigners in Egypt. God confirmed this choice by leading them out of Egypt by a high arm (mighty power; see Exodus 6:1, 6; Psalm 136:11, 12). That is, God increased their number during the time of persecution and protected them from the plagues.

Then Paul only mentioned that God endured the manners (ways, disposition)[9] of the people during 40 years in the wilderness. Then Joshua's conquest and the time of the Judges are quickly summarized, as is the reign of Saul.

The seven nations of verse 19 are the tribes of Canaanites and others that were in Palestine. (See Deuteronomy 7:1.) The 450 years (a round number) of verse 20 refers not merely to the time of the Book of Judges, but to the whole time after they entered the land up to the beginning of David's reign.[10]

The climax of this historical account is reached when Paul says God bore witness to David that he was a man after His own heart who would do all God's will. (See 1 Samuel 13:14; Psalm 89:20.)

---

[9]Several ancient manuscripts read a word with only one letter different. It means "carried them" (as a nurse would). Deuteronomy 1:31 in the Greek Septuagint Version has the same variant.

[10]Some manuscripts apply the 450 years to the 400 years in Egypt plus the time of the conquest up to the dividing of the land in Joshua chapter 14. It should be noted that the rules of the Judges overlapped in many cases.

Note also that the 40 years of Saul's reign are not given in the Old Testament. In fact 1 Samuel 13:1 reads literally, "Saul was a son of ? year in his reigning (when he began to reign), and he reigned two years over Israel." This follows the usual formula for giving a king's reign, like that found in 2 Kings 14:2; 16:2; 18:2. It probably means that early in the process of copying the Books of Samuel the actual age of Saul was accidentally left out and so was the length of his reign. Many Bible scholars conjecture that Saul was 40 years old when he began to reign and that he reigned 32 years. Paul, however, was including in Saul's reign the seven and one-half years when David reigned in Hebron and Saul's son continued Saul's reign and kingdom. Jews in those days usually rounded off the last half year or part year of a reign and added it as a year to the total, thus giving 40 years here. However, some writers follow Josephus who says Saul reigned 20 years and Samuel judged 20 years, together making the 40. Still other writers conjecture that Saul reigned 42 years and that Paul rounded it off here to 40 years.

The purpose and desire to do all God's will is, of course, the thing that made David a man after God's own heart.

Now the people in Paul's audience knew God's promise to David (2 Samuel 7:12; Psalm 89:29-34). They also knew the prophecies that God would raise up a greater seed to David (Isaiah 9:6, 7; 11:1-5), as well as the prophecy that He would give David's throne to the One whose right it is (Ezekiel 21:27). Thus Paul declares that God had fulfilled His promise and from the seed (descendants) of David raised up to Israel a Saviour, Jesus (Matthew 1:21).

Paul further identified Jesus as the One John the Baptist recognized as the One to come.[11] John the Baptist's ministry was well-known to Jews everywhere; his denial that he was the one to come, the promised Messiah and Saviour, was also well-known. John's testimony to Jesus was therefore important. For John to say that he was not worthy to loose (unloose, take off) the shoes (or sandals), a most menial service, indicates how far above him John considered Jesus.

The second part of the sermon (13:26-37) deals with the death and resurrection of Jesus and with the witness of the apostles as well as the witness of the Scriptures.

In verse 26 Paul emphasizes that this message of salvation was sent out to them personally (through those commissioned by the Lord Jesus), and not only to the Jews present, but to the Gentile God-fearers among them as well.

Then Paul shows that the death of Jesus was the fulfillment of God's prophetic Word and that it was carried out by Jerusalem dwellers and their rulers.

It is important to notice here that Paul didn't blame the death of Jesus on the Jews in general, but only on those in Jerusalem who were actually involved. He also recognizes that they did it because they were ignorant of Him and of the voices of the prophets read every Sabbath (in their synagogues). The Greek word used here sometimes implies willful ignorance or a deliberate ignoring of the truth. Since they did know these prophecies, willful ignorance is indeed meant here.

---

[11]The baptism of (because of) repentance (verse 24) was the baptism which declared and symbolized a repentance which had already taken place. (See Matthew 3:8.)

Paul also says they found no cause, no real grounds, for death, yet they asked Pilate to have Jesus killed. But after the prophecies of Christ's death were fulfilled, they (Jerusalem dwellers) took him from the "tree" (the cross; compare Deuteronomy 21:23 and Galatians 3:13) and laid Him in a tomb. (Nicodemus and Joseph of Arimathea were the ones who actually did this, John 19:38, 39.) Then God raised Jesus from the dead. His disciples, Galileans who came up with Him to Jerusalem, were witnesses of this.

This was the glad tidings (good news) which Paul and Barnabas were bringing. The promise made to the Old Testament fathers was now fulfilled to their children by God's raising Jesus from the dead. Paul confirmed this by quoting Psalm 2:7 where "This day I have begotten thee" means "I am declaring this day that I have begotten you, or rather, I am your father." This was declared to one who was already a king's son. Most today believe it was a formula by which a king made a public declaration that he was at that particular time raising his son to share the throne as king, as his associate and equal. Thus, in the Psalm it refers to Jesus being declared by God to be His Son. God did this first when Jesus began His ministry and God sent His Spirit upon Him (Luke 3:22). Then He did it even more unmistakably when He raised Jesus from the dead. As Romans 1:3, 4 says, Jesus, who was "made of the seed of David according to the flesh" was "declared to be the Son of God with power, according to the spirit of holiness [or, by means of the Holy Spirit], by the resurrection from the dead." Since Luke is even here condensing a sermon that took a long time to preach, it is probable that Paul explained these things more fully to his audience.

Next Paul pointed out further Scripture references, mentioning first Isaiah 55:3 which refers to the sure mercies of David, in a passage that speaks of pardon and salvation. He then assumed those mercies to include Psalm 16:10 which says God will not permit (give) His Holy One to see corruption (decay or dissolution of the body). Furthermore, David, after he served his own generation in the will of God, died, and his body did see corruption. In contrast to David, the One God raised up (Jesus) did not see corruption. (Compare Acts 2:29. Paul saw the same truth as Peter did, but presented it in a little different way. Clearly, Paul preached the same gospel the other apostles did. See Galatians 1:8, 9; 2:2, 9; 1 Corinthians 15:11.)

The final part of this sermon (13:38-41) gives exhortation. "Through this man is preached [proclaimed, announced] unto you forgiveness of sins." By this One also all believers are justified (made righteous, acquitted, treated as if they had never sinned; and therefore freed from the guilt and punishment of their sin). The believers are even forgiven and delivered from the guilt of all those things for which the Law of Moses was not able to provide justification (or could not treat one as righteous).[12]

Paul then concluded the sermon with a warning using language taken from Habakkuk 1:5 (in the Greek Septuagint version). "Perish" (verse 41) means to be removed. Paul wanted his audience to be on their guard for fear an even greater judgment come on them than on the rebels to whom Habakkuk spoke.

Turning to the Gentiles (13:42-49)

[42]And when the Jews were gone out of the synagogue, the Gentiles besought that these words might be preached to them the next sabbath. [43]Now when the congregation was broken up, many of the Jews and religious proselytes followed Paul and Barnabas; who, speaking to them, persuaded them to continue in the grace of God.

[44]And the next sabbath day came almost the whole city together to hear the word of God. [45]But when the Jews saw the multitudes, they were filled with envy, and spake against those things which were spoken by Paul, contradicting and blaspheming. [46]Then Paul and Barnabas waxed bold, and said, It was necessary that the word of God should first have been spoken to you: but seeing ye put it from you, and judge yourselves unworthy of everlasting life, lo, we turn to the Gentiles. [47]For so hath the Lord commanded us, *saying,* I have set thee to be a light of the Gentiles, that thou shouldest be for salvation unto the ends of the earth.

[48]And when the Gentiles heard this, they were glad, and glorified the word of the Lord: and as many as were ordained to eternal life believed. [49]And the word of the Lord was published throughout all the region (Acts 13:42-49).

---

[12]The Greek word order is, "even from all which you were not able to be justified by the Law of Moses, in this One every one believing is justified." Some take this to mean that the Law provided justification for some things and the gospel provides justification for the rest. But the meaning is rather that the Law could not really provide justification at all, and the gospel provides justification for everything. Cf. Bruce, *op. cit.,* pp. 278, 279.

As the people were leaving the synagogue they asked that these words (this message) continue to be spoken to them the next Sabbath.[13]

Afterward, many of both Jews and worshiping (God-fearing) proselytes (converts to Judaism) followed Paul and Barnabas. They spent some time speaking to them and persuaded them to remain in the grace of God. This means they believed and accepted the grace of God that brings salvation, and they were encouraged to continue in it.

The God-fearing Gentiles spread the word so effectively that the next Sabbath nearly the whole city assembled to hear God's Word (the gospel). The sight of the crowd filled the Jews with jealousy, and they proceeded to speak against what Paul said. They even blasphemed (not God, but Paul). That is, they used abusive language against Paul. This implies they were afraid of losing their influence over those Gentiles who had been looking to them for teaching. It may also imply that they had a zeal for a Judaism that had no room for blessing on Gentiles who did not first become Jews.

Paul and Barnabas responded by speaking boldly and freely that it was necessary (that is, necessary in order to fulfill God's plan) to speak God's Word first to "you Jews." But since the Jews had scornfully thrust it away (rejected it) and thus judged themselves unworthy of eternal life (by their conduct), "behold" the two apostles were turning (at that moment) to the Gentiles. ("Behold" indicates that this turning to the Gentiles was something unexpected and surprising to the Jews.)

Turning to the Gentiles was not really the apostles' own idea. Rather it was obedience to the prophetic Word given in Isaiah 49:6 concerning the Messiah, God's Servant. (See also Isaiah 42:6; Luke 2:30-32. Christ and His Body, the Church, the believers, share in bringing the light of the gospel to the world.)

Hearing this, the Gentiles rejoiced and glorified the Word of the Lord. "And as many as were ordained to eternal life believed." This may sound as if the Bible is teaching arbitrary predestination

[13]A number of ancient manuscripts leave out the word "Gentiles" and indicate that as Paul and Barnabas were going out the people as a whole asked them this. Sir William Ramsay gives good reasons for seeing this as the correct picture. See Ramsay, *op. cit.*, pp. 307, 308.

here. However, it is not said that God "ordained" them. The word "ordained" here can mean "fixed on." That is, these Gentiles accepted the truth of eternal life through Jesus and did not let the Jews' contradiction move them from it.[14] The result was that the Word of the Lord (Jesus) was carried (by these believers) throughout the whole region.

Paul and Barnabas Expelled (13:50-52)

[50]But the Jews stirred up the devout and honorable women, and the chief men of the city, and raised persecution against Paul and Barnabas, and expelled them out of their coasts. [51]But they shook off the dust of their feet against them, and came unto Iconium. [52]And the disciples were filled with joy, and with the Holy Ghost (Acts 13:50-52).

The unbelieving Jews then proceeded to urge on devout (worshiping, God-fearing) women of honorable position in society[15] and the chief men of the city government. By their means the unconverted Jews aroused persecution to the point that Paul and Barnabas were thrown out of the district. (See 1 Thessalonians 2:15, 16.)

In response, Paul and Barnabas simply shook off the dust of their feet as a testimony against them (compare Matthew 10:14; Mark 6:11; Luke 9:5; 10:11). Then they went on to Iconium (a Phrygian city in the southern part of the Roman province of Galatia).

The persecutors did not destroy the Church in Pisidian Antioch, however. They were true disciples of the Lord and were filled with joy and with the Holy Spirit. (Compare Matthew 5:11, 12; Romans 14:17; 15:13.) Once again we see that Acts does not tell everything every time. Though Luke does not mention it here, we can be sure that these believers were also baptized in water as well as in the Holy Spirit.

[14]*The New English Bible* suggests that because they accepted the truth of the gospel they were "marked out" for eternal (resurrection) life. Cf. Packer, *op. cit.*, p. 112.

[15]These may have been the wives of the city government leaders. In Pisidian Antioch women also held important positions, however.

ACTS
CHAPTER
14

The preaching at Pisidian Antioch, the greater response of the Gentiles, and the persecution that followed set a pattern. Much or all of this was repeated at practically all of the cities Paul visited on his missionary journeys.

ICONIUM, LYSTRA, DERBE (14:1-7)

[1]And it came to pass in Iconium, that they went both together into the synagogue of the Jews, and so spake, that a great multitude both of the Jews and also of the Greeks believed. [2]But the unbelieving Jews stirred up the Gentiles, and made their minds evil affected against the brethren. [3]Long time therefore abode they speaking boldly in the Lord, which gave testimony unto the word of his grace, and granted signs and wonders to be done by their hands. [4]But the multitude of the city was divided: and part held with the Jews, and part with the apostles. [5]And when there was an assault made both of the Gentiles, and also of the Jews with their rulers, to use *them* despitefully, and to stone them, [6]they were ware of *it,* and fled unto Lystra and Derbe, cities of Lycaonia, and unto the region that lieth round about: [7]and there they preached the gospel (Acts 14:1-7).

Iconium was about 60 miles east and a little south of Pisidian Antioch on a plateau of 3,370 feet elevation. Arriving there, Paul and Barnabas went to the synagogue first. As usual, they were given opportunity to speak. Luke does not record their sermon. He simply indicates that they spoke so (thus), in their usual manner; that is, just as they did in Pisidian Antioch.[1]

The results were similar. A very large number of both Jews and Greeks (Greek-speaking Gentiles) believed (and, of course, were

[1]Cf. Packer, *op. cit.,* p. 115.

baptized in water and in the Holy Spirit). Then, as before, unbelieving (disobedient, rebellious)[2] Jews in their zeal and jealousy aroused the Gentiles and badly affected their minds (soul, self, desire) against the brethren (the new believers who were now disciples of Jesus and fellow-members of His Body).

The Jews in this case, however, were not able initially to get much support from the Gentiles. Therefore Paul and Barnabas stayed in Iconium a considerable length of time. With bold freedom they spoke for (or, in) the Lord Jesus (relying on Him). As they did so the Lord bore witness to the Word (message) of His grace[3] by giving miraculous signs and wonders to be done by their hands. They were thus recognized as Christ's agents doing His work by His authority.[4]

In time, however, the city crowd became sharply divided. Some were with the (unbelieving) Jews. Some held with the apostles.[5] Then both Gentiles and Jews with their synagogue rulers joined together with hostile intent. They purposed to treat the apostles outrageously and stone them to death. The Greek, however, does not mean there was any actual assault, but only the intent and instigation of one.

The apostles became aware of the plot, however, and fled. This was not because they were afraid, but because there were other places that needed their ministry. Thus, they went on to Lystra and Derbe, Lycaonian cities in the southern part of the Roman province of Galatia. Lystra, like Iconium, had the status of Roman military colonies and was responsible to safeguard the interests of Rome and guard the Roman roads. At Lystra the apostles continued (were continuing) to preach the gospel (tell the good news). What follows gives us an example of how Paul preached to Gentiles who had no knowledge of the Scriptures.

---

[2]As translated in 1 Peter 2:8. Note that belief in the gospel was not optional, but was a matter of obedience to God's Word and will.

[3]That is, the whole gospel with all the provisions of His grace in salvation, healing, the baptism in the Holy Spirit, the gifts of the Spirit, and our future inheritance and new bodies which will be ours when Jesus comes again were witnessed to.

[4]Bruce, *op. cit.*, p. 287 points out that Paul in Galatians 3:5 shows that these miracles were evidence to the gospel of grace, not to the works of the Law.

[5]Note that Paul and Barnabas are both called apostles here. Barnabas was thus a witness of the resurrection of Jesus and was commissioned by Jesus. Possibly, he was part of the 120 in the Upper Room. See also 1 Corinthians 9:6; Galatians 2:9, 10.

A Cripple Healed (14:8-18)

[8]And there sat a certain man at Lystra, impotent in his feet, being a cripple from his mother's womb, who never had walked: [9]the same heard Paul speak: who steadfastly beholding him, and perceiving that he had faith to be healed, [10]said with a loud voice, Stand upright on thy feet. And he leaped and walked. [11]And when the people saw what Paul had done, they lifted up their voices, saying in the speech of Lycaonia. The gods are come down to us in the likeness of men. [12]And they called Barnabas, Jupiter; and Paul, Mercurius, because he was the chief speaker. [13]Then the priest of Jupiter, which was before their city, brought oxen and garlands unto the gates, and would have done sacrifice with the people. [14]*Which* when the apostles, Barnabas and Paul, heard *of*, they rent their clothes, and ran in among the people, crying out, [15]and saying, Sirs, why do ye these things? We also are men of like passions with you, and preach unto you that ye should turn from these vanities unto the living God, which made heaven, and earth, and the sea, and all things that are therein: [16]who in times past suffered all nations to walk in their own ways. [17]Nevertheless he left not himself without witness, in that he did good, and gave us rain from heaven, and fruitful seasons, filling our hearts with food and gladness. [18]And with these sayings scarce restrained they the people, that they had not done sacrifice unto them (Acts 14:8-18).

At Lystra Paul did not go to a synagogue as was his usual custom. Perhaps there was none. Instead, it seems he went to the market place or to an open square just inside the city gates (as verse 13 indicates); there he began to preach. Among those nearby was a cripple. To draw attention to the hopelessness of his case the Bible uses repetition. He was unable to use his feet since birth, and he had never walked. Paul fixed his eyes on the man as he kept listening and saw that he had faith to be healed.[6] Paul encouraged the man's faith to action by commanding him in a very loud voice to stand up straight (erect) on his feet.

Paul's command caught the attention of the crowd. When they saw the man leap up and walk, they began shouting. However, though they knew the Greek Paul was using, in their excitement they reverted to their native Lycaonian language, which Paul and Barnabas did not understand.[7]

---

[6]Greek, *sothenai* from the verb *sozo* which is ordinarily translated "saved," but also means to rescue from danger or from severe situations and thus to be restored or made whole.

[7]This sort of thing is a common occurrence. Usually, when a person is educated to use a second language, he will fall back into his native language, the language of his childhood when excited.

The miracle made the people (who were pagan Gentiles) believe that the Greek gods had come down, being made like human beings. Thus they began to call Barnabas *Dia* (or, *Dios*), a form of the Greek sky god Zeus, who was identified by the Romans with their god Jupiter and by this people with the chief Lycaonian god. Then, since Paul was the chief speaker ("the leader of the word"), they called him *Hermen* (Hermes), the messenger and herald of the gods, especially of *Dios* (Zeus, Jupiter). Hermes was identified by the Romans with their god Mercurius (Mercury).

Accordingly, the people took what they thought was appropriate action. They contacted the priest of the *Dios* whose temple was in front of the city. He brought oxen (bulls, the mostly costly victims they could offer in sacrifice). These were decorated with garlands (wreaths) and brought to the gates where the crowds gathered, wanting to sacrifice.

In verses 12 and 14 Barnabas is again named first because as *Dios* (Zeus, Jupiter) he was the leading one for whom the sacrifice was to be made. Finally someone probably explained to them in Greek what was going on. When the apostles heard and understood this, they tore apart their outer garments (as a sign of grief and dismay). As they did so, they rushed out (sprang out) into the crowd crying out, trying to stop them by declaring they were human beings with feelings like theirs (implying a nature like theirs). They had come to preach the gospel (good news) to turn them from these vain (unreal, useless, unfruitful) things to the living God.

Since these Gentiles had no knowledge of the Scriptures, Paul did not identify God as the God of Israel, nor did he appeal to the Old Testament prophecies of the Messiah. He did use Scriptural language, however, and took them back to the time of the creation. God is the God who made all things, who in past generations permitted all nations (all the Gentiles) to go their own way (in contrast to God's ways). Yet He did not leave himself without witness. He did good deeds, giving us rain from heaven and fruitbearing seasons, filling our hearts with food and gladness.

Even with this, the apostles had difficulty stopping the crowd from carrying out their intention to sacrifice to them.

Paul Stoned (14:19, 20)

[19]And there came thither *certain* Jews from Antioch and Iconium,

who persuaded the people, and, having stoned Paul, drew *him* out of the city, supposing he had been dead. [20]Howbeit, as the disciples stood round about him, he rose up, and came into the city: and the next day he departed with Barnabas to Derbe (Acts 14:19, 20).

Verse 20 indicates Paul and Barnabas stayed in Lystra long enough for a number to believe and become disciples (and, as always, to be baptized in water and in the Holy Spirit according to Acts 2:4). But Jews from Pisidian Antioch (about 100 miles away) who had thrown him out of their city, and some from Iconium (about 30 miles away) who had wanted to stone him to death, heard of Paul's success at Lystra. They came and persuaded the heathen crowds to help them, or at least permit them, to carry out their plot. (Some of the heathen may have felt they were disgraced when Paul and Barnabas did not let them sacrifice to them; so they listened to Paul's enemies.)

This time they did stone Paul and dragged his body out of the city, thinking he was dead. It is clear that he was not actually dead, though he was unconscious and must have been severely bruised all over his body. Undoubtedly he had broken bones as well.[8]

As soon as the crowd left, the believing disciples surrounded Paul. Undoubtedly they were looking to God, and God did not disappoint them. Suddenly, in what must have seemed like a resurrection, Paul rose up, obviously completely healed, and went back into the city with them. But, knowing the mood of the crowds, he and Barnabas left the next day for Derbe (now identified as a ruin about 60 miles southeast of Lystra near the border of the Roman province of Galatia).

Confirming Believers (14:21-25)

[21]And when they had preached the gospel to that city, and had taught many, they returned again to Lystra, and *to* Iconium, and Antioch, [22]confirming the souls of the disciples, *and* exhorting them to continue in the faith, and that we must through much tribulation enter into the kingdom of God. [23]And when they had ordained them elders in every church, and had prayed with fasting, they commended them to the Lord, on whom they believed. [24]And after they had passed through Pisidi-

[8]See 2 Corinthians 11:25 where he includes this stoning between beatings and shipwrecks as calamities he endured. There is no hint here that he died. He refers to his scars also in Galatians 6:17.

a, they came to Pamphylia. [25]And when they had preached the word in Perga, they went down into Attalia (Acts 14:21-25).

At Derbe also, there was apparently no synagogue. Thus Paul and Barnabas must have preached the gospel much as they did at Lystra, but without the Jewish opposition since Paul's enemies thought he was dead.

After they made a considerable number of disciples, and thus established a growing church, they courageously returned to Lystra, Iconium, and Pisidian Antioch. This time, however, they did not stir up the Jews. Apparently they did no evangelistic work, leaving that to the local believers. Their ministry this time was to the Church. In each place, they confirmed (strengthened and established) the souls of the disciples. They also challenged and encouraged them to continue in the faith. The Greek is very strong here. They told the people they must maintain the faith, standing by it, that is, living by the principles of the gospel.

They also challenged them to share the suffering of the apostles and to accept the fact that through much tribulation (persecution, affliction, distress) it was necessary to enter the kingdom (come under the rule and authority of God).

Because the believers needed organization to be able to work together and carry on the work of the Lord, the apostles then "ordained" elders (overseers, superintendents, presidents of the congregation or assembly) in each place. This, however, was not an ordination in the modern day sense. The Greek for "ordained" is *cheiratonesantes* where *cheir* is the Greek word for hand; the whole word means they conducted an election by a show of hands.

When the seven were chosen in chapter 6, the apostles laid down the qualifications, and the people did the choosing of the deacons. We can be sure the same thing happened here. Paul must have given the qualifications which he recorded later in 1 Timothy 3:1-7 and Titus 1:6-9. Then the people of the local assembly made the choice by an election (undoubtedly after a time of prayer during which they sought the leading of the Holy Spirit to help them decide who best fulfilled these qualifications).

At the beginning the elders were Spirit-filled men chosen from among the members of the local congregation.[9] Not until many

---

[9]Cf. Lenski, *op. cit.,* pp. 585, 586.

years later did the churches begin to feel that they needed to bring in pastor-teachers who could also be the administrative head of the assembly and who would combine the office of elder (also called bishop and presbyter) with the God-called ministry of pastor-teacher. Elders in the first century were expected to be "apt to teach," and they were responsible to see that the teaching was done. But they could bring in others who had the pastor-teacher ministry from the Lord and the Spirit's gifts to go with it. They did not have to do the teaching themselves. The fact that Paul says, "Let the elders that rule well be counted worthy of double honor (honorarium), especially they who labor in the word and doctrine [teaching]" (1 Timothy 5:17) shows that not all did labor or work in the Word and teaching. But as time went on, they became more and more aware of the need for consistent teaching ministry in the local church, and it was natural for them to look to these teachers for leadership. Thus, the modern idea of a pastor who is also an administrator developed gradually.

Before Paul and Barnabas went on to the next city, they always spent time in prayer and fasting with the believers. Then they entrusted them (as something precious and valuable) to the care and keeping of the Lord (Jesus) in whom they had believed (and continued to believe). The initial believing, of course, took place on Paul's previous visit.

From Pisidian Antioch they went on through Pisidia back to Pamphylia and Perga, evangelizing wherever possible as they went. At Perga they preached the Word apparently without opposition or mistreatment. Evidently, they had not preached there when they first landed and Mark deserted them. After establishing the church there, they went to Attalia, Perga's seaport.

Reporting at Syrian Antioch (14:26-28)

> [26] . . . and thence sailed to Antioch, from whence they had been recommended to the grace of God for the work which they fulfilled. [27] And when they were come, and had gathered the church together, they rehearsed all that God had done with them, and how he had opened the door of faith unto the Gentiles. [28] And there they abode long time with the disciples (Acts 14:26-28).

From Attalia they sailed away to Syrian Antioch. There they had been given over to the grace of God to do the work which they had now completed. At this visit, Paul and Barnabas felt they had fulfilled the ministry for which the Spirit sent them out in Acts 13:2-4.

Therefore, they gathered the Church together and reported how much God had done with them. That is, they told what great things God did as they worked as fellow laborers with Him. To the Gentiles also He had opened a door of faith. (The Greek has "a door," not "the door" here.) Then the two apostles remained "not a little time" with the disciples. That is, they resumed a ministry of teaching and help in the assembly of believers for several months, possibly as much as a year.

ACTS

CHAPTER

15

The Jerusalem Conference dealt with in this chapter is another important turning point in the history of the Church. The Jerusalem Church leaders were satisfied by Peter's account of the Lord's accepting uncircumcised Gentiles in Caesarea and baptizing them in the Holy Spirit. Then, according to Galatians 2:1-10, when Paul visited Jerusalem and presented the gospel he preached among the Gentiles, they gave their approval to his message and did not require Titus to be circumcised.

A little later (Galatians 2:11-16), when Peter came to Syrian Antioch, he enjoyed table fellowship and ate nonkosher food with the Gentiles as he had in the house of Cornelius.[1] But then some Jewish believers came up from James (not sent officially, but sent to help and encourage the believers). However, they were probably converted Pharisees who were still strict about Jewish believers keeping the traditional customs. For fear of them, Peter quit eating with the Gentiles and withdrew from their fellowship; his example affected the other Jewish believers in Antioch. Even Barnabas was carried away with this hypocrisy. Paul therefore took a strong stand against Peter and faced him with the hypocrisy of what he was doing (Galatians 2:14).

---

[1]See Bruce, *op. cit.*, pp. 298-300 for an excellent presentation of conclusive reasons showing that Galatians was written to the churches in South Galatia visited by Paul on his first missionary journey. This makes Galatians the earliest of Paul's Epistles. Its whole attitude shows that the controversy was heated, just as it was immediately before the Jerusalem council. This view of the authorship of Galatians and of a date of A.D. 49 for the Book of Galatians and the Jerusalem Council was developed by Sir William Ramsay in *A Historical Commentary on St. Paul's Epistles to the Galatians.* See also Bruce's note 5 on p. 287. Merril C. Tenney of Wheaton College, Wheaton, Illinois, has also made statements in his lectures in favor of this dating.

Paul and Barnabas Sent to Jerusalem (15:1-5)

[1]And certain men which came down from Judea taught the brethren, *and said,* Except ye be circumcised after the manner of Moses, ye cannot be saved. [2]When therefore Paul and Barnabas had no small dissension and disputation with them, they determined that Paul and Barnabas, and certain other of them, should go up to Jerusalem unto the apostles and elders about this question. [3]And being brought on their way by the church, they passed through Phoeni'cia and Samaria, declaring the conversion of the Gentiles: and they caused great joy unto all the brethren. [4]And when they were come to Jerusalem, they were received of the church, and *of* the apostles and elders, and they declared all things that God had done with them. [5]But there rose up certain of the sect of the Pharisees which believed, saying, That it was needful to circumcise them, and to command *them* to keep the law of Moses (Acts 15:1-5).

Later, after Peter's visit, other unnamed Jewish believers came from Judea to Antioch and went a step further.[2] They began teaching the Gentile brethren that unless they were circumcised according to the custom of Moses, they could not be saved.[3]

These teachers, who later are called Judaizers, did not deny that these Gentiles were believers baptized in the Holy Spirit. But the salvation they had in mind was the ultimate salvation whereby we shall receive our new bodies (at the rapture) and be changed. (Compare Romans 13:11, "Now is our salvation nearer than when we believed.") As 1 John 3:2; Romans 8:17, 23, 24; and 1 Corinthians 15:57 show, we are already sons of God, but we do not yet have all God has promised. Not until Jesus comes again and we see Him as He is will our bodies be changed and become like His glorified body. God's promise also includes our reigning with Christ and making our ultimate home in the New Jerusalem and the new heaven and the new earth (2 Peter 3:13; Revelation 21:1, 2).

Thus, what these Judaizers were really saying was that the Gentile believers must be circumcised and come under the Old Covenant of Moses' Law; otherwise, they could not be heirs of the promises that are yet to come. By this they also implied that they

[2]Bruce, *op. cit.,* p. 303, suggests that these were the same ones who "came from James" in Galatians 2:12, and they took things into their own hands when they saw so many Gentile believers.

[3]They obviously represented themselves to be gifted teachers of the Church. This teaching was later continued by the Ebionite heresy.

would lose what they had already received if they did not become Jews and be circumcised.

This has often been the cry of false teachers: You will lose your salvation if you do not accept our pet teaching. Some still say that a person is not really or fully saved unless they go through certain prescribed rites or ceremonies. All these fail to recognize that salvation is by grace through faith alone, as is clearly taught in Romans 10:9, 10 and Ephesians 2:8, 9.

This Judaizing teaching brought no little dissension (disturbance, discord, upheaval) and disputation (questioning) between them (or, more probably, between the brethren) and Paul and Barnabas. They (the brethren) then assigned Paul, Barnabas, and some others to go to Jerusalem to the apostles and elders about this question.

It is probable that these teachers had already gone on to try to spread their teaching in the other churches Paul had established in South Galatia. Since Paul had to go to Jerusalem, he could not go to these churches and set them straight. Thus it seems evident that at this time (A.D. 48, 49) the Spirit directed and inspired Paul to write the Epistle to the Galatians.

The whole church turned out to escort Paul and Barnabas and the others for a little distance on the way. By this the Church showed they still loved them, respected them, and had confidence in them in spite of the questions these Judaizing teachers had raised.

Paul took the road south through Phoenicia and the province of Samaria, stopping to visit churches all along the way.[4] In each place he gave a complete account of the Gentiles turning to the Lord. This caused great joy among all the brethren. Though made up of Jewish believers in Phoenicia and Samaritan believers in Samaria, the churches all accepted the word of God among the Gentiles without question.

In giving a full report, Paul undoubtedly included an account of the persecution as well as the miracles. We can be sure also that he told of the baptism in the Holy Spirit and the confirmation of the faith of these believers.

---

[4]Phoenicia at this time extended south to Mount Carmel on the Mediterranean coast, so it was not necessary to go through Galilee. From Mount Carmel they took the inland route through Samaria to Jerusalem.

In Jerusalem, also, the Church welcomed them, and the apostles and elders gave them a favorable reception. They all listened to the report of how much God had done along with them (with them as His fellow-laborers). They gave God all the glory; he had been with them; He had really done the work. (Compare 1 Corinthians 3:5-7.)

It was not long, however, before some converted Pharisees rose up out of the assembly in Jerusalem. They forcefully expressed the view that it was (and continued to be) necessary both to circumcise the Gentiles and to command them to keep (observe) the Law of Moses.

The Question Considered (15:6-12)

[6]And the apostles and elders came together for to consider of this matter. [7]And when there had been much disputing, Peter rose up, and said unto them, Men *and* brethren, ye know how that a good while ago God made choice among us, that the Gentiles by my mouth should hear the word of the gospel, and believe. [8]And God, which knoweth the hearts, bare them witness, giving them the Holy Ghost, even as *he did* unto us; [9]and put no difference between us and them, purifying their hearts by faith. [10]Now therefore why tempt ye God, to put a yoke upon the neck of the disciples, which neither our fathers nor we were able to bear? [11]But we believe that through the grace of the Lord Jesus Christ we shall be saved, even as they.

[12]Then all the multitude kept silence, and gave audience to Barnabas and Paul, declaring what miracles and wonders God had wrought among the Gentiles by them (Acts 15:6-12).

The apostles and elders then assembled to consider the matter. It was not a closed meeting, however. Verse 12 indicates a multitude (a crowd) was present.

At first there was much disputing, not in the sense of arguing, but rather there was a great deal of questioning and discussion as they tried to probe into the subject. Wisely, the leaders allowed the people to present various points of view.

Finally, after a long period of debate, Peter rose and reminded them that by God's choice he took the gospel to the Gentiles (in Caesarea) and they believed. Then God, who saw the faith in their hearts, bore witness to the fact they were believers by giving them the Holy Spirit, just as He did to all the Jewish believers. God thus did not distinguish between or make a separation between the

Gentile and Jewish believers in any way "having purified [cleansed] their hearts by faith." That is, God had already cleansed their hearts by faith when He showed there was no distinction by baptizing them in the Holy Spirit.[5] In other words, not circumcision, not keeping the Law of Moses, but a heart cleansed by faith was all that was necessary for God to bear witness to that faith by pouring out His Spirit.

Peter then asked why they would tempt God (put God to the test) by disregarding what He had done and made plain at Caesarea, thus stirring His anger. To put a yoke on the necks of these Gentile disciples which neither the Jewish Christians nor their Jewish ancestors had strength to bear would indeed put God to the test after His gracious revelation at Caesarea.

Then Peter concluded by declaring that through the grace of the Lord Jesus Christ the Jewish disciples keep believing in order to keep on being saved in exactly the same way as those Gentiles. That is, by grace, apart from the heavy yoke of the Law and the legalistic bondage encouraged by the Pharisees (who were very severe at this time), they all continued in their relation to Christ.

These words of Peter quieted down the crowd, and they listened in silence as Barnabas and Paul related (and explained) how many signs and wonders God did through them among the Gentiles.[6] By this they implied that the miracles showed God's concern for winning these Gentiles to Christ and establishing them in the faith. As Paul later wrote to the Corinthians, he preached to them in the demonstration of the Spirit and of mighty, miracle-working power, that their faith might not stand in the wisdom of men, but in the power of God (1 Corinthians 2:4, 5).

A Word of Wisdom (15:13-29)

[13]And after they had held their peace, James answered, saying, Men *and* brethren, hearken unto me: [14]Simeon hath declared how God at the

---

[5]Some writers point out that both the giving (verse 8) and the cleansing (verse 9) are Greek aorists which these writers claim are simultaneous here. But the cleansing is clearly prior to the "making no distinction" and is definitely not simultaneous with it. Cf. Horton, *op. cit.*, pp. 159-161 for the use of the aorist participle in relation to the main verb of a Greek sentence.

[6]Note that Barnabas is mentioned first again, for he was known and respected by the Jerusalem leaders and believers. This time he was the spokesman.

first did visit the Gentiles, to take out of them a people for his name. [15]And to this agree the words of the prophets; as it is written, [16]After this I will return, and will build again the tabernacle of David, which is fallen down; and I will build again the ruins thereof, and I will set it up: [17]that the residue of men might seek after the Lord, and all the Gentiles, upon whom my name is called, saith the Lord, who doeth all these things. [18]Known unto God are all his works from the beginning of the world.

[19]Wherefore my sentence is, that we trouble not them, which from among the Gentiles are turned to God: [20]but that we write unto them, that they abstain from pollutions of idols, and *from* fornication, and *from* things strangled, and *from* blood. [21]For Moses of old time hath in every city them that preach him, being read in the synagogues every sabbath day.

[22]Then pleased it the apostles and elders, with the whole church, to send chosen men of their own company to Antioch with Paul and Barnabas; *namely*, Judas surnamed Barsabas, and Silas, chief men among the brethren: [23]and they wrote *letters* by them after this manner; The apostles and elders and brethren *send* greeting unto the brethren which are of the Gentiles in Antioch and Syria and Cilicia: [24]Forasmuch as we have heard, that certain which went out from us have troubled you with words, subverting your souls, saying, *Ye must* be circumcised, and keep the law; to whom we gave no *such* commandment: [25]it seemed good unto us, being assembled with one accord, to send chosen men unto you with our beloved Barnabas and Paul, [26]men that have hazarded their lives for the name of our Lord Jesus Christ. [27]We have sent therefore Judas and Silas, who shall also tell *you* the same things by mouth.

[28]For it seemed good to the Holy Ghost, and to us, to lay upon you no greater burden than these necessary things; [29]that ye abstain from meats offered to idols, and from blood, and from things strangled, and from fornication: from which if ye keep yourselves, ye shall do well. Fare ye well (Acts 15:13-29).

After Barnabas and Paul finished, the crowd waited until James broke the silence by asking them to listen. But in this request he speaks as a brother, not as one who had superior authority. First he drew attention to what Peter said, calling Peter by his Hebrew name, Simeon. He summarized this by saying that God, at the house of Cornelius (before other Gentiles were saved), first visited the Gentiles (intervened to bring them blessing) to take out of the Gentiles (the nations) a people for His name, that is, a people who would honor His Name and be His people.

James then gave grounds for this in the prophets, quoting Amos 9:11, 12 from the Greek Septuagint version. This differs from the Hebrew by substituting "men (mankind, human beings)" for Edom. Actually, the Hebrew could also be read "man" (Hebrew, *adam*) instead of Edom.[7]

Apparently also James took the setting up of the fallen tabernacle (tent) of David to be parallel to the prophecy that the Messiah would come as a new shoot or branch out of the stump of Jesse and the root of David. Though David's glory would be gone and his kingdom fallen, God would raise up the Messiah from David's descendants and restore the hope, not only of Israel, but of the Gentiles who would accept the Messiah and become part of God's people. This was, as the prophets said, the work of the Lord who has known all these things from the beginning of the world (or, age), that is, from the beginning of time.

"My sentence is" (verse 19) is better translated, "I think it good." Wycliffe's translation, the first major translation of the Bible in English, reads, "I deem." James was not acting as a judge here, nor as a leading elder of the Church. In verse 28 we read, "It seemed good to the Holy Spirit and to us," not, "to James and to us." In this situation James was simply a Christian brother, a member of the Body, who gave a word of wisdom as the Spirit willed. (See 1 Corinthians 12:8, 11.)

The Spirit's Word of Wisdom was that they not trouble further (in addition, as a further requirement to the faith and practice of) the Gentile believers. Let them instead write a letter that they (directing the Gentile believers to) abstain (keep away) from the pollutions of idols (everything connected with idol worship), from fornication (the various types of heterosexual and homosexual immorality habitually practiced by so many Gentile heathen), from things strangled (killed without draining out the blood), and from blood.[8]

These things were to be asked of the Gentiles, not to put them

[7]This difference involves only a slight change in the vowels, which the ancient Hebrew did not write anyway. In fact, Hebrew was written only in consonants until several hundred years after Christ. Note also that Edom in Amos is parallel to the heathen (the nations, the Gentiles). At least, Edom is representative of the Gentiles. But some Bible scholars believe the vowels for Edom were added by later Jews to change the meaning because they knew the Book of Acts used this verse to uphold the acceptance of uncircumcised Gentiles.

[8]Some ancient manuscripts leave out "things strangled" and interpret blood as bloodshed or murder. But the evidence is in favor of the usual text given above.

under a burden or list of rules. Rather, it was for the sake of the Jewish believers and for the sake of the testimony of the synagogues in every city (in city after city) where they had been for generations, going back to ancient times.

The first two requests to keep away from pollutions or polluted things of idolatry and from all forms of sexual immorality were for the sake of the Jewish witness to the one true God and to the high moral standards a holy God requires. Gentiles should not keep around anything from their former idol worship, not even as family heirlooms, and even though they now knew these things were meaningless and harmless. Their idolatrous neighbors would misinterpret this and suppose the worship of God could be mixed with heathen worship or heathen ideas.

The Gentile believers also had to be reminded of the high moral standards God requires. They came from a background where immorality was accepted and even encouraged in the name of religion. It took considerable teaching to make them realize that the things everyone else was doing were wrong. In several of Paul's epistles he had to deal very sternly with the problems of immorality.[9] (See Romans 6:12, 13, 19-23; 1 Corinthians 5:1, 9-12; 6:13, 15-20; 10:8; Galatians 5:19-21; Ephesians 5:3, 5; Colossians 3:5, 6; 1 Timothy 1:9, 10.)

The second two requests were for the sake of promoting fellowship between Jewish and Gentile believers. If there was anything that would turn a Jewish believer's stomach, it was to eat meat from which the blood had not been drained, or to eat blood itself. If the Jewish believers were going to give up a lot by eating nonkosher food in Gentile believers' homes, then the Gentile believers could give a little and avoid serving and eating those things which no Jew, no matter how long he had been a Christian, could stomach.

There was precedent for these last two requests because long

[9]See Bruce, *op. cit.,* p. 315. Some writers take fornication here to mean the prohibited degrees of marriage in Leviticus 18:6-18. First Corinthians 5:1 might be an example of fornication used in that sense, but it seems rather to be just an example of one kind of fornication. Paul goes on to use fornication to mean immorality in a more general sense in 1 Corinthians 5:9-11. It seems clear also that here in Acts the word is used in the more general sense including all forms of sexual immorality both before and after marriage. Certainly the kind of fornication mentioned in 1 Corinthians 5:1 was not common among the Gentiles, as that verse itself indicates.

before Moses' time, long before the Law was given, God told Noah not to eat blood because it represented the life. The same restriction in Moses' law treated blood as a type that pointed ahead to the blood of Christ and showed its importance. James, however, did not bring out this typology. Primarily it was concern for fellowship between Jews and Gentiles that was involved. This was the kind of wisdom James speaks of in his Epistle (James 3:17, 18). It was pure, peaceable, and gentle.

The apostles and elders together with the whole church thought it good to send men they chose out from among themselves to go with Paul and Barnabas to Antioch to present this decision and this letter. Those chosen were Judas Barsabas and Silas (short for Silvanus; 2 Corinthians 1:19), leading men among the brethren of the Jerusalem Church.

The letter stated clearly that the Jerusalem church gave no command that the Gentile believers must be circumcised and keep the Law. Their decision to send chosen men with their beloved ones, Barnabas and Paul, came as they were assembled in one accord. In other words, the decision was unanimous. Moreover, both Barnabas and Paul were loved by them. ("Beloved" is plural in the Greek.) Thus they recommended them to the Gentile believers in Antioch as men who had pledged themselves (their souls, their lives) for the name of our Lord Jesus Christ (that is, for all that His name expresses: His love, His salvation, His grace, His Person, etc).

Judas and Silas would personally confirm this. Only the necessary things which seemed good to the Spirit and to the Jerusalem believers would be asked of them. If they would keep themselves safe from these things, they would do well. "Fare ye well" is literally, "Make yourselves strong," but had become a common phrase used at the end of a letter to mean farewell or goodbye.

Rejoicing at Antioch (15:30-35)

[30]So when they were dismissed, they came to Antioch: and when they had gathered the multitude together, they delivered the epistle: [31]*which* when they had read, they rejoiced for the consolation. [32]And Judas and Silas, being prophets also themselves, exhorted the brethren with many words, and confirmed *them.* [33]And after they had tarried *there* a space, they were let go in peace from the brethren unto the apostles. [34]Notwithstanding it pleased Silas to abide there still. [35]Paul also and Barnabas

continued in Antioch, teaching and preaching the word of the Lord, with many others also (Acts 15:30-35).

When Paul and his company arrived and read the letter to the whole crowd of the believers in Antioch, they (the whole Body) rejoiced greatly for the consolation (encouragement, exhortation). Clearly, Paul also accepted and rejoiced in the decision of the Jerusalem Council.[10]

Judas and Silas then did more than confirm the facts of the letter. They were prophets (speakers for God, used by the Holy Spirit in the gift of prophecy for the edification, exhortation, and comfort or encouragement of the believers). By the Spirit they exhorted (encouraged and challenged) the brethren with many (Spirit-given) words. Through these words they confirmed (upheld, supported) them. That is, they gave them solid encouragement to forget the arguments of the Judaizers and to maintain their faith in Christ and in the gospel they had received, the gospel of salvation by grace through faith alone (apart from the works of the Law), as Paul emphasizes in his epistles to the Romans and Galatians.

After a time, the brethren (the believers at Antioch) released Judas and Silas with a farewell blessing of peace (and well-being) to go back to those who had sent them, that is, to the whole Church in Jerusalem, as the Greek shows. Judas Barsabas did return, but Silas chose to remain.[11]

Paul and Barnabas also remained in Antioch to teach and preach the gospel, along with many others; the Lord had raised up many other teachers and spreaders of the gospel in the still growing church. These may have included some others that came from Jerusalem and elsewhere. But undoubtedly the majority were people from the local assembly. They too were entering into the work of ministry for the edifying (building up) of the Body of Christ. Paul later wrote that all saints (all dedicated believers) should receive from Christ and thus edify the Body (Ephesians 4:12, 15, 16).

[10]Cf. Longenecker, *op. cit.*, pp. 254-260.

[11]Some writers take this to be a contradiction to verse 33. However, the church only released them to go. The Bible does not say they went. Many modern versions do omit verse 34 and suppose Silas went back to Jerusalem and returned later.

PAUL AND BARNABAS SEPARATE (15:36-41)

[36]And some days after, Paul said unto Barnabas, Let us go again and visit our brethren in every city where we have preached the word of the Lord, *and see* how they do. [37]And Barnabas determined to take with them John, whose surname was Mark. [38]But Paul thought not good to take him with them, who departed from them from Pamphylia, and went not with them to the work. [39]And the contention was so sharp between them, that they departed asunder one from the other: and so Barnabas took Mark, and sailed unto Cyprus; [40]and Paul chose Silas, and departed, being recommended by the brethren unto the grace of God. [41]And he went through Syria and Cilicia, confirming the churches (Acts 15:36-41).

After certain days (which could mean a considerable time) Paul suggested to Barnabas that they visit the brethren in the churches established during the first missionary journey in Cyprus and South Galatia. Paul throughout his ministry maintained a love and concern that kept him praying for the churches and believers to whom he had ministered. His epistles are evidence of this.

When Barnabas decided to (willed to, purposed to) take along John Mark, Paul did not think Mark worthy. Mark had left them in the lurch at an important point when they needed him for the work. Paul evidently did not believe that it would be good to bring into these young churches a person who might not set a good example of faith and diligence. Barnabas, however, was determined to give his cousin another chance.

Both Paul and Barnabas felt so strongly about this that they felt temporary irritation, perhaps indignation. The Greek indicates sharp feelings between them. But they did not let this hinder the work of the Lord; they came up with a peaceful settlement. They decided it was best to separate and divide up the responsibility of visiting and encouraging the believers. Barnabas therefore took his cousin Mark and went to Cyprus to visit the churches founded on the first part of the first journey. This was wise, for Cyprus was familiar territory to Mark. He had been faithful there. It was better to take him back to the area where he had been a success.

That Barnabas was right in wanting to give Mark a second chance is shown by the fact that Paul later asked Timothy to bring Mark with him because he was useful for ministry (2 Timothy 4:11). Mark was also with Peter on his visit to Babylon (1 Peter

5:13).[12] Early tradition says also that Mark wrote down the preaching of Peter in his Gospel. So we have both Barnabas and Peter to thank that Mark was in a position where the Holy Spirit could direct and inspire him to write the second Gospel.

Paul then chose Silas, who was a mature believer, a prophet already used by the Spirit to challenge and encourage the churches. Silas would be an excellent helper to Paul in his effort to encourage the churches in South Galatia who were in a most difficult environment.

Since Silas was an outstanding member of the Jerusalem church, this would also help to show the Galatian churches the unity between Paul and the Jerusalem leaders and would thus further put to rest the arguments of the Judaizers.[13] It was helpful also that Silas was, like Paul, a Roman citizen. (See Acts 16:37, 38.)

The brethren at Antioch then released them and committed them anew to the grace of God. And so they went on their way through Syria and Cilicia, confirming the churches. These would include assemblies in cities north of Antioch in Syria and Paul's home city of Tarsus in Cilicia.[14]

[12]Some writers take Babylon here to mean Rome. But Babylon had one of the largest orthodox Jewish communities outside of Palestine. (The Jewish community at Alexandria was probably larger, but they were Hellenistic rather than strictly orthodox). It would be strange if Peter, the apostle to the circumcision (Galatians 2:7) did not visit this large Jewish community. Peter's visit to Babylon probably took place before Paul went to Rome.

[13]Cf. Longenecker, *op. cit.*, p. 226.

[14]Codex Bezae (D) and other ancient manuscripts add that they delivered the injunctions of the elders, that is, the instructions given in the letter of Acts 15 from the Jerusalem church.

ACTS

CHAPTER

16

From Cilicia Paul and Silas went through the Taurus mountains by way of a famous pass called the Cilician Gates.[1] Coming from this direction they would arrive at Derbe first and then Lystra.

TIMOTHY CHOSEN (16:1-5)

[1]Then came he to Derbe and Lystra: and, behold, a certain disciple was there, named Timothy, the son of a certain woman, which was a Jewess, and believed; but his father *was* a Greek: [2]which was well reported of by the brethren that were at Lystra and Iconium. [3]Him would Paul have to go forth with him; and took and circumcised him because of the Jews which were in those quarters: for they knew all that his father was a Greek. [4]And as they went through the cities, they delivered them the decrees for to keep, that were ordained of the apostles and elders which were at Jerusalem. [5]And so were the churches established in the faith, and increased in number daily (Acts 16:1-5).

At Lystra Paul came across a young disciple named Timothy (short for Timotheus). His mother was a believing Jewess named Eunice. His grandmother Lois was also a very godly believer. (See 2 Timothy 1:5; 3:14, 15.) His father, however, was a Greek, probably a member of a prominent and wealthy family, but apparently still unconverted.

Fortunately, the faith and training given by his mother and grandmother had more effect on young Timothy than the unbelief of his father. They trained him in the Scriptures from his earliest childhood. Then, when he accepted Christ, he made

[1]Sir William Ramsay describes this pass in *Pauline and Other Studies* (London; 1906), pp. 273 ff., cited by Bruce, *op. cit.*, p. 321.

great progress in the Christian life. Verse 2 means he was witnessed to by the believing brethren at Lystra and in the next town, Iconium. This clearly means that God had given him a spiritual ministry in both cities and that both his life and ministry were a blessing to the assemblies there.

It is probable also that he was converted under Paul's ministry during one of Paul's previous visits to Lystra. However, when Paul calls him "my son" later, he was probably using the term "son" to mean "student" as well as younger fellow-worker. (See 1 Timothy 1:2, 18; 2 Timothy 1:2.)

Paul wanted to take Timothy out of the church at Lystra for further training as well as to help in the ministry of these missionary journeys. But when he decided to do this, he did something very unusual. He circumcised Timothy. Paul makes quite a point in Galatians 2:3-5 that the Jerusalem leaders did not require Titus to be circumcised. Why, then, did he circumcise Timothy?

Titus was a Gentile. To circumcise him would have been to yield to the Judaizers who said Gentiles must become Jews to keep their salvation. Timothy, however, was brought up in the Jewish traditions by his Jewish mother and grandmother. Jews even today accept a person as a Jew if his mother is Jewish even if his father is a Gentile. They rightly understand that the mother has the greatest influence on the values and religious attitudes of a young child. We can be sure that the Jews in Paul's day also would consider Timothy a Jew.

Paul still went to the Jew first in every new city that he visited. For him to take an uncircumcised Jew into a synagogue would be like taking a traitor into an army camp. It would be intolerable to the Jews; none of them would listen to him. As a result, Paul took Timothy and circumcised him for the sake of his witness to his own people.[2]

Perhaps 1 Corinthians 9:20-23 gives a little further insight into Paul's reasoning. Paul did not go against the cultural norms of the people to whom he ministered unless they were immoral or idolatrous. Thus he brought everything into line with the promotion of the gospel and the salvation of souls. Everyone knew Timothy's father was a Greek, so Paul had to confirm Timothy's

---

[2]Cf. Hackett, *op. cit.*, pp. 181, 182. Note also that Paul in Galatians 5:6; 6:15; and 1 Corinthians 7:19 shows that circumcision and uncircumcision in themselves mean nothing.

Jewish heritage before they could go on. First Timothy 4:14 indicates that the elders of the local assembly accepted this, prayed for Timothy, and sent him out with their blessing.

As Paul, Silas, and Timothy went on their way through South Galatia, they handed over copies of the decrees or regulations from the letter of Acts 15 for the Gentile believers to keep. These regulations they recognized as decided by the apostles and elders in Jerusalem. But we can be sure also they gave attention to Acts 15:28, "It seemed good to the Holy Spirit and to us."

The result was that the upsetting teachings of the Judaizers were counteracted. What had been a critical issue was now no longer a threat or a cause of division; everyone accepted the decision of the Jerusalem counsel. Undoubtedly, the Epistle to the Galatians had helped to prepare the way for this.

Then the assemblies in the various cities were all strengthened, not only in faith, but in the faith; that is, they grew in their understanding of the truth of the gospel and their obedience to its teachings and precepts. Because of this, the assemblies continued to grow, increasing in number day by day.

The Macedonian Call (16:6-10)

[6]Now when they had gone throughout Phrygia and the region of Galatia, and were forbidden of the Holy Ghost to preach the word in Asia, [7]after they were come to Mysia, they assayed to go into Bithynia: but the Spirit suffered them not. [8]And they passing by Mysia came down to Troas. [9]And a vision appeared to Paul in the night; There stood a man of Macedonia, and prayed him, saying, Come over into Macedonia, and help us. [10]And after he had seen the vision, immediately we endeavored to go into Macedonia, assuredly gathering that the Lord had called us for to preach the gospel unto them (Acts 16:6-10).

After Paul and his company went through the region of Phrygia and Galatia it would have been logical to go next into the Roman province of Asia. Its great city of Ephesus was a challenge. But it was not God's time. The Holy Spirit had already forbidden them to speak the Word in Asia. The Bible does not say how the Spirit did this. He may have done it by a word of wisdom given to one of Paul's company, or perhaps given by a Spirit-filled believer in one of the churches.[3]

---

[3]Bruce, *op. cit.*, p. 326, suggests that this may have come through a prophet in Lystra.

Since they were forbidden to enter Asia, they moved north along the eastern border of Mysia and made an attempt to enter Bithynia to the northeast along the Black Sea.[4] Paul was never one to sit around and do nothing when he did not know where God wanted him to go or what God wanted him to do next. He was always conscious of the missionary burden laid upon him. So when he was checked by the Spirit from going in one direction, he would take a step in another, trusting the Holy Spirit to confirm or check that direction too.

Again the Spirit[5] would not let them go into Bithynia. Only one direction was left, so they took it, turning west and going to Troas. To do this they had to go through Mysia. But the Greek says literally that they bypassed Mysia. That is, they were not given permission to minister in Mysia either, and they bypassed it as far as preaching the gospel was concerned.

Think of what this must have meant to the Apostle Paul, who said, "Woe is unto me if I preach not the gospel" (1 Corinthians 9:16). How he must have been burdened as he passed city after city, still forbidden to preach the Word. But because he was obedient God brought him to Troas when He wanted him there.

At Troas, a harbor city of Mysia across the Aegean Sea from Macedonia, came another important turning point in Paul's ministry and missionary travels. Had he gone into Bithynia, he might have continued eastward and never gone to Greece or Rome. But God had new centers He wanted to establish in Europe. It was left for other apostles and believers to go eastward.[6]

The call westward was made clear in a night vision given to Paul in which a (pagan) Macedonian stood beseeching him to cross over to Macedonia and help them. Immediately Paul and his

---

[4]Bithynia had important Jewish settlements, especially in the Greek-speaking cities of Nicaea and Nicomedia. First Peter 1:1 shows that Bithynia was later evangelized by others.

[5]Some ancient manuscripts have the Spirit of Jesus here, which is, of course, another title of the Holy Spirit, the Spirit of God. It may mean simply that Jesus checked him by the Holy Spirit.

[6]There is strong tradition in South India that the apostle Thomas went there. Some believe it was another Thomas, but it is not impossible that the apostle himself went.

company (which now included Luke)[7] sought to go out to Macedonia, concluding that God had called them out to preach the gospel to the people there.

An Open Door in Philippi (16:11-15)

[11]Therefore loosing from Troas, we came with a straight course to Samothracia, and the next *day* to Neapolis; [12]and from thence to Philippi, which is the chief city of that part of Macedonia, *and* a colony: and we were in that city abiding certain days. [13]And on the sabbath we went out of the city by a river side, where prayer was wont to be made; and we sat down, and spake unto the women which resorted *thither*. [14]And a certain woman named Lydia, a seller of purple, of the city of Thyatira, which worshiped God, heard *us:* whose heart the Lord opened, that she attended unto the things which were spoken of Paul. [15]And when she was baptized, and her household, she besought *us*, saying, If ye have judged me to be faithful to the Lord, come into my house, and abide *there*. And she constrained us (Acts 16:11-15).

A sailing ship took them about 125 miles in two days to Neapolis, the harbor town of Philippi, by way of the mountainous island of Samothrace. The wind must have been very favorable. Later, the journey in the other direction took five days (Acts 20:6).

Philippi, named for the father of Alexander the Great, was a great city of the first division of the Roman province of Macedonia, north of Greece. The city also was a Roman "colony." That is, the Romans had settled a garrison of Roman soldiers there who were citizens of Rome and who followed Roman laws and customs.[8] It was an important city also because it was located at the eastern end of the famous Roman road, the Egnatian Way.

There was no Jewish synagogue in the city, which means it lacked the ten Jewish men necessary to have one. Probably by making inquiries, they heard that there was a place for prayer about a mile outside the city gate on the bank of the Gangites River.[9] There they sat down and proceeded to talk to a group of women who met together there.

---

[7]This is the first of the "we passages" where Luke lets us know he was with Paul and was an eyewitness to these events.

[8]Cf. Richard B. Rackham, *The Acts of the Apostles* (Grand Rapids: Baker Book House, 1964 reprint from 1901), p. lvii.

[9]The King James Version gives the correct translation of the Greek of verse 13. Cf. Bruce, *op. cit.*, p. 329.

One of them, Lydia, was a wealthy businesswoman, a seller of purple-dyed cloth.[10] She was a God-fearing Gentile from Thyatira in the Roman province of Asia, a city famous for its dyes. She kept listening to Paul. Soon the Lord opened her heart to give full attention to the things Paul was saying. The result was she believed the gospel and was baptized in water along with her entire household, that is, her staff and servants. By her influence they also believed, and together they became the first body of believers in Europe.

This took place over a period of time. By winning her household to the Lord, Lydia demonstrated her own faithfulness to the Lord. On this basis she besought Paul and his entire company to make her large home their home and headquarters. Then she kept urging them until they finally did so.

A Demon Cast Out (16:16-18)

[16]And it came to pass, as we went to prayer, a certain damsel possessed with a spirit of divination met us, which brought her masters much gain by soothsaying: [17]the same followed Paul and us, and cried, saying, These men are the servants of the most high God, which show unto us the way of salvation. [18]And this did she many days. But Paul, being grieved, turned and said to the spirit, I command thee in the name of Jesus Christ to come out of her. And he came out the same hour (Acts 16:16-18).

One day as Paul, Silas, Timothy, and Luke were going to the place for prayer a demon possessed slave girl met them. The Greek says she had a spirit of ventriloquism. That is, a demon spirit used her in spite of herself to speak through her and to practice soothsaying. The Greek also calls her a "pythoness." The python was the symbol of the Greek god, Apollo. Her masters claimed that her fortune telling was the voice of Apollo. This kind of fortune telling brought much gain (much money) to her masters. It may be implied also that they used her to attract people to other businesses they carried on.

This slave girl kept following Paul and his company shouting out, practically shrieking, in a high-pitched voice over and over: "These men are slaves of the most high God who are announcing

[10]The ancient "royal" purple referred to here was actually a deep shade of red, later called "Turkey red." It was the product of the shellfish murex and was very expensive.

to you a way of salvation."[11] This she kept doing for (during) many days. That is, she did not do it continuously, but during part of every day she would follow them, shouting out the same thing.

The slave girl's shrieks and cries must have attracted a great deal of attention. It surely let the city know Paul and his company were there. But it was not the kind of witness that brings real glory to God, nor did it proclaim the whole truth. Paul was greatly troubled by her unpleasant shrieking. It really became a burden to him, and he undoubtedly felt it was hindering the work of the Lord. Finally, he turned and spoke, not to the woman, but to the evil spirit, commanding it in the name (authority) of Jesus Christ to come out of her. In this he was following the example of Jesus who also spoke directly to the demons who possessed people. It came out of her in that hour, which really means immediately.[12]

Paul and Silas in Prison (16:19-26)

[19]And when her masters saw that the hope of their gains was gone, they caught Paul and Silas, and drew *them* into the market place unto the rulers, [20]and brought them to the magistrates, saying, These men, being Jews, do exceedingly trouble our city, [21]and teach customs, which are not lawful for us to receive, neither to observe, being Romans. [22]And the multitude rose up together against them; and the magistrates rent off their clothes, and commanded to beat *them.* [23]And when they had laid many stripes upon them, they cast *them* into prison, charging the jailer to keep them safely: [24]who, having received such a charge, thrust them into the inner prison, and made their feet fast in the stocks.

[25]And at midnight Paul and Silas prayed, and sang praises unto God: and the prisoners heard them. [26]And suddenly there was a great earthquake, so that the foundations of the prison were shaken: and immediately all the doors were opened, and every one's bands were loosed (Acts 16:19-26).

The slave girl's masters were quite upset when they saw the hope of their gain was gone. So they seized Paul and Silas and dragged (pulled) them into the marketplace (Greek, *agora*) before the rulers (governors, leading men), that is, before the two praetors or chief Roman magistrates of the city.

---

[11]The Greek has no article: "a way," rather than "the way." Satan still does not mind calling the gospel "a way" of salvation as long as we do not say it is the only way.

[12]Codex Bezae (D) adds the word "immediately."

In their accusation they did not mention the real reason they brought Paul and Silas there. Instead, they called them big Jewish troublemakers who were proclaiming things that were not lawful for Romans to welcome or practice. Though Judaism was a legal religion in the Roman Empire, it was only tolerated by the majority of the people and was not looked on with any real favor by the government.

The people were ready to believe that Jews could be troublemakers. This accusation stirred up the crowd in the marketplace; they joined together in an outbreak of mob violence. The chief magistrates then, to satisfy the mob, tore off the clothes from Paul and Silas and ordered them to be beaten (flogged) with a rod—a common Roman punishment. (See 2 Corinthians 11:25.)

After many blows, the magistrates had them thrown into prison and ordered the jailer to guard them securely. To make sure they could not escape, the jailer then threw them into the inner prison and fastened their feet securely in wooden stocks, with their legs painfully forced apart so they could not move them.

After all this rough treatment, to be put into such an uncomfortable position must have indeed been most painful. The inner prison was probably damp, cold, and insect infested. Yet Paul and Silas did not complain. We can be sure they did not feel like singing at this point either. But they prayed and sang praises to God anyway. Undoubtedly, as they did so God brought them a sense of peace and victory.

About midnight Paul and Silas were still praying and singing and the rest of the prisoners were listening to them. Suddenly a great earthquake shook the foundations of the prison. As the walls shook back and forth all the doors flew open and all the prisoners' chains were broken loose. (They were probably fastened into the wall.)

The Jailer Converted (16:27-34)

[27]And the keeper of the prison awaking out of his sleep, and seeing the prison doors open, he drew out his sword, and would have killed himself, supposing that the prisoners had been fled. [28]But Paul cried with a loud voice, saying, Do thyself no harm: for we are all here. [29]Then he called for a light, and sprang in, and came trembling, and fell down before Paul and Silas, [30]and brought them out, and said, Sirs, what must I do to be

saved? [31]And they said, Believe on the Lord Jesus Christ, and thou shalt be saved, and thy house. [32]And they spake unto him the word of the Lord, and to all that were in his house.

[33]And he took them the same hour of the night, and washed *their* stripes; and was baptized, he and all his, straightway. [34]And when he had brought them into his house, he set meat before them, and rejoiced, believing in God with all his house (Acts 16:27-34).

The earthquake woke up the jailer. It seems he immediately rushed to the prison, saw all the doors were open, and jumped to the conclusion that all the prisoners had escaped. He knew the penalty that would be his if this were so. Rather than face the trial, shame, and disgraceful death that he expected to come, he drew his sword, intending to commit suicide.

From the deep darkness of the prison, Paul could see what the jailer was doing even though the jailer could not see into the prison. Immediately he shouted out, telling the jailer not to harm himself, for all the prisoners were still there.

After asking for lights, the jailer rushed into the prison. Trembling with fear, he fell down beside Paul and Silas. That is, he was completely overcome by fear and awe because of what had happened.

Then, recovering his composure,[13] he brought Paul and Silas out of the prison and asked them what he must do that he might be saved. This might seem a strange question from a pagan Roman. But he must have remembered the words of the ventriloquist spirit that possessed the slave girl. These men could tell him the way of salvation.

Paul's answer was simple. "Believe on the Lord Jesus Christ and thou shalt be saved, and thy house." By this Paul did not mean that the jailer's household would be saved simply because the jailer was. Paul wanted the jailer to know, however, that the offer was not limited to him, but the same kind of faith would bring salvation to all who believed. He undoubtedly could see that the earthquake and its results had affected them all. He wanted to see them all saved, not just one.[14]

Paul and Silas then proceeded to give the Word of God (the gospel) to all who were in the household. Thus he explained to

---

[13]Codex Bezae (D) adds that he first secured the other prisoners. This was undoubtedly true.

[14]Cf. Hackett, *op. cit.,* p. 191.

them all what it meant to believe in Jesus and what it meant to be saved.

Then the jailer took the apostles and washed their stripes (the wounds from the beating), and immediately he and all his were baptized in water. This was probably done in a pool in the courtyard of his house. After this he took the apostles back inside the house and set before them a table loaded with food. The whole household was then full of joy because they believed in God with a faith that was strong and continuing.

Some writers try to use this passage as an argument for infant baptism since the entire household was baptized in water. But when we examine the passage more carefully it is easy to see that everyone in the household heard the Word of God, everyone believed, and everyone was full of joy. Clearly, no infants were included. It is possible that the jailer had no small children. He was actually the "governor" of the prison and was probably an older man before being appointed to this position. It is probable too that Roman custom would not consider babies or small children as part of the household until they reached a certain age.

The joy was so great that we might translate it they jumped for joy. Again, Luke does not tell everything every time. We can be sure that part of the reason for that great joy was the fact they were also baptized in the Holy Spirit and spoke in other tongues as the early believers did on the Day of Pentecost (Acts 2:4) and at the house of Cornelius. After all, would God do any less for these believers than He did for Cornelius?

Paul and Silas Released (16:35-40)

[35]And when it was day, the magistrates sent the sergeants, saying, Let those men go. [36]And the keeper of the prison told this saying to Paul, The magistrates have sent to let you go: now therefore depart, and go in peace. [37]But Paul said unto them, They have beaten us openly uncondemned, being Romans, and have cast *us* into prison; and now do they thrust us out privily? nay verily; but let them come themselves and fetch us out. [38]And the sergeants told these words unto the magistrates: and they feared, when they heard that they were Romans. [39]And they came and besought them, and brought *them* out, and desired *them* to depart out of the city. [40]And they went out of the prison, and entered into *the house of* Lydia: and when they had seen the brethren, they comforted them, and departed (Acts 16:35-40).

The rejoicing probably continued the rest of the night. It would be hard to sleep after such experiences. In the morning the chief magistrates sent officers called lictors, who were orderlies or attendants, to tell the jailer to let Paul and Silas go. The jailer passed the word to them to go out of the prison area and to proceed in peace.

Paul knew, however, that the crowds still had a wrong idea about them and about both Jews and Christians. Paul therefore refused to sneak away like a beaten criminal. The magistrates had beaten them publicly, without any semblance of a trial, even though they were Roman citizens, and then had thrown them publicly into prison. Were they now going to throw them out of prison secretly? Let them come themselves and lead the apostles out. In this way the city would know that the charges were false and that Paul and Silas were restored to good standing in the community.

When this was reported to the chief magistrates, they knew they were wrong in yielding to the mob and not questioning Paul and Silas. They were afraid, too, because Roman citizens had rights to trial before punishment, rights that could not be ignored with impunity. They knew also what could happen to them if Paul and Silas were to lodge a complaint with the government in Rome. So they came very humbly and besought Paul and Silas (not to bring charges against them). Then they led them out of the prison compound publicly. (Paul and Silas had returned from the jailer's house to the prison itself.)

The magistrates then asked them to leave the city. This was not because they were unwilling to have the gospel preached in Philippi. But they were afraid that Paul and Silas might change their minds. Or, perhaps they were afraid that the sympathies of the people would now swing to Paul and Silas and against them. So they asked the apostles to leave for the sake of peace in the city. We can be sure also that there was no more persecution of the believers as long as these magistrates were in power.

Before leaving the city, Paul and Silas went to Lydia's house where a large courtyard (or upper room) was full of believers who were gathered, undoubtedly praying for Paul and Silas. Then, after seeing and exhorting the brethren, the apostles left town.[15]

At this point it is evident that Luke did not leave with them. The next chapter (17:14) shows that Timothy did leave with them. But Luke no longer says "We." He obviously stayed in Philippi to give further encouragement and teaching to the assembly there. He was still in Philippi in Acts 20:6.

---

[15]Note that the believers were no longer limited to a few women. Brethren took the leadership, though in Hebrew usage "brethren" included the sisters. (Just as the "children of Israel" in Hebrew is literally the "sons of Israel" but included both men and women.)

ACTS

CHAPTER

17

After Paul, Silas, and Timothy left Philippi, they proceeded westward on the Egnatian Road. The next two towns of any size, each about a days' journey apart, apparently had no Jewish synagogue; and so they pushed on 100 miles from Philippi to Thessalonica, the most important city of ancient Macedonia and still important today. It was founded in 315 B.C. and named by Cassander, its founder, for his wife, who was a step-sister of Alexander the Great.

To the Jew First (17:1-9)

[1]Now when they had passed through Amphipolis and Apollonia, they came to Thessalonica, where was a synagogue of the Jews: [2]and Paul, as his manner was, went in unto them, and three sabbath days reasoned with them out of the Scriptures, [3]opening and alleging, that Christ must needs have suffered, and risen again from the dead; and that this Jesus, whom I preach unto you, is Christ. [4]And some of them believed, and consorted with Paul and Silas; and of the devout Greeks a great multitude, and of the chief women not a few.

[5]But the Jews which believed not, moved with envy, took unto them certain lewd fellows of the baser sort, and gathered a company, and set all the city on an uproar, and assaulted the house of Jason, and sought to bring them out to the people. [6]And when they found them not, they drew Jason and certain brethren unto the rulers of the city, crying, These that have turned the world upside down are come hither also; [7]whom Jason hath received: and these all do contrary to the decrees of Caesar, saying that there is another king, *one* Jesus. [8]And they troubled the people and the rulers of the city, when they heard these things. [9]And when they had taken security of Jason, and of the others, they let them go (Acts 17:1-9).

Again Luke draws attention to Paul's custom of going to the Jew first and taking advantage of their background and of the opportunities given by the synagogue to teach. For three successive Sabbaths, Paul preached to them, undoubtedly following the same pattern as in Pisidian Antioch (Acts 13:16-41). As always he opened out the Scriptures that prophesied the Messiah, explaining them fully. That is, he set them out in such a way that they clearly showed it was God's divine purpose for the Messiah to suffer and rise again from the dead. As in Antioch also, he showed that none of these prophecies could apply to anyone but Jesus. Therefore, "this Jesus" truly is the Messiah, the Christ, God's anointed Prophet, Priest, and King.

Some of the Jews were persuaded (believed in Jesus and obeyed the gospel; thus they were baptized in water and in the Holy Spirit). These threw in their lot with Paul and Silas. So did a large crowd of God-fearing Greeks, including not a few of the wives of the chief men of the city. Thus the Gentile converts far outnumbered the Jewish believers.

First Thessalonians 2:1-13 gives a further description of the ministry of Paul and Silas at this time. Their preaching and ministry were very effective. Even though they were treated outrageously at Philippi, this did not cause them to be timid or fearful. At Thessalonica they preached in a bold, free, open, fearless manner with pure motives as servants of Jesus Christ. They were gentle to the new converts also, giving them all kinds of tender loving care. Yet they were firm in their stand for righteousness and encouraged every one of them to live in a manner worthy of the God who called them to His own kingdom and glory.

The Jews who rejected Paul's message soon became frustrated by the increasing numbers of Gentiles who were accepting the gospel. These Jews rebelled against what God was doing and even went so far as to forbid (hinder, prevent) Paul and his company from speaking (or even talking) to Gentiles with a view to their salvation (1 Thessalonians 2:14-16).

When they saw that the Gentiles continued to respond to the gospel and paid no attention to them, these unbelieving Jews proceeded to stir up a riot. First, they took to themselves a group of marketplace loungers who were always ready to join any agitators who came along. Then, with their help, they gathered a crowd and set up a disturbance that threw the whole city into a panic. Then they went to the house of Jason, taking Jason by surprise and seeking to bring out Paul and Silas to the rabble. But evidently the word had already gotten to the apostles and they had left for another part of the city.

Because Paul and Silas were not there, the mob dragged Jason and some of his fellow believers before the rulers (politarchs).[1] There were five or six of these, and they were the chief magistrates of the city.

As usual, the accusation did not reveal the real reason for wanting to get rid of Paul and Silas. The unbelieving Jews and their coconspirators accused them of turning the inhabited world upside down. This was a phrase used of political agitators or revolutionaries who had caused trouble elsewhere and who upset not only the status quo, but everything. They also accused Jason of welcoming these "troublemakers" to his house and joining with them to practice things contrary to the decrees of Caesar, speaking of another king (really, a rival emperor), Jesus.

The crowd and the politarchs were disturbed by these things. Part of their problem may have been that they knew Jason and many of the other converts and had not seen any evidence of political activity. It is probable, also, that the believers who were wives of the chief men included the wife of one or more of these politarchs.

Apparently the politarchs did not take the charges seriously, but to satisfy the crowd they took security (surety) from Jason and the rest who had been brought before them. This probably means Jason and his friends provided bail as a guarantee that Paul and Silas would leave the city and not come back lest there be further disturbance.[2] This was later used by Satan to hinder Paul's return. (See 1 Thessalonians 2:17, 18.)

Paul probably refers to this also when he says the Thessalonians "received the Word in much affliction, with joy of the Holy Spirit" (1 Thessalonians 1:6). The unbelieving Jews had apparently begun causing trouble some time before the incident with Jason. In fact, Paul indicates that from the beginning he spoke the gospel (good news) of God to them "in much conflict" (1 Thessalonians 2:2). Then, when Paul wanted to return, Satan hindered him, probably by bringing up the question of the security

[1]Archaeologists have found inscriptions referring to these politarchs.
[2]Cf. Hackett, *op. cit.*, p. 196.

or surety. Thus Paul was not able to return when he wanted to do so.

NOBLE BEROEANS (17:10-15)

[10]And the brethren immediately sent away Paul and Silas by night unto Beroea: who coming *thither* went into the synagogue of the Jews. [11]These were more noble than those in Thessalonica, in that they received the word with all readiness of mind, and searched the Scriptures daily, whether those things were so. [12]Therefore many of them believed; also of honorable women which were Greeks, and of men, not a few. [13]But when the Jews of Thessalonica had knowledge that the word of God was preached of Paul at Beroea, they came thither also, and stirred up the people. [14]And then immediately the brethren sent away Paul to go as it were to the sea: but Silas and Timothy abode there still. [15]And they that conducted Paul brought him unto Athens: and receiving a commandment unto Silas and Timothy for to come to him with all speed, they departed (Acts 17:10-15).

The Christian brethren saw how bitter and determined the unbelieving Jews were. So they took no chances. By night they sent Paul and Silas out to Beroea, about 50 miles to the southwest on the road to Greece. This was off the main Egnatian Road they had been following, and the believers may have thought they would be safer there.

The Beroeans did respond quite differently. Instead of reacting against Paul's message, they welcomed the Word with all kinds of eagerness, zeal, and enthusiasm. Even more important, they examined the Scriptures daily, searching it out like lawyers investigating a case, to see whether these things were so.

Because of their attitude and their searching of the Scriptures, the Bible says they were more noble than the Jews in Thessalonica. In Thessalonica some of the Jews believed. Others just let their old prejudices guide them, and they reacted against the gospel. In Beroea, however, many of the Jews believed, probably the majority of them. There was no opposition stirred up among them.

Because they searched the Scriptures these Beroeans not only set an example for us all, but Paul did not have to correct them later, as he did so many other churches.[3]

---

[3]They searched the Scriptures, not looking for proof texts to uphold their own preconceived ideas, but seeking to find the meaning intended by the Holy Spirit who inspired the Scriptures.

Many Gentiles also believed, both of women who had an honorable position in society, and men as well.

Though the synagogue at Beroea caused no trouble, the news of Paul's effective proclamation of the gospel there reached the Jews of Thessalonica. They came to Beroea then and did the same sort of thing they did at home. They shook up and disturbed the crowds, trying to rouse mob violence against Paul.

Before they could do any damage, the Beroean Christian brethren hurried Paul off in the direction of the Aegean Sea, probably intending to send him away by ship. Silas and Timothy stayed behind to teach and encourage the believers further.

Those who were conducting Paul then changed directions, possibly because the Thessalonian Jews were plotting something else and they got wind of it. So they (or a part of the group) took Paul to Athens. He then sent them back with a command for Silas and Timothy to come to him as quickly as possible.

Waiting in Athens (17:16-21)

[16]Now while Paul waited for them at Athens, his spirit was stirred in him, when he saw the city wholly given to idolatry. [17]Therefore disputed he in the synagogue with the Jews, and with the devout persons, and in the market daily with them that met with him. [18]Then certain philosophers of the Epicureans, and of the Stoics, encountered him. And some said, What will this babbler say? other some, He seemeth to be a setter forth of strange gods: because he preached unto them Jesus, and the resurrection. [19]And they took him, and brought him unto Areopagus, saying, May we know what this new doctrine, whereof thou speakest, *is?* [20]For thou bringest certain strange things to our ears: we would know therefore what these things mean. [21](For all the Athenians, and strangers which were there, spent their time in nothing else, but either to tell or to hear some new thing.) (Acts 17:16-21).

Athens was famous for its Acropolis and all its temples. By this time, however, it had lost its former glory. It was no longer politically important. Its old leadership in culture and education had been taken over by Alexandria in Egypt. But Athens still nurtured the memory of its past. Its temples were still beautiful examples of the best in Greek architecture. But everywhere Paul looked the city was full of idols, and this caused his spirit to be provoked (almost "angered") within him.

As always, Paul first went to the synagogue on the Sabbath day and preached to the Jews and the godly Gentiles there. But he was concerned about the rest of the Gentiles too. Every day he talked to those he happened to meet in the marketplace. There some Epicurean and Stoic philosophers engaged him in a discussion.

Epicureans were followers of Epicurus (342-270 B.C.). He said that Nature is the supreme teacher and provides sensations, feelings, and anticipations for the testing of truth. By feelings he meant pleasure and pain. These he said could be used to distinguish between the good and the evil around us. He also taught that the gods were incapable of wrath, indifferent to human weakness, and did not intervene or participate in human affairs. Thus he denied the possibility of miracles, prophecy, and divine providence.[4] In the beginning Epicurus by "pleasure" meant real happiness. At first his followers merely sought a quiet life free from fear, pain, and anger. Later, some made sensual pleasures the goal of life.

Stoics were followers of Zeno of Citium (335-263 B.C.). He believed in a creative power and made duty, reason (or accordance with divine reason), and self-sufficiency the goal of life. He encouraged his followers to accept the laws of nature and conscience and to try to be indifferent to pleasure, pain, joy, and grief.

Some of these philosophers were quite contemptuous of Paul's gospel and called him a babbler, literally, a seed-picker. This term was also used as slang for parasites and ignorant plagiarists. Then, because he preached the good news of Jesus and the resurrection, they said he seemed to be proclaiming not merely strange gods, but foreign demons.

Apparently, they felt Paul's teaching was dangerous to their ideas and philosophies, so they seized him and brought him before the Council of the Areopagus, the supreme court of Athens. This court formerly met on the Hill of Ares (Mars' Hill) a rocky ridge facing the Acropolis. There is some evidence it met in a colonnade in the public marketplace in New Testament times, but it retained the same name.

The Council politely requested to know the meaning of this new teaching that was bewildering them. This was not an unusual

[4]Cf. Norman W. DeWitt, *St. Paul and Epicurus* (Minneapolis: University of Minnesota Press, c1954), pp. 9, 10, 20.

request. The Athenians as a whole, as well as the resident aliens, spent their (leisure) time telling and hearing something new.

Message to the Council of Mars' Hill (17:22-34)

[22]Then Paul stood in the midst of Mars' hill, and said, *Ye* men of Athens I perceive that in all things ye are too superstitious. [23]For as I passed by, and beheld your devotions, I found an altar with this inscription. TO THE UNKNOWN GOD. Whom therefore ye ignorantly worship, him declare I unto you. [24]God that made the world and all things therein, seeing that he is Lord of heaven and earth, dwelleth not in temples made with hands; [25]neither is worshipped with men's hands, as though he needed any thing, seeing he giveth to all life, and breath, and all things; [26]and hath made of one blood all nations of men for to dwell on all the face of the earth, and hath determined the times before appointed, and the bounds of their habitation; [27]that they should seek the Lord, if haply they might feel after him, and find him, though he be not far from every one of us: [28]for in him we live, and move, and have our being; as certain also of your own poets have said, For we are also his offspring. [29]Forasmuch then as we are the offspring of God, we ought not to think that the Godhead is like unto gold, or silver, or stone, graven by art and man's device. [30]And the times of this ignorance God winked at; but now commandeth all men every where to repent: [31]because he hath appointed a day, in the which he will judge the world in righteousness by *that* man whom he hath ordained; *whereof* he hath given assurance unto all *men,* in that he hath raised him from the dead.

[32]And when they heard of the resurrection of the dead, some mocked: and others said, We will hear thee again of this *matter.* [33]So Paul departed from among them. [33]Howbeit certain men clave unto him, and believed: among the which *was* Dionysius the Areopagite, and a woman named Damaris, and others with them (Acts 17:22-34).

Standing in the midst of the Council, Paul wisely began in a positive way. The translation that says they were "too superstitious" sounds as if he was intending to insult them. Though the words can bear that meaning, it is better to translate them here with the meaning of "very religious," in the sense of very respectful to their gods.

Then Paul used an inscription on an altar in Athens to give him an opportunity to speak about the one true God in contrast to their many gods. The "unknown God" of their altar, whom they worshiped without knowing Him, is the Creator and Lord of heaven and earth. He therefore is too great to dwell in sanctuaries made by human hands. This was a truth understood by Solomon also (1 Kings 8:27) and by the prophets (Isaiah 57:15; 66:1). What a contrast to the little gods of Athens whose idols they washed and pretended to feed!

The true God does not need to be cared for (attended, treated, as a physician would tend a patient) by human hands as if He needed anything. How could He need anything or any care? He is the true Source of and Giver of all life, breath, and all things. As James 1:17 points out, every good gift and every perfect gift is from above, from Him.

God also has made out of one (that is, from Adam; from one blood line) every nation of mankind to dwell on the whole face of the earth. (Some ancient manuscripts omit the word "blood" in verse 26.) We are all part of Adam's race and no one has room for any special pride of ancestry or of race. God also fixed the limit of mankind's appointed seasons (times, occasions, opportunities) and boundaries of mankind's dwelling (habitation); that is, by separating the dry land from the waters (Genesis 1:9, 10).

By this Paul does not mean mankind could not or should not move from one place to another. All peoples have done that to a greater or lesser extent. Rather, Paul meant that God brought mankind to the places and times where they would have opportunities to seek God, "If perhaps they might touch Him and find Him." (Compare Romans 1:20, 21.)

Actually, it should not be hard to find Him, for, as Paul went on to say, He is not far from each one of us. "For in Him we live, and move, and are (exist, have our being)." This statement is a quotation from one of the ancient poets, possibly Minos or Epimenedes of Crete.[5] As one of their own poets (Aratus of Cilicia) had said, "For we are His offspring."

Being the offspring of the true God (in the sense of being created in His image), man would be totally unreasonable to think of the divine nature as gold or silver or stone, an engraved work of the art and meditations or thoughts of a human being. This is one of the strong points of Old Testament teaching. See Psalm 115:4-8; 135:15-18; Isaiah 40:18-22; 41:24; 44:9-17.

All of this idolatry showed ignorance of what God is really like. The times (time periods) of this ignorance God in mercy and longsuffering overlooked. But now He (through the gospel) was

---

[5]Cf. Charles W. Carter and Ralph Earle, *The Acts of the Apostles* (Grand Rapids: Zondervan Publishing House, 1959), p. 261.

announcing to all human beings everywhere that they should repent, that is, change their minds and attitudes toward God by turning to Him through Christ and the gospel. This repentance is imperative because God has set up a day in which He is about to judge the inhabited earth in righteousness by a Man whom He has designated. That is, there is a judgment day coming and God has revealed who the Judge will be. (Compare Daniel 7:13; John 5:22, 27.) That this day is actually coming and that there will be no escape from it God guaranteed to all by the fact He raised that Man (Jesus) out from the dead.

The mention of the resurrection of the dead brought immediate mockery from some, especially from the Epicureans, we can be sure. They refused to believe that any God could show wrath, and they did not believe in miracles either. Many therefore mocked Paul by scoffing words and gestures. Others, who seemed to have a desire for the truth, said, "We shall hear you concerning this even again."

These sessions of the Council of the Areopagus were open to the public. Some men did respond and join themselves to Paul, believing the gospel. Among them was Dionysius, a member of the Council and thus a very important person in Athens. A (prominent) woman named Damaris along with others also joined with them and believed.

This is the second recorded sermon of Paul given to Gentiles who had no background in or knowledge of the Old Testament Scriptures. In Lystra Paul used a similar approach, drawing attention to God as the Creator (Acts 14:15-17). But here more details of his approach are given.

With the Jews who claimed to believe the Scriptures, Paul always based his reasoning on the Old Testament. But with Gentiles like these, he was guided by the Holy Spirit to use a different approach. His reasoning was still based on Scripture, but he started where the people were and led them to the point where he could introduce the gospel. Missionaries in recent times have sometimes had to do the same sort of thing. One missionary to Amazon jungle Indians found he could not start with John 3:16. They had no word for love. The only world they knew was the valley and tributary river where they lived. So he started with creation and gradually led them to the point where they could understand about Jesus.

Some writers suppose that Paul was disappointed in the results of this approach.[6] They say that his disappointment caused him to say to the Corinthians, "I determined not to know any thing among you, save Jesus Christ, and Him crucified" (1 Corinthians 2:2). But this does not mean Paul said nothing about other truths. Rather, he meant he would see, experience, and live out the crucified Christ.

It seems probable also that some of the Jews and godly Gentiles in the synagogue at Athens believed and that these others who believed joined with them. Paul later referred to the household of Stephanas as the firstfruits of Achaia (1 Corinthians 16:15), but this may be because Athens was considered a free, independent city, not part of Achaia (Greece).[7]

Luke does not give any more details, but it is clear that Paul left at least a small body of believers, an assembly, behind him in Athens. Tradition says Dionysius the Areopagite was its first pastor (elder, bishop).

---

[6]Cf. Rackham, *op. cit.,* p. 320. N. B. Stonehouse, *The Areopagus Address* (London: 1949), pp. 39 ff. has a good answer to this opinion (cited by Bruce, *op. cit.,* p. 365).

[7]Cf. Carter and Earle, *op. cit.,* p. 263.

ACTS
CHAPTER
18

Why did Paul leave Athens when he had intended to wait for Silas and Timothy there? The Bible does not tell us. But Paul did leave a number of believers behind, and the Greek indicates he separated himself from them with regret.

It may be that one reason he left Athens was that he found no opportunity to carry on his trade of tentmaking there. Athens was not a commercial center. Paul included among his sufferings for the Lord's sake times when he did not have enough to eat, that is, enforced fasting for financial reasons (2 Corinthians 11:27).

Another reason for leaving Athens may have been the great need in Corinth. Corinth was a commercial center and a very prosperous city. It was destroyed in 146 B.C. and was not rebuilt until Julius Caesar took an interest in it one hundred years later. He made it a Roman colony, and it again became prosperous. But it was also a center of idolatry and licentiousness. The Greeks even invented a new word to express extreme sexual immorality and profligacy, "to Corinthianize." The Corinthians were encouraged in this immorality by their worship of the so-called goddess of love, Aphrodite.

Priscilla and Aquila (18:1-4)

[1]After these things Paul departed from Athens, and came to Corinth; [2]and found a certain Jew named Aquila, born in Pontus, lately come from Italy, with his wife Priscilla, (because that Claudius had commanded all Jews to depart from Rome,) and came unto them. [3]And because he was of the same craft, he abode with them, and wrought: (for by their occupation they were tentmakers.) [4]And he reasoned in the synagogue every sabbath, and persuaded the Jews and the Greeks (Acts 18:1-4).

At Corinth Paul met a husband and wife who were to become some of his most faithful friends and fellow laborers in the gospel. The husband, Aquila, was a Jew from a family of the Roman province of Pontus (located in northern Asia Minor east of Bithynia on the Black Sea). Since Aquila was a common slave name in Rome, there is some speculation that when the Romans took Pontus his family was captured and sold or given as slaves in Rome. Later many of the Jewish slaves were set free. There was a large class of freedmen in Rome who were set up in business by their former masters or who carried on trades.

Aquila's wife's name, Priscilla, a diminutive or familiar form of Prisca (2 Timothy 4:19), indicates that she was a Roman lady of one of the upper classes of society. It is at least possible that she was the daughter of Aquila's former master. He may have helped her to believe in the one true God, the God of Israel. Then, when he was set free he married her.

They had recently come to Corinth from Italy. The fourth Roman Emperor, Claudius,[1] had commanded all the Jews to leave Rome. Paul came to them and found in their home a place to live and to carry on his trade, for they also were tentmakers and had been able to establish their business in Corinth successfully.[2]

There is nothing to indicate that Priscilla and Aquila were Christians before Paul met them, though it is possible they knew something about the gospel. If they were not believers already, Paul soon won them to the Lord. They became faithful followers of Christ. We can be sure they accompanied him to the synagogue every Sabbath and encouraged him as he sought to persuade both Jews and Greeks.

Turning to the Gentiles (18:5-11)

[5]And when Silas and Timothy were come from Macedonia, Paul was

---

[1]Tiberius Claudius Caesar Augustus Germanicus ruled A.D. 41-54. Bruce, *op. cit.*, p. 368, prefers the date of A.D. 49-50 for this expulsion. Paul probably arrived in Corinth in the fall of A.D. 50.

[2]Some writers believe they were also leather workers and makers of felted cloth for tents. Cf. Packer, *op. cit.*, p. 152. Paul's native province of Cilicia was, however, famous for its goats' hair cloth, most of which was used for tentmaking, and tentmaking would be an obvious trade for him, as a future rabbi, to learn. Jewish rabbis were expected to learn a trade; most did not believe in taking money for their teaching. Many also believed that hard work would help to keep them from sin. Cf. Bruce, *op. cit.*, p. 367.

pressed in the spirit, and testified to the Jews *that* Jesus *was* Christ. [6]And when they opposed themselves, and blasphemed, he shook *his* raiment, and said unto them, Your blood *be* upon your own heads; I *am* clean: from henceforth I will go unto the Gentiles. [7]And he departed thence, and entered into a certain *man's* house, named Justus, *one* that worshiped God, whose house joined hard to the synagogue. [8]And Crispus, the chief ruler of the synagogue, believed on the Lord with all his house; and many of the Corinthians hearing believed, and were baptized.

[9]Then spake the Lord to Paul in the night by a vision, Be not afraid, but speak, and hold not thy peace: [10]for I am with thee, and no man shall set on thee to hurt thee: for I have much people in this city. [11]And he continued *there* a year and six months, teaching the word of God among them (Acts 18:5-11).

After Silas and Timothy came to Corinth from Macedonia, Paul was pressed by the Word. He wrote 1 Thessalonians shortly after they came, for they brought good news. In 1 Thessalonians 3:6-10 he speaks of this. Timothy brought good news of the faith and love of the Thessalonian believers. The enemies of the gospel had not been able to turn them away from the Lord or from Paul. During his painful circumstances and crushing pressure or persecution, the wonderful report of their faith and continuance in the gospel cheered him and relieved the pressure of his passionate concern for them, giving him new courage to go on.

Apparently, up to this point there had been no great response to the gospel in Corinth. Now he felt such pressure from the Word that he gave witness with greater and greater intensity and zeal. Everywhere he declared the fact that Jesus is the Messiah, God's anointed Prophet, Priest, and King.

In the synagogue this increased intensity on Paul's part caused most of the unbelieving Jews to cease their indifference and line up against the gospel. They even blasphemed (not God, but Paul), using abusive language as they resisted Paul and spoke evil against him and the gospel.

This was too much for Paul. So he shook off his outer garments (robes) against them as a sign that he was rejecting their blasphemy. Then he called down their blood on their own heads. That is, he declared they would be responsible for the judgment God would send on them. Paul had warned them, and he was clean. They would understand, of course, that he was referring to the responsibility God put on Ezekiel to warn the people (Ezekiel

3:16-21). Paul had done his part with respect to warning the Jews. From now on (at Corinth) he would go to the Gentiles.

Paul then left the synagogue and went next door to the house of a God-fearing Gentile named Titus (or Titius) Justus.[3] There he began to preach the gospel.

Paul, Silas, and Timothy were not the only ones to leave the synagogue. The ruler of the synagogue, Crispus, made a decision to believe in the Lord, and his entire household followed his example and made the same decision. (See 1 Corinthians 1:14.) Many of the Gentile Corinthians also believed and were baptized.

The Lord confirmed to Paul that he had done the right thing. In a night vision He (Jesus) told Paul not to be afraid. The form of the Greek used here indicates Paul was beginning to be afraid he would have to leave Corinth as he had so many other cities when persecution began. But Jesus told him that he should keep on speaking the Word in Corinth and not be silent; the Lord was with him and would not allow anyone to lay hands on him or harm him, for He had much people in Corinth. That is, many would yet come to Jesus and become part of the true people of God.

With this encouragement Paul remained in Corinth a year and six months, teaching the Word of God among them. During all this time there was no violence and no one harmed Paul, just as the Lord promised.

Brought Before Gallio (18:12-17)

[12]And when Gallio was the deputy of Achaia, the Jews made insurrection with one accord against Paul, and brought him to the judgment seat, [13]saying, This *fellow* persuadeth men to worship God contrary to the law. [14]And when Paul was now about to open *his* mouth, Gallio said unto the Jews, If it were a matter of wrong or wicked lewdness, O *ye* Jews, reason would that I should bear with you: [15]but if it be a question of words and names, and *of* your law, look ye *to it;* for I will be no judge of such *matters.* [16]And he drave them from the judgment seat. [17]Then all the Greeks took Sosthenes, the chief ruler of the synagogue, and beat *him* before the judgment seat. And Gallio cared for none of those things (Acts 18:12-17).

[3]His Roman name indicates he was a Roman citizen. Sir William Ramsay and others have suggested that his full name was Gaius Titius Justus and that he was the Gaius mentioned in Romans 16:23 and 1 Corinthians 1:14. Cf. Bruce, *op. cit.,* p. 371.

In the spring of A.D. 52 a new proconsul named Gallio was appointed by the Roman Senate to govern the province of Achaia (Greece).[4] The unbelieving Jews apparently thought they could take advantage of the new governor's lack of knowledge of the situation. So they rose up with one mind against Paul and brought him before the governor's judgment seat (tribunal). Archaeologists have discovered this judgment seat (*bema* throne) built of blue and white marble.

To Gallio they accused Paul of persuading men to worship God in a way contrary to the law. Since they were before a Roman court, they probably meant contrary to Roman law. Since Roman law allowed Judaism as a legal religion, these unbelieving Jews were now saying that Christianity was different from Judaism and therefore illegal.

Paul was about to speak when Gallio answered the Jews. He had sense enough to realize that no crime or wicked act of immorality was involved. Because it seemed to him that the case against Paul involved nothing but questions about words and names and their own Jewish Law, he told them they could see to that for themselves. He did not want to be a judge of such matters. Then he drove them (or had them driven) from the tribunal, which was probably set up in an open public square.

This pleased the crowd, for the Jews were not popular with them. They then took advantage of Gallio's attitude and seized Sosthenes, the new ruler of the synagogue, striking him down before he could leave the tribunal. Gallio, as the people expected, paid no attention. He considered the whole matter outside his jurisdiction.[5] Thus, the Jews who hoped to turn the governor against Paul found the tables turned. It had looked at first as if the promise Jesus gave Paul that he would not be harmed in Corinth could not be fulfilled. But Paul's enemies, not Paul, were the ones who were harmed.

This must have had a deep effect on Sosthenes. After this Paul

---

[4]Lucius Iunus Gallio became proconsul in the spring of A.D. 52 according to some scholars. Others say he began a little earlier in July of A.D. 51. Cf. Packer, *op. cit.*, p. 153; Bruce, *op. cit.*, p. 374. He was given his name by adoption; he was born Lucius Annaeus Novatus and was the brother of the famous Stoic philosopher, Seneca. A man of great personal charm or great graciousness, he remained in office until the spring of A.D. 53.

[5]Cf. Harrison, *op. cit.*, p. 280.

continued in Corinth for a considerable time. Finally Sosthenes must have yielded to the truth of the gospel. In 1 Corinthians 1:1 Brother Sosthenes joins Paul in greeting the Corinthians. Though we cannot prove it for sure, this must be the same Sosthenes. It would be unlikely that there would be another prominent Sosthenes who was well known to the Corinthian church. Truly the grace of God is marvelous! The leader of the opposition, a man who must himself have blasphemed Paul and the gospel, became a brother in the Lord. With this victory before Gallio and the conversion of Sosthenes, there must have been more freedom than ever for the Christians to witness for Christ in Corinth.

RETURNING TO ANTIOCH (18:18-22)

[18]And Paul *after this* tarried *there* yet a good while, and then took his leave of the brethren, and sailed thence into Syria, and with him Priscilla and Aquila; having shorn *his* head in Cenchreae: for he had a vow. [19]And he came to Ephesus, and left them there: but he himself entered into the synagogue, and reasoned with the Jews. [20]When they desired *him* to tarry longer time with them, he consented not; [21]but bade them farewell, saying, I must by all means keep this feast that cometh in Jerusalem: but I will return again unto you, if God will. And he sailed from Ephesus. [22]And when he had landed at Caesarea, and gone up, and saluted the church, he went down to Antioch (Acts 18:18-22).

After some time (probably several months) Paul sailed for Syria in the final part of his second missionary journey.

He took Priscilla and Aquila with him. As is usually the case, Priscilla is named first. She seems to have been gifted by the Spirit for ministry, but we always find Aquila working with her. They must have been a wonderful team!

At Cenchraea, the port of Corinth, Paul had his hair cut, for he had taken a vow.[6] This is not explained but it was probably a modified Nazarite vow, a vow that expressed total dedication to God and to His will. The hair was always cut at the conclusion of the period of the vow. (See Numbers 6:1-21.)

When they came to the great city of Ephesus, Paul left Priscilla

[6]A few scholars take the Greek to mean that Aquila rather than Paul had taken the vow. Cf. Lenski, *op. cit.,* pp. 762, 763.

and Aquila.[7] This time the Holy Spirit did not check him from preaching there. So he went to the synagogue and found Jews willing to listen to his reasoned presentation of the gospel. In fact, they wanted him to stay longer, but he did not consent. However, in his farewell he promised to return, "God willing."

After landing at Caesarea, he went up to Jerusalem and paid his respects to the church there. He probably let them know he had been faithful to carry out the instructions of the council of Acts 15. He also wanted to maintain a good relationship with them.

From Jerusalem he went to Antioch of Syria, thus ending the second missionary journey.

Paul's Third Missionary Journey Begins (18:23)

And after he had spent some time *there,* he departed, and went over *all* the country of Galatia and Phrygia in order, strengthening all the disciples (Acts 18:23).

Paul spent some time in Antioch encouraging and teaching the church. Then he went north by land on a 1,500 mile journey into the regions of Galatia and Phrygia. One after another he visited the churches established in his first and second journeys. Paul never founded churches and forgot them. Always he sought to go back to give further teaching and to establish and strengthen the disciples. That is, he was always as much or more concerned with following up the new believers as he was in getting them saved in the first place.

Apollos of Alexandria (18:24-28)

[24]And a certain Jew named Apollos, born at Alexandria, an eloquent man, *and* mighty in the Scriptures, came to Ephesus. [25]This man was instructed in the way of the Lord; and being fervent in the spirit, he spake and taught diligently the things of the Lord, knowing only the baptism of John. [26]And he began to speak boldly in the synagogue: whom when Aquila and Priscilla had heard, they took him unto *them,* and expounded unto him the way of God more perfectly. [27]And when he was

[7]They stayed several years in Ephesus, the capital of the Roman province of Asia. Its population was over 300,000 and it was a very prosperous center of trade and commerce.

disposed to pass into Achaia, the brethren wrote, exhorting the disciples to receive him: who, when he was come, helped them much which had believed through grace: [28]for he mightily convinced the Jews, *and that* publicly, showing by the Scriptures that Jesus was Christ (Acts 18:24-28).

Alexandria, located on the north coast of Egypt west of the mouth of the Nile River, was the second largest city of the Roman Empire, an important seaport, and the empire's greatest cultural and educational center. It has a large Jewish population in the northeast part of the city. They were hellenistic (Greek-speaking) and had produced the famous Greek Septuagint Version of the Old Testament.

From Alexandria to Ephesus came an eloquent Jew named Apollos (short for Apollonius). Not only was he eloquent, he was well-educated, a real scholar, and powerful in his use of the Scriptures. He had already been instructed orally in the way of the Lord Jesus, probably in his home city of Alexandria. So enthusiastic was he about Jesus that his spirit literally was boiling over as he spoke.

His teaching was accurate also. He had all the facts straight about Jesus' life and ministry, as well as about His death and resurrection. But he must have heard the facts from one of the witnesses of Christ's resurrection who, like many of the over 500 (1 Corinthians 15:6), did not come to Jerusalem and were not present at the outpouring of the Holy Spirit on the Day of Pentecost. He was excited about what he knew, however, and began to speak boldly (showing that Jesus is the Messiah) in the synagogue at Ephesus.

Priscilla and Aquila were present and heard him. They did not say anything to him in the synagogue but took him aside to give him further instruction. The Greek also implies that they welcomed him and probably took him home with them. Then they explained God's way to him more precisely. Just what they said the Bible does not tell here, but the next chapter deals with 12 disciples who were in the same position, with the same need for instruction, and the details are given there.

It is interesting to note here that John Chrysostom ("John of the golden mouth"), the chief pastor of the church in Constantinople about 400 A.D. recognized that Priscilla took the lead in giving this instruction to Apollos. The best Greek scholars today agree. Apollos was a man of culture and education. She also must have been well-educated and a very gracious woman. Paul's epistles also show she was, along with her husband, a fellow-worker, fellow-teacher, and missionary.[8]

Looking ahead, we can see that Apollos must have been baptized in water on the authority of Jesus (as in Matthew 28:18, 19). Then they must have prayed for him to be baptized in the Holy Spirit as in Acts 2:4.

That Apollos responded is shown by the letters of recommendation the Christian brethren in Ephesus wrote for him when he wanted to go over to Greece. In Greece also his ministry was effective. He became a channel of God's grace to help the believers. He also powerfully and utterly refuted the arguments of the unbelieving Jews, showing by the Scriptures that Jesus is the Messiah, the Christ. As Paul says in 1 Corinthians 3:6, Apollos watered what Paul had planted, but all along it was God who was giving the increase.

[8]Cf. Carter and Earle, *op. cit.*, p. 264.

ACTS
CHAPTER
19

In this chapter we come to an important question. Today its interpretation has become controversial. But the King James translators had no doubts about its meaning. They were good scholars and they said it well: "Have ye received the Holy Ghost since ye believed?"

This is a question that still needs to be asked. These disciples had no positive answer until the Holy Spirit did come upon them. Then they spoke in tongues and prophesied; then they knew by experience the right answer to the question Paul asked.

Twelve Disciples at Ephesus (19:1-7)

[1]And it came to pass, that, while Apollos was at Corinth, Paul having passed through the upper coasts came to Ephesus; and finding certain disciples, [2]he said unto them, Have ye received the Holy Ghost since ye believed? And they said unto him, We have not so much as heard whether there be any Holy Ghost. [3]And he said unto them, Unto what then were ye baptized? And they said, Unto John's baptism. [4]Then said Paul, John verily baptized with the baptism of repentance, saying unto the people, that they should believe on him which should come after him, that is, on Christ Jesus. [5]When they heard *this*, they were baptized in the name of the Lord Jesus. [6]And when Paul had laid *his* hands upon them, the Holy Ghost came on them; and they spake with tongues, and prophesied. [7]And all the men were about twelve (Acts 19:1-7).

After Paul visited the churches founded on the First Journey in the cities of South Galatia, he went through the higher central plateau of North Galatia. In the meantime, Apollos went to Corinth where he "watered" the churches planted by Paul (1 Corinthians 3:6).

Then Paul came to Ephesus and found a group of twelve

disciples. Some writers believe these were disciples of John the Baptist. But everywhere else in the Book of Acts where Luke mentions disciples he always means disciples of Jesus, believers in Jesus, followers of Jesus. Some believe these were converted by Apollos before Priscilla and Aquila instructed him. Undoubtedly, like Apollos, they knew the facts about the life, death, resurrection, and ascension of Jesus.

Though Paul sensed there was something lacking in their experience, he did not question the fact that they were believers. In fact, he recognized that they were. The question he asked shows rather that they lacked the freedom and spontaneity in worship that always characterized Spirit-filled believers.

Modern versions generally translate "since ye believed" as "when you believed." But this translation is based on their theological presuppositions. The Greek is literally, "Having believed, did you receive?" "Having believed" *(pisteusantes)* is a Greek aorist (past) participle. "Did you receive" *(elabete)* is the main verb, also in the aorist. But the fact that they are *both* in the aorist is not significant here. The fact that the participle "having believed" is in the past is what is important, for the tense of the participle normally shows its relation to the main verb. Because this participle is in the past, this normally means that its action precedes the action of the main verb. That is why the King James translators, as good Greek scholars, translated the participle "since ye believed." They wanted to bring out that the believing must take place before the receiving. This also brings out the fact that the baptism in the Holy Spirit is a distinct experience following conversion.

Some modern Greek scholars do claim that the aorist participle may sometimes indicate an action occurring at the same time as the main verb, especially if it is also in the aorist as it is in Acts 19:2.[1] The examples given are not really applicable to this verse, however.

The chief example, "answered and said," is idiomatic (usually a

[1]One writer, Dunn, says that anyone who suggests that the aorist participle in Acts 19:2 indicates action prior to the receiving is only showing that he (along with the King James translators, of course) has an inadequate grasp of Greek grammar. But Dunn later contradicts himself and admits that the aorist participle usually indicates action prior to that of the main verb. See James D. G. Dunn, *Baptism in the Holy Spirit* (London: SCM Press, 1970), pp. 86, 158, 159.

Hebraism), a formula used to indicate the continuation of a discourse. It does not help at all in the interpretation of other passages. In the few passages where the action of the verb does seem to be coincident, the participle defines what is meant by the main verb. For example: *"This He did once for all, having offered up himself"* (Hebrews 7:27). *"I have sinned, having betrayed innocent blood"* (Matthew 27:4). *"You have done well, having come"* (Acts 10:33). (Italicized passages are author's own translation.) But "having believed" is hardly a definition of what is meant by receiving the Spirit. Luke makes it clear, as in other passages, that the receiving of the Spirit involves a definite baptism in the Spirit, a definite outpouring on those who are already believers.

Many other passages in the New Testament do show that the action of the aorist participle normally precedes the action of an aorist main verb. One is: *"Having fallen asleep in Christ, they perished"* (1 Corinthians 15:18). That is, after they fell asleep they perished if Jesus did not rise from the dead.

Another example is Matthew 22:25. Speaking of seven brothers the Sadducees said of the first, *"Having married a wife, he died."* Obviously, even though the King James Version translates this, "When he had married a wife," it does not mean the marrying and the dying were the same thing, or even that they happened at the same time. They were distinct events and the marrying clearly preceded the dying, probably by some time.

Other examples can be found in Acts 5:10, *"Having carried her [Sapphira] out, they buried her"*; Acts 13:51, *"Having shaken the dust off their feet, they came to Iconium"*; Acts 16:6, *"And they went through the Phrygian and Galatian region having been forbidden by the Spirit to speak the Word in Asia"*; Acts 16:24, *"Having received the orders, he threw them into the inner prison."* In these cases and many more the action of the participle clearly precedes the action of the main verb.

Thus, though there are some cases in which the aorist participle is coincident with that of the aorist main verb, this is not the rule. The whole impression of Acts 19:2 is that since these disciples claimed to be believers, the baptism in the Holy Spirit should have been the next step, a distinct step after the believing, though not necessarily separated from it by a long time.

The disciples' reply, "We have not so much as heard whether

there be any Holy Ghost," may be translated, "But we have not even heard if the Holy Spirit is." The meaning, however, does not seem to be that they had never heard of the existence of the Holy Spirit. What godly Jew or interested Gentile would or could have been so ignorant? It is more likely that the phrase compares with John 7:39. There, the condensed phrase, *"it was not yet Spirit,"* means the age of the Spirit with its promised mighty outpouring had not yet come.[2]

From this we see that these disciples were really saying they had not heard that the baptism in the Holy Spirit was available.[3] In fact, several ancient manuscripts and versions of the New Testament[4] actually read, "We have not even heard if any are receiving the Holy Spirit." Obviously, they were not taught about this when they were converted.

Paul then inquired further and found these disciples had been baptized only into John the Baptist's baptism. This, Paul explained, was only preparatory, a baptism of repentance (because of repentance).[5] John himself told the people that they should believe in the Coming One, Jesus. This means, of course, that they would not only accept Him as Messiah and Saviour, but would obey Him and follow His directions that they should ask for and receive the Spirit. (See Luke 11:9, 13; 24:49; Acts 1:4, 5; 11:15, 16.)

Because of Paul's explanation, the twelve were baptized in the name (into the worship and service) of the Lord Jesus. Then, after they were baptized in water, Paul laid hands on them and the Holy Spirit came upon them with the same evidence given on the Day of Pentecost. They began to speak (and continued to speak) in tongues (languages) and prophesied. Though Luke does not say "other" tongues here, it is clearly the same gift as was given on the Day of Pentecost and as was exercised in the Corinthian Church.[6]

---

[2]Cf. Horton, *op. cit.*, p. 116.

[3]Cf. J. H. E. Hull, *The Holy Spirit in the Acts of the Apostles* (London: Lutterworth Press, 1967), p. 110.

[4]Including Codex Bezae (D), p[38] (a papyrus from the third or fourth century A.D., p[41], plus Syriac and Sahidic versions originating in the second and third centuries A.D.

[5]Cf. Horton, *op. cit.*, p. 84.

[6]*Ibid.*, pp. 229, 230.

It needs to be emphasized, therefore, that their baptism in the Spirit here came not only after they believed, but in this case after they were baptized in water. Paul also laid hands on them, but as at Samaria, the laying on of hands did not cause them to receive the Spirit. Rather, it encouraged their faith and preceded, or at least was distinct from, the Spirit's coming upon them. Then the speaking in tongues gave them further assurances that the Holy Spirit's presence and power were real.[7]

Two Years in Ephesus (19:8-10)

> [8]And he went into the synagogue, and spake boldly for the space of three months, disputing and persuading the things concerning the kingdom of God. [9]But when divers were hardened, and believed not, but spake evil of that way before the multitude, he departed from them, and separated the disciples, disputing daily in the school of one Tyrannus. [10]And this continued by the space of two years; so that all they which dwelt in Asia heard the word of the Lord Jesus, both Jews and Greeks (Acts 19:8-10).

As always, Paul went to the synagogue, starting with the Jew first when he arrived in Ephesus. In this case also, he was fulfilling his promise to return (Acts 18:21). For three months he was able to speak boldly and freely, reasoning of the things concerning the kingdom (rule, authority) of God (as revealed in Jesus, now ascended to the right hand of the Father [Acts 2:30-33]).

It took a little longer than usual here, but eventually some of the unconverted Jews became hardened (obstinate, unyielding) and disobedient (rebellious). They showed their rebellious spirit by publicly speaking evil of the Way, that is, of the Christian faith and way of life, before the crowds who gathered to hear the gospel and packed out the synagogue.

Paul therefore withdrew from them. He found a separate place for the disciples to meet in the schoolroom or lecture hall of Tyrannus. There, instead of meeting only on the Sabbath, Paul preached and taught the gospel daily for two years.

As Paul later indicates (Acts 20:34), he continued his usual practice. He worked at his tentmaking trade from dawn until about 11 a.m. in order to support his evangelistic party. Then,

---

[7]Cf. Harrison, *op. cit.*, p. 289.

after Tyrannus finished his lectures, Paul from 11 a.m. to 4 p.m. (as stated by Codex Bezae and other ancient manuscripts) taught those whom his fellow workers brought in. They had been witnesses, going among the crowds on the streets and in the marketplaces all morning, and they brought in their converts for further teaching.

In the evenings (after 4 p.m.) Paul would go to various homes to teach and establish the believers and to help win their friends and neighbors to the Lord. (See Acts 20:20.)

The result was that the whole of the Roman province of Asia was evangelized; both Jews and Gentiles heard the Word. There is no evidence that Paul himself left the city of Ephesus during this period. Yet, it is evident that the seven churches of Asia mentioned in the Book of Revelation were founded at this time.

Many other churches were established too. Since Ephesus was a great center, people from all over the province came there for business or other reasons. Many of them were converted, filled with the Spirit, and taught by Paul. Then they went back to their home cities and towns where they became powerful witnesses for Christ, and churches grew up around them.

Special Miracles (19:11-20)

[11]And God wrought special miracles by the hands of Paul: [12]so that from his body were brought unto the sick handkerchiefs or aprons, and the diseases departed from them, and the evil spirits went out of them. [13]Then certain of the vagabond Jews, exorcists, took upon them to call over them which had evil spirits the name of the Lord Jesus, saying, We adjure you by Jesus whom Paul preacheth. [14]And there were seven sons of *one* Sceva, a Jew, *and* chief of the priests, which did so. [15]And the evil spirit answered and said, Jesus I know, and Paul I know; but who are ye? [16]And the man in whom the evil spirit was leaped on them, and overcame them, and prevailed against them, so that they fled out of the house naked and wounded.

[17]And this was known to all the Jews and Greeks also dwelling at Ephesus; and fear fell on them all, and the name of the Lord Jesus was magnified. [18]And many that believed came, and confessed, and showed their deeds. [19]Many of them also which used curious arts brought their books together, and burned them before all *men:* and they counted the price of them, and found *it* fifty thousand *pieces* of silver. [20]So mightily grew the word of God and prevailed (Acts 19:11-20).

An important factor in this spread of the gospel in Roman Asia was the fact God did special miracles by the hand of Paul. The

Greek really means the Lord made miracles an everyday occurrence. So powerfully was the Lord working through Paul that people did not want to wait for him to minister to them in the lecture hall of Tyrannus. They would come to his workroom where he was busy at his tentmaking and would carry off handkerchiefs (actually, the sweat cloths he used to wipe away perspiration while he was working) and work aprons that had been in contact with his body (his skin). These they laid upon the sick who were then freed from their diseases. Even evil spirits came out of those who were possessed.

All this caught the attention of a group of seven traveling Jewish exorcists who went about claiming to be able to cast out evil spirits. These seven were sons of Sceva, a chief priest (one of the chief priests associated with Annas and Caiphas in Jerusalem). Possibly following the example of other Jewish exorcists, they took it upon themselves to use the name of Jesus in a sort of formula: "I adjure by Jesus whom Paul preaches." But their attempt failed. The evil spirit answered, "Jesus I know (know about) and Paul I know (I understand who he is), but as for you, who are you?" Then the demon-possessed man leaped upon them and overpowered all of them.[8] In fact, he used his strength in such a way against them that the seven brothers fled out of that house naked and wounded.

The news of this soon spread throughout Ephesus and a fear (an awe inspired by the supernatural) fell upon Jews and Gentiles alike. This caused them to magnify the name (character, person, and authority) of Jesus.

All this had an important effect on the believers also. Many of them came confessing and publicly reporting their deeds. The Greek indicates they now came out and out for the Lord (with a total commitment). They realized their need for holiness and righteousness as well as for salvation.

Another result was the fact that they now realized that the true power over evil was only in Jesus. Ephesus was also a center for the practice of magical arts, especially the putting of spells on people or things. A considerable number of the new believers had

[8]Some ancient manuscripts have *amphoteron* which in earlier Greek usage (before New Testament times) meant "both." In New Testament times, however, it was often used in everyday speech to mean "all." Many ancient Greek papyrus manuscripts confirm this.

practiced magic, including attempts at foretelling or influencing the future. Most of them still had the book they used in their homes. (Some of the books of this kind have been discovered by archaeologists.)

Now the believers saw that these books with their formulas, spells, and astrological forecasts were of no value whatsoever. In fact, they were purely heathen, even demonic, in their origin. So they brought together all their books and burned them publicly. Books were very expensive in those days, and when they reckoned up the total price of the books it came to 50,000 pieces of silver. This was as much as 200 day laborers or soldiers would earn in a year.

With this Luke concludes the story of the success of the gospel in Ephesus. But it was the Word of the Lord (the Word concerning Jesus) that grew mightily (with divine might and power) and prevailed (in a healthy, vigorous way). The fact that later (20:17) there were a number of elders in the Church at Ephesus shows that there were many house churches and that the whole Church there continued to grow in a healthy way.

Paul's Purpose to Visit Rome (19:21, 22)

[21]After these things were ended, Paul purposed in the spirit, when he had passed through Macedonia and Achaia, to go to Jerusalem, saying, After I have been there, I must also see Rome. [22]So he sent into Macedonia two of them that ministered unto him, Timothy and Eras'tus; but he himself stayed in Asia for a season (Acts 19:21, 22).

Paul himself felt that these things brought not just an end, but a fulfillment to his ministry in Ephesus. "Ended" is literally "fulfilled" and indicates he had carried out the ministry he came to accomplish. The tremendous growth of the church in the previous more than two years and the training of the people and their leaders meant that he could leave them now with confidence and go on to another place of ministry.

Paul's epistles show there had been problems. He says he fought with "beasts" at Ephesus (1 Corinthians 15:32). This probably means he risked his life opposing "beasts" in human form, men who acted like beasts. He also says he suffered such affliction in Asia (that is, in Ephesus) that he despaired of life, but was delivered by God (2 Corinthians 1:8-10). Luke says nothing about this since, apparently, it affected Paul personally, but not the church.

Now that everything was going well, Paul purposed (set firmly) in the spirit (or, in the Holy Spirit) to see Rome. But he would first revisit Macedonia, Greece, and Jerusalem. (See Romans 1:11, 14, 15; 15:22-25.)

It is not clear in the Greek whether Paul's purpose was set firmly in his own spirit or in the Holy Spirit. In the spirit usually does mean in the Holy Spirit. (In New Testament times the Greek did not distinguish between capital and small letters.) We can be sure also that his own spirit was in harmony with, and submissive to, the Holy Spirit. His purpose thus was a holy purpose, a God-planned purpose.

This is further confirmed by his statement "I must see Rome." The Greek indicates a divine necessity was laid upon him. It is the same sort of expression as is found in John 4:4 where Jesus felt the divine imperative to go through Samaria. That Paul's purpose to go to Rome was indeed pleasing to the Lord was confirmed later by Jesus himself (Acts 23:11) and by an angel (27:23, 24).

Thus we see Paul was being led by the Spirit and was given a vision of the next step in God's plan for his ministry. However, it was not a full vision. He did not yet know how God was going to get him to Rome. But from this point to the end of the Book of Acts, Rome is the objective in view.

He did not go to Rome directly, however, because he felt a responsibility to visit the churches in Macedonia and Greece again and also to take their offering to the Church in Jerusalem (Acts 24:17, Romans 15:26; 1 Corinthians 16:1-4).

Later he wrote to the Roman believers recognizing there was an established church in Rome, but one which obviously had never been visited by an apostle (Romans 1:10-13). By the time he wrote Romans also, he hoped to go on from Rome to Spain (Romans 15:28).

To prepare the churches in Macedonia for his visit, Paul sent Timothy and Erastus on ahead. But he himself stayed for a time in Ephesus. As he told the Corinthians, a great door and an effectual one was still open to him, but there were many adversaries (1 Corinthians 16:8, 9).

Silversmiths Stir a Riot (19:23-29)[9]

[23]And the same time there arose no small stir about that way. [24]For a certain *man* named Demetrius, a silversmith, which made silver shrines for Diana, brought no small gain into the craftsmen; [25]whom he called together with the workmen of like occupation, and said, Sirs, ye know that by this craft we have our wealth. [26]Moreover ye see and hear, that not alone at Ephesus, but almost throughout all Asia, this Paul hath persuaded and turned away much people, saying that they be no gods, which are made with hands: [27]so that not only this our craft is in danger to be set at nought; but also that the temple of the great goddess Diana should be despised, and her magnificence should be destroyed, whom all Asia and the world worshippeth.

[28]And when they heard *these sayings*, they were full of wrath, and cried out, saying, Great *is* Diana of the Ephesians. [29]And the whole city was filled with confusion: and having caught Gaius and Aristarchus, men of Macedonia, Paul's companions in travel, they rushed with one accord into the theater (Acts 19:23-29).

Just how many adversaries there were in Ephesus soon became apparent. Luke speaks of it as no small disturbance concerning the (Christian) way. It was started by a silversmith named Demetrius. His chief product, like that of most silversmiths in Ephesus, was a miniature silver shrine of Artemis containing a miniature image of this many-breasted fertility goddess of Ephesus.

The Ephesian goddess actually had no relation to the other Artemis, the Artemis of Greece known as the maiden huntress and identified by the Romans with their goddess Diana. The Artemis of Ephesus was worshiped primarily in that city (in spite of their claims) and was not at all like the Roman goddess Diana. The names were the same, but the goddesses were different.

The demand for these shrines ordinarily kept the silversmiths quite busy and brought them a great deal of profit. Now sales were falling off. So Demetrius gathered all these craftsmen together and made a speech pointing out that Paul's message had permeated practically the whole province of Asia. Multitudes were believing the truth that there were no gods made with hands, in other words, that idols were nothings. Thus, the sales of

[9]Recent archaeological studies show that these silversmiths were not a commercial guild. They belonged to a religious guild attached to the Temple of Artemis. They were temple silversmiths, directly connected with the worship of the goddess. See T. D. Proffitt, III, "Mycenaen Tablets and Demetrius the Silversmith, Acts 19:23-28," pp. 59-62 in *Near East Archaeological Bulletin,* No. 14, 1979.

the shrines were diminishing and the trade of idol shrine making was in danger of falling into disrepute (rejection, refutation). Not only so, Demetrius claimed that the temple of the goddess Artemis was in danger of being accounted as nothing. The goddess itself was also in danger of being deposed, or rather, of having her divine majesty (or magnificence) diminished (or destroyed). Then Demetrius made the exaggerated claim that not only the whole province of Asia, but all the (inhabited) world (that is, the entire Roman Empire as they viewed it) worshiped it.

Demetrius unwittingly bore witness to the great success of the spread of the gospel. He also succeeded in his purpose to touch his hearers with respect to their pocketbooks and with respect to their civic pride in the temple of Artemis. This, as he hoped, brought an outburst of passionate wrath among the silversmiths. They cried out with great emotion, "Great is Artemis of the Ephesians!" The Greek indicates they kept this up and their chant filled the whole city with confusion and disturbance. The result was that they all rushed into the theater (a Greek-style amphitheater or arena open to the sky with room for 25,000 people).

First, however, they seized Gaius and Aristarchus, Macedonians, who were among Paul's traveling companions. Aristarchus was from Thessalonica (Acts 20:4). Their presence shows Paul's company was considerably larger on this third missionary journey than on his earlier travels. These two were seized and dragged into the amphitheater, not for their own sake, but because the crowd's anger was stirred against Paul.

Total Confusion (19:30-34)

[30]And when Paul would have entered in unto the people, the disciples suffered him not. [31]And certain of the chief of Asia, which were his friends, sent unto him, desiring *him* that he would not adventure himself into the theater. [32]Some therefore cried one thing, and some another: for the assembly was confused; and the more part knew not wherefore they were come together. [33]And they drew Alexander out of the multitude, the Jews putting him forward. And Alexander beckoned with the hand, and would have made his defense unto the people. [34]But when they knew that he was a Jew, all with one voice about the space of two hours cried out, Great *is* Diana of the Ephesians (Acts 19:30-34).

When Paul wanted to go in among the tumultuous crowd, the disciples would not let him. Some of the Asiarchs (officials connected with Roman worship in the Province of Asia) who were his friends urged him not to offer himself in the amphitheater. No doubt, they thought the crowd might tear him to pieces.

In the crowd some were crying out one thing, some another. The assembly (Greek, *ekklesia,* the same word usually translated "church") was in a state of total confusion; the majority did not know why he had come together.

At this point the Jews put forward Alexander out of the crowd with the intention of instructing them. That is, they wanted him to explain that the Jews were not responsible for what the Christians were doing. He came down to the front and waved his hand to get their attention and give his defense before the crowd. But when they recognized that he was a Jew, the whole crowd went wild. With one voice they kept crying for about two hours, "Great is Diana (Artemis) of the Ephesians." The possession of this image and temple was a great source of civic pride for the people of the city.

The Crowd Quieted (19:35-41)

[35]And when the townclerk had appeased the people, he said, *Ye* men of Ephesus, what man is there that knoweth not how that the city of the Ephesians is a worshipper of the great goddess Diana, and of the *image* which fell down from Jupiter? [36]Seeing then that these things cannot be spoken against, ye ought to be quiet, and to do nothing rashly. [37]For ye have brought hither these men, which are neither robbers of churches, nor yet blasphemers of your goddess. [38]Wherefore if Demetrius, and the craftsmen which are with him, have a matter against any man, the law is open, and there are deputies: let them implead one another. [39]But if ye inquire any thing concerning other matters, it shall be determined in a lawful assembly. [40]For we are in danger to be called in question for this day's uproar, there being no cause whereby we may give an account of this concourse. [41]And when he had thus spoken, he dismissed the assembly (Acts 19:35-41).

Finally, the town clerk (the secretary of the city)[10] quieted (subdued) the crowd and asked the Ephesians, "Who is there of mankind who does not know the city of Ephesus is the temple-keeper (literally, the templesweeper) of the great Artemis, even the one fallen from the sky (or, from the sky gods)?" The town

[10]A citizen of Ephesus who was their official contact or liaison with the Roman government officials in Ephesus.

clerk thus argued that there was no reason to be so upset and excited since these things, in his opinion, were undeniable. Therefore, it was their duty to quiet down. It would be wrong to do anything rash (impulsive, reckless, in thoughtless haste).

The town clerk also pointed out that the men they had brought into the amphitheater were neither temple robbers (or sacrilegious), nor were they blasphemers of their goddess. It is important to note here that Paul had been nearly three years in Ephesus, but there was no evidence that either he or the Christians ever said anything against the temple or Artemis. They were not iconoclasts. They simply kept preaching the good news of Jesus Christ in a positive way, and the sale of the images and shrines automatically fell off.

The clerk also called for law and order. The court days were kept regularly in the marketplace; the proconsuls were available.[11] That is, the governor appointed by the Roman Senate would be there to give judgment. If Demetrius and his fellow craftsmen had a case against anyone, let them bring their charges against one another (in the lawful way). Then, if anyone wanted to seek anything beyond that, it should be explained in the legal (duly constituted) assembly (Greek, *ekklesia,* the word usually translated "church"), that is, not in a riotous gathering *(ekklesia)* like this.

The clerk was actually upset about this riot for it put the city in danger of having a charge of sedition (or, revolution) brought against it. There would be no reason or excuse in the Roman rulers' eyes for the events of this day; they could give no account for this crowding together, which the Romans could take as a seditious meeting or a conspiracy. With this the clerk permitted the assembly (Greek, *ekklesia*) to depart.

The use of the Greek *ekklesia* for this assembly is an important help to the understanding of the meaning of the word as it was used in New Testament times. It shows that the word had lost its old meaning of "called out" and was used of any assembly of gathering, including an illegal assembly or rushing together of citizens such as this gathering in the amphitheater. Thus the word

[11]The plural is general and does not mean there was more than one at a time.

ekklesia, usually translated "church," is properly translated "assembly" with the connotation that it was any assembly of citizens. It is used in this passage of an assembly of the citizens of Ephesus. When it is used of the believers, the proper translation is also *assembly,* with the connotation that it is an assembly of believers who are "fellow-citizens with the saints" (Ephesians 2:19).[12]

[12]It should be noted also that the word *ekklesia* in the New Testament is never used of a building or an organization as such. It is always people.

ACTS
CHAPTER
20

Part of the pressure on Paul in Ephesus was his care or deep concern for all the churches. His letters to the Corinthians show he was especially concerned about those in Macedonia and Greece. (See 2 Corinthians 11:28; 12:20; 13:6). He had already sent Timothy and Erastus to Macedonia. Now it was time for Paul to go too.

Macedonia and Greece Revisited (20:1-6)

[1]And after the uproar was ceased, Paul called unto *him* the disciples, and embraced *them,* and departed for to go into Macedonia. [2]And when he had gone over those parts, and had given them much exhortation, he came into Greece, [3]and there abode three months. And when the Jews laid wait for him, as he was about to sail into Syria, he purposed to return through Macedonia. [4]And there accompanied him into Asia Sopater of Beroea; and of the Thessalonians, Aristarchus and Secundus; and Gaius of Derbe, and Timothy; and of Asia, Tychicus and Trophimus. [5]These going before tarried for us at Troas. [6]And we sailed away from Philippi after the days of unleavened bread, and came unto them to Troas in five days; where we abode seven days (Acts 20:1-6).

After the riot and all the noise ceased, Paul sent for the disciples (the Ephesian believers) and exhorted (encouraged) them (to live holy lives and to be faithful to the Lord, as the practical sections of his epistles show). Then, after farewell greetings, he went to Macedonia. This was probably the last time he would see this body of believers. When he passed by Ephesus on the way to Jerusalem later, he saw only the elders of the church.

It is probable that he went to Macedonia by way of Troas hoping to find Titus there (2 Corinthians 2:13). Not finding him, he went on to Philippi (2 Corinthians 2:12, 13). There Titus did come with good news (2 Corinthians 7:6, 7).

During the summer and fall Paul went through the various churches in Macedonia giving them much exhortation (and encouragement), or, as the Greek says, he exhorted (encouraged) them with much discourse. Probably he also visited the cities west of those visited on the previous journey since in Romans 15:19 he says he fully preached the gospel as far as Illyricum (Dalmatia) on the northwest side of Macedonia.

Then he went down into Greece where he spent the three winter months of A.D. 56, 57. Most of this time was probably spent in Corinth. Tradition says he wrote the Epistle to the Romans there just before he left.

Just as he was about to go to Syria, the unbelieving Jews formed a plot against him. So Paul changed his plans. Instead of taking a ship from Greece he was counseled to return through Macedonia.

Seven men who were accompanying Paul into Asia apparently took the ship as originally planned. They went on ahead of Paul to Troas and waited for him there. These seven included Sopater (also called Sosipater) of Beroea, Aristarchus and Secundus of Thessalonica, Gaius of Derbe, and Timothy, and Tychicus, and Trophimus of Asia (Ephesus). Many writers believe they took this journey to represent the churches who gave money as an offering for the poor among the Jerusalem Christians. They had the responsibility to see what was done with the money and report back to their home churches. The Early Church was very careful to keep good financial accounts and just as careful to make them known to the members of the congregation.

After the seven days of the Feast of Unleavened Bread in April, Paul sailed from Philippi with Luke accompanying him. At Troas they met the others and remained there for seven days.

Eutychus Raised (20:7-12)

[7]And upon the first *day* of the week, when the disciples came together to break bread, Paul preached unto them, ready to depart on the morrow; and continued his speech until midnight. [8]And there were many lights in the upper chamber, where they were gathered together. [9]And there sat in a window a certain young man named Eutychus, being fallen into a deep sleep: and as Paul was long preaching, he sunk down with

sleep, and fell down from the third loft, and was taken up dead. [10]And Paul went down, and fell on him, and embracing *him* said, Trouble not yourselves; for his life is in him. [11]When he therefore was come up again, and had broken bread, and eaten, and talked a long while, even till break of day, so he departed. [12]And they brought the young man alive, and were not a little comforted (Acts 20:7-12).

At Troas Paul probably went to the synagogue on the Sabbath day as was his custom. Then, on the day following, the believers gathered with Paul and his company to break bread. This means they all brought food, shared a fellowship meal, and concluded with an observance of the Lord's Supper.

Paul took the opportunity to preach. Since he was going to leave the next day, he prolonged his discourse until midnight. He could do this, for there were plenty of olive-oil lamps in the upper room where they were meeting.

A young man, Eutychus, was sitting on the window sill listening. About midnight he was borne down (overcome) with deep sleep. Everyone's attention was on Paul, so no one noticed. As Paul kept on preaching, the young man, brought down by sleep, fell from the third story and was taken up dead. This means he was really dead. Luke, as a physician, would be able to determine this.

Immediately, Paul went down (probably by an outside stairway), fell on him, and put his arms around him tightly. We can be sure he prayed as he did so. (Compare 1 Kings 17:21; 2 Kings 4:34 where Elijah and Elisha had similar experiences.) Then Paul said, "Don't panic, for his life is in him." That is, his life had returned to him.[1]

After that Paul went back up, broke bread, ate ("tasted") with enjoyment, and kept on talking with the believers until daylight. Then he left. The boy was also brought before them alive (and fully recovered), and they were very greatly encouraged.

Jerusalem by Pentecost (20:13-16)

[13]And we went before to ship, and sailed unto Assos, there intending to take in Paul: for so had he appointed, minding himself to go afoot. [14]And when he met with us at Assos, we took him in, and came to Mitylene.

---

[1]"Life" is the Greek *psyche* which also means soul or person but which here does mean physical life.

[15]And we sailed thence, and came the next *day* over against Chios; and the next *day* we arrived at Samos, and tarried at Trogyllium; and the next *day* we came to Miletus. [16]For Paul had determined to sail by Ephesus, because he would not spend the time in Asia: for he hasted, if it were possible for him, to be at Jerusalem the day of Pentecost (Acts 20:13-16).

Luke and the rest of Paul's company did not stay until daylight. They went on ahead to the ship and set sail for Assos in Mysia south of Troas where they expected to take Paul on board. He had directed them to do this. The ship would go a longer distance around a peninsula (Cape Lectum) while Paul walked the shorter distance to Assos by land.

Luke does not tell us why Paul did this; for some reason he wanted to be alone. A little later he told the Ephesian elders that in every city the Holy Spirit bore witness to him that bonds (chains) and affliction (persecution, distress) awaited him in Jerusalem. No doubt, Paul needed this time alone to settle it with God about going to Jerusalem.

By sailing along the coast of Asia Minor, stopping at Mitylen, the capital of the island of Lesbos, and touching (passing over by) the island of Samos, they came to Miletus on the coast of Asia near Ephesus.

Paul had decided to sail past Ephesus. He did not want to take too much time there. He had indeed settled it with God, and now he was in a hurry to get to Jerusalem by the Day of Pentecost (in May) if possible. This would be a time when the Jewish believers in Palestine would be together and the offering from Greece and Macedonia would be most helpful.

Paul's Faithful Service (20:17-21)

[17]And from Miletus he sent to Ephesus, and called the elders of the church. [18]And when they were come to him, he said unto them, Ye know, from the first day that I came into Asia, after what manner I have been with you at all seasons, [19]serving the Lord with all humility of mind, and with many tears, and temptations, which befell me by the lying in wait of the Jews: [20]*and* how I kept back nothing that was profitable *unto you,* but have showed you, and have taught you publicly, and from house to house, [21]testifying both to the Jews, and also to the Greeks, repentance toward God, and faith toward our Lord Jesus Christ (Acts 20:17-21).

Paul did not bypass Ephesus because of any lack of concern for the church there. To show his concern and care for them, he called the elders of the church to come to Miletus. This was a very serious occasion for him because he believed it would be the last time he would ever see them.

He began, therefore, by reminding them how all the time he was with them he served the Lord with all meekness (humility), with tears, and with testings brought by the plots of the (unbelieving) Jews. At the same time, he did not let danger cause him to shrink from telling them anything that was beneficial, teaching them publicly and in their homes. To both Jews and Greeks he bore witness to their need of repentance (a change of mind and attitude) toward God and faith in our Lord Jesus.

Willing to Die (20:22-24)

[22]And now, behold, I go bound in the spirit unto Jerusalem, not knowing the things that shall befall me there: [23]save that the Holy Ghost witnesseth in every city, saying that bonds and afflictions abide me. [24]But none of these things move me, neither count I my life dear unto myself, so that I might finish my course with joy, and the ministry, which I have received of the Lord Jesus, to testify the gospel of the grace of God (Acts 20:22-24).

Paul then told the elders that he was going to Jerusalem, not of his own will, but already bound by the Spirit to go. That is, the Spirit had made it clear to him that divine necessity was still upon him to go to Jerusalem. He did not know the things he would encounter there, except that the Holy Spirit in city after city gave solemn witness (undoubtedly through the gift of prophecy) that bonds (chains) and affliction (persecution, distress) awaited him there. (See also Romans 15:31.)

This witness of the Holy Spirit was not intended to stop Paul from going, for he was still bound by the Spirit to go. In fact, he was willing to go. On no account did he make his life valuable (precious) to himself in comparison with finishing his run (as in a race), accomplishing the ministry (the service) which he received from the Lord Jesus, giving serious witness to the good news of the grace of God.

The Challenge of Paul's Example (20:25-35)

[25]And now, behold, I know that ye all, among whom I have gone

preaching the kingdom of God, shall see my face no more. [26]Wherefore I take you to record this day, that I *am* pure from the blood of all *men.* [27]For I have not shunned to declare unto you all the counsel of God. [28]Take heed therefore unto yourselves, and to all the flock, over the which the Holy Ghost hath made you overseers, to feed the church of God, which he hath purchased with his own blood. [29]For I know this, that after my departing shall grievous wolves enter in among you, not sparing the flock. [30]Also of your own selves shall men arise, speaking perverse things, to draw away disciples after them. [31]Therefore watch, and remember, that by the space of three years I ceased not to warn every one night and day with tears.

[32]And now, brethren, I commend you to God, and to the word of his grace, which is able to build you up, and to give you an inheritance among all them which are sanctified. [33]I have coveted no man's silver, or gold, or apparel. [34]Yea, ye yourselves know, that these hands have ministered unto my necessities, and to them that were with me. [35]I have showed you all things, how that so laboring ye ought to support the weak, and to remember the words of the Lord Jesus, how he said, It is more blessed to give than to receive (Acts 20:25-35).

Paul next let the elders know that this was a final farewell. They would never see him again. For this reason he bore witness that he was pure (clean) from the blood of all. Ezekiel was appointed a watchman and a warner to the people of Israel who were in exile by the Chebar Canal in Babylon. If he failed to warn the people and they died in their sins, their blood would be required at his hand (Ezekiel 3:18, 20; 33:6, 8). Paul recognized he had the same heavy responsibility toward the people to whom the Lord sent him to minister.

No one could say Paul had failed to give warning. Even more important, he never shrank from telling all the counsel (wise counsel, wise purpose) of God. Nor did he stop now. He proceeded (verse 28) to give further warning to the elders themselves. Let them attend to (give attention to) themselves and to all the flock among whom the Holy Spirit had made them bishops (overseers, superintendents, ruling elders, presidents of the local congregations) to feed (shepherd) the assembly (Greek *ekklesia,* as in 19:41) of God,[2] which He (Jesus) made His own through His

---

[2]Several ancient manuscripts read "the assembly of the Lord (Jesus)." But "assembly of God" is the better reading. Note that Paul moves from God the Father to God the Son in this sentence. Cf. Rackham, *op. cit.,* p. 393. Note also that the terms, elder and bishop are used interchangeably here, and Paul expects them to exercise a ministry as shepherd or pastor.

own blood, that is, through the shedding of His blood when He died in agony on Calvary (Ephesians 1:7; Titus 2:14; Hebrews 9:12, 14; 13:12, 13).

Here we see that Paul expected the elders to have the office of overseer and be the executive or administrative head of the local congregation. They were, as Acts 14:23 shows, elected to this office by Spirit-filled people who were led by the Spirit. Thus, the Holy Spirit really gave them the office. More important, they were dependent on the Holy Spirit for the gifts of administration (governments) and ruling necessary for the carrying out of their office (1 Corinthians 12:28; Romans 12:8).[3] Through the Holy Spirit they could give wise counsel, manage the business affairs of the church, give spiritual leadership, and show the people the kind of love, concern, and care that Jesus showed for His disciples when He was on earth.

In addition, Paul expected the elders to shepherd the church as the assembly of God. The chief duty of the shepherd was to lead the sheep to food and water. The elders thus needed to have the Christ-given, Spirit-anointed, Spirit-gifted ministry of pastor and teacher. This was a great responsibility. They were not simply leading and teaching their church but the Lord's assembly, an assembly made His own by a tremendous price, the shedding of the precious blood of Jesus. Service, not domineering leadership, was required of them.

Another part of the work of a shepherd was to protect the sheep from enemies. The shepherd's staff guided. The shepherd's rod broke the bones of the wolves who came to destroy the sheep. Paul therefore warned these elders that after his departure grievous (heavy, difficult to handle) wolves would come in among them, not sparing the little flock,[4] but injuring them severely.

Not all of these wolves would come in from the outside. (See Matthew 7:15.) From among the believers, even from among the elders themselves, some would rise up. By speaking perverted things, that is, by using half-truths or by twisting the truth, they would seek to draw away a following for themselves from the disciples (the members of the local assemblies). This indicates that

---

[3]Cf. Horton, *op. cit.*, pp. 279, 281.

[4]See Luke 12:32 where the same word is used of Jesus' disciples.

their real purpose would be to build up themselves rather than to build up the assembly. They would also attempt to draw away disciples who were already believers; they would have little interest in winning the lost for Christ, nor would they desire to build up the churches that were already established. The elders needed to be on their guard against wolves such as these. (Compare 1 Timothy 1:19, 20; 4:1-10; 2 Timothy 1:15; 2:17, 18; 3:1-9; Revelation 2:2-4.)

Paul set them an example in this too. For the nearly three-year period he was with them night and day, he never ceased warning each one of them with tears. That is, he was instant in season and out of season and was always moved by tender love for them. From what we read in Paul's epistles, we see also that during those years he was opposed by many wolves and false brethren.

Paul always did more than warn. He also commended (entrusted) them to God and to His gracious Word which was able to edify them (build them up) and give them the inheritance among all those who are sanctified (holy, set apart to follow Jesus, treated as a holy people, saints of God).

Paul also set them an example of selfless service. He did not desire, he did not even want, anyone's silver, gold, or clothing. They well knew that by his own hands he served (ministered to) his own needs and the needs of those who were with him. As Paul told the Thessalonians, he worked night and day that he might not be a burden on any of them (1 Thessalonians 2:9).

He did tell Timothy that elders who rule well should be given a double honorarium, for the laborer is worthy of his hire (1 Timothy 5:17, 18). But this applied to established, growing, well-taught churches. When Paul came into a new area he was careful to show them that he was not preaching the gospel in order to gain material benefits. The love of Christ constrained him (2 Corinthians 5:14).

Paul worked with his hands, also, to set an example for all. The object of every believer should be to give, not just to receive. We should become mature and strong, and work hard so we can give to help the weak (including the physically sick or weak, as well as those who are spiritually weak).[5] In doing this they would be

[5]Compare Ephesians 4:28 where he urges working with one's hands in order to be able to give to those in need. See also 2 Thessalonians 3:10, 12.

remembering the words of Jesus: "it is more blessed to give than to receive!"

This saying of Jesus is not recorded in any of the four Gospels. Paul, in Galatians, says he did not receive his gospel from men but directly through revelation by Jesus Christ (Galatians 1:11, 12). That is, even the sayings of Jesus were given him by Jesus himself. In a number of instances in his epistles, he indicates he has a word or saying of Jesus to confirm what he says. Here he uses one of these sayings of Jesus to reinforce his counsel to these Ephesian elders.

A Sad Farewell (20:36-38)

[36]And when he had thus spoken, he kneeled down, and prayed with them all. [37]And they all wept sore, and fell on Paul's neck, and kissed him, [38]sorrowing most of all for the words which he spake, that they should see his face no more. And they accompanied him unto the ship (Acts 20:36-38).

When Paul finished speaking he and the elders went to their knees and prayed together. Praying on the knees was common in the Early Church (Acts 9:40; 21:5). But they also prayed standing and sitting.

After prayer there was a considerable amount of weeping from them all as they fell on (pressed on) Paul's neck and kissed him (probably on both cheeks). They were filled with acute pain and sorrow, most of all because Paul said they would see his face no more. Then, as a mark of their affection and respect, they escorted him to the ship.

ACTS

CHAPTER 21

The farewell at Miletus must have been very hard for Paul. Nor did things get easier as he continued his journey toward Jerusalem. There were more sad farewells all along the way.

A Prophecy at Tyre (21:1-6)

[1]And it came to pass, that after we were gotten from them, and had launched, we came with a straight course unto Coos, and the *day* following unto Rhodes, and from thence unto Patara: [2]and finding a ship sailing over unto Phoenicia, we went aboard, and set forth. [3]Now when we had discovered Cyprus, we left it on the left hand, and sailed into Syria, and landed at Tyre: for there the ship was to unlade her burden. [4]And finding disciples, we tarried there seven days: who said to Paul through the Spirit, that he should not go up to Jerusalem.

[5]And when we had accomplished those days, we departed and went our way; and they all brought us on our way, with wives and children, till *we were* out of the city: and we kneeled down on the shore, and prayed. [6]And when we had taken our leave one of another, we took ship; and they returned home again (Acts 21:1-6).

The first day took Paul and his company to the island of Cos, the next to the island of Rhodes, then they went on to land at Patara on the coast of the Roman province of Lycia. There they found a ship crossing over to Phoenicia, which took them to Tyre. At Tyre they had seven days to wait while the ship unloaded cargo.

Paul did not know where the Christians were in Tyre. But he sought them out and spent the time with them. Here, as in many places before, the Spirit warned of what was going to happen to Paul in Jerusalem. The Bible does not say how the Spirit did this, but from what happened a little later in Caesarea, we can be sure the warning came through a prophecy.

We read that the believers "through the Spirit" said (kept saying) to Paul not to go up to Jerusalem. This does not mean, however, that the Spirit did not want Paul to go to Jerusalem. The word "through" (Greek, *dia*) is not the word used in previous passages for the direct agency of the Spirit. (See Acts 13:4, where the Greek is *hupo,* a word used for direct or primary agency.) Here the Greek is better translated "in consequence of the Spirit," that is, because of what the Spirit said. The Spirit himself definitely did not forbid Paul to go on.[1] The Spirit was constraining Paul to go (Acts 20:22). Paul knew the Holy Spirit does not contradict himself. It was not the Spirit but their love for Paul that made them say he should not go.[2] In other words, because of prophecy of bonds and imprisonment the people voiced their feeling that he should not go. But Paul refused to let them force their feelings on him. So he still obeyed what the Holy Spirit directed him personally to do, that is, go on to Jerusalem.

Within the seven days all the believers came to know and love Paul. Thus, when the week was up, all of them, along with their wives and children, escorted Paul to the level, sandy beach outside the city. There they all knelt and prayed before giving parting greetings and returning to their homes.

PROPHECY AT CAESAREA (21:7-14)

[7]And when we had finished *our* course from Tyre, we came to Ptolemais, and saluted the brethren, and abode with them one day. [8]And the next *day* we that were of Paul's company departed, and came unto Caesarea; and we entered into the house of Philip the evangelist, which was *one* of the seven; and abode with him. [9]And the same man had four daughters, virgins, which did prophesy. [10]And as we tarried *there* many days, there came down from Judea a certain prophet, named Agabus. [11]And when he was come unto us, he took Paul's girdle, and bound his own hands and feet, and said, Thus saith the Holy Ghost, So shall the Jews at Jerusalem bind the man that owneth this girdle, and shall deliver *him* into the hands of the Gentiles.

[12]And when we heard these things, both we, and they of that place, besought him not to go up to Jerusalem. [13]Then Paul answered, What mean ye to weep and to break mine heart? for I am ready not to be bound

[1]Cf. Bruce, *op. cit.*, p. 385; also Joseph A. Alexander, *Commentary on the Acts of the Apostles* (Grand Rapids: Zondervan Publishing House, 1956 reprint from 1875 3rd ed.), p. 222.

[2]Cf. David Thomas, *Acts of the Apostles* (Grand Rapids: Baker Book House, 1956 reprint from 1870), p. 359.

only, but also to die at Jerusalem for the name of the Lord Jesus. [14]And when he would not be persuaded, we ceased, saying, The will of the Lord be done (Acts 21:7-14).

After stopping midway at Ptolemais (the Old Testament Accho mentioned in Judges 1:31, now called Acre or Akka), where they spent the day with the Christians, the ship brought them to Caesarea. There they stayed at the home of Philip the evangelist, one of the seven (Acts 6:5). He now had four virgin daughters who prophesied.[3]

The mention of these daughters seems to be significant. It shows that Philip's family served the Lord and that he encouraged them to seek and exercise gifts of the Spirit. It seems also that their ministry in this gift of prophecy must have brought encouragement and blessing to Paul. (Compare 1 Corinthians 14:3.) At Miletus he was anxious to hurry on his way. But here the blessing of the Lord was so rich that he stayed a considerable number of days. It is probable also that Philip gave Luke much information concerning the early days of the Church at Jerusalem.

Then the prophet Agabus, the same one who prophesied the famine in Acts 11:28, came down from Judea. Taking Paul's belt (probably one made of cloth), he bound his own feet and hands as an object lesson. Then he gave the prophecy from the Holy Spirit that the Jews would bind (or be the cause of binding) Paul and give him over into the hands of the Gentiles (that is, into the hands of the Roman rulers).

Because of this prophecy, those who were meeting in Philip's house along with Paul's companions all begged him not to go up to Jerusalem. This was undoubtedly like what happened at Tyre. The people, when they heard the Spirit's message, expressed their own feelings.

Paul, however, said, "What are you doing, weeping and making me feel crushed to pieces." Breaking (crushing to pieces) the heart was a phrase used to mean breaking the will, weakening the purpose, or causing a person to "go to pieces" so that he could accomplish nothing. To get them to stop their weeping Paul

[3]The church historian Eusebius (260-340 A.D.) quotes Papias as saying that these daughters moved to Asia, lived long lives, and continued to minister and witness to the Early Church. Cf. Bruce, *op. cit.*, p. 424.

declared he was ready not only to be bound, but to die in Jerusalem for the sake of the name of the Lord Jesus. He knew it was God's will for him to go. Then the others finally said, "The will of the Lord be done." (Compare Luke 22:42.) Finally, they recognized it really was the Lord's will for Paul to go to Jerusalem.

It was actually very important for the Christians to know it was God's will for Paul to be bound. There were still a number of Judaizers around who opposed the gospel Paul preached. They were still trying to demand that Gentiles become Jews before they could become Christians. In effect, they were saying the Gentile believers would lose their salvation and would never inherit the future blessings God had purposed for them.

Had Paul gone to Jerusalem without all these warnings to let the Church know what was going to happen, the Judaizers would have been quick to take his arrest as the judgment of God. They would have said, "See, did we not tell you? Paul's preaching is all wrong." This could have brought great confusion into the churches. But the Holy Spirit bore witness to Paul and the gospel he preached through these prophecies. At the same time, the Church itself was protected from forces which could have caused division. Truly, the Holy Spirit is the Guide and Protector we need.

Welcomed at Jerusalem (21:15-19)

[15]And after those days we took up our carriages, and went up to Jerusalem. [16]There went with us also *certain* of the disciples of Caesarea, and brought with them one Mnason of Cyprus, an old disciple, with whom we should lodge. [17]And when we were come to Jerusalem, the brethren received us gladly. [18]And the *day* following Paul went in with us unto James; and all the elders were present. [19]And when he had saluted them, he declared particularly what things God had wrought among the Gentiles by his ministry (Acts 21:15-19).

"We took carriages" probably means they saddled up horses. Some writers, however, believe it means they packed their bags (their luggage). Perhaps both meanings are included. At least, they made ready. Then Paul and his company along with some of the disciples from Caesarea went up to Jerusalem. These believers from Caesarea knew a believer from Cyprus, Mnason, who, like Barnabas, was one of the old (original) disciples, that is, one of the 120. (He was not necessarily "old" in age.) He was known as one who delighted to entertain strangers (foreigners). Like Barnabas also, he would be sympathetic to Paul and would not object to entertaining Gentile believers.[4]

At Jerusalem the brethren (including Mnason) welcomed them joyfully, and, as the Greek indicates, entertained them hospitably. The next day Paul took Luke and the rest of his company to see James, the brother of Jesus. All the elders of the Jerusalem church were also present. But it is something worth noting that the apostles are not mentioned. Probably, as much Early Church tradition says, they were already scattered, spreading the gospel in many different directions.

After greeting these elders, Paul gave them a detailed account of what God had done among the Gentiles through his ministry. This must have been a step-by-step rehearsal of his second and third missionary journeys. Specifically, he told them everything that happened since he was with them at the Council of Acts 15.

Encouraging Jewish Believers (21:20-26)

[20]And when they heard *it,* they glorified the Lord, and said unto him, Thou seest, brother, how many thousands of Jews there are which believe; and they are all zealous of the law: [21]and they are informed of thee, that thou teachest all the Jews which are among the Gentiles to forsake Moses, saying that they ought not to circumcise *their* children, neither to walk after the customs. [22]What is it therefore? the multitude must needs come together: for they will hear that thou art come. [23]Do therefore this that we say to thee: We have four men which have a vow on them; [24]them take, and purify thyself with them, and be at charges with them, that they may shave *their* heads: and all may know that those things, whereof they were informed concerning thee, are nothing; but *that* thou thyself also walkest orderly, and keepest the law. [25]As touching the Gentiles which believe, we have written *and* concluded that they observe no such thing, save only that they keep themselves from *things* offered to idols, and from blood, and from strangled, and from fornication.

[26]Then Paul took the men, and the next day purifying himself with them entered into the temple, to signify the accomplishment of the days of purification, until that an offering should be offered for every one of them (Acts 21:20-26).

---

[4]Some translations indicate that Mnason was visiting in Caesarea at the time Paul was there and came up with them to Jerusalem. But it is more likely that the Caesarean believers simply brought Paul and his company to Mnason's house in Jerusalem.

James and the other elders all glorified God because of all He was doing among the Gentiles. But there was another matter of deep concern that was affecting the Jerusalem Church. Thousands, literally tens of thousands (Greek, *myriades*), among the Jews in the Jerusalem area believed on Jesus as their Messiah, Lord, and Saviour. Yet they were still zealots of the Law (eagerly devoted to the Law of Moses). False teachers had come among them, probably Judaizers or else unconverted Jews from Asia Minor, Macedonia, or Greece. These told (deliberately taught) the Jerusalem believers again and again that Paul was teaching all the Jews who lived among the Gentiles (the nations outside Palestine) not to circumcise their children. They also said Paul taught them to stop walking (conducting their lives) according to their (Jewish) customs. This was nothing but slander. Paul had circumcised Timothy; he had recently taken a vow himself.

The elders recognized that these accusations were false. But everyone in Jerusalem had heard them again and again. Now, since all in Jerusalem would surely hear that Paul had come, what should be done? James and the elders had a suggestion. They saw one way to stop the rumors and show they were false. Four of the Jewish believers had taken a vow upon themselves, obviously a temporary Nazarite vow. By this vow any Israelite man or woman could declare their total dedication to God and to His will. Usually the vow was taken for a limited period of time. At the close of the period they had chosen, they would offer rather expensive sacrifices, including a male and female lamb, a ram, and other offerings. Then they would shave their heads as a sign that the vow was completed (Numbers 6:14-20).

Paul did not have to take the vow himself. But he was asked to go through ceremonies of purifying himself along with them and pay for the sacrifices so they could complete the vow and shave their heads.[5] This would show the believers and everyone in Jerusalem that Paul did not teach Jewish believers to go against the customs of their fathers. It would also answer all the false

[5]It is possible these four had defiled themselves in some way and were now undergoing seven days of purification (Numbers 6:9). Cf. Bruce, *op. cit.,* pp. 430, 431.

things said about Paul and would demonstrate that Paul himself walked a straight line and was an observer of the Law.

Then James and the elders confirmed the decision of the Council of Acts 15, a decision Paul had already carried to the Gentile believers. That is, though they wanted Paul, as a Jewish believer, to show he did not ask Jews to live like Gentiles, they were still willing to accept Gentile believers without asking them to become Jews.

The next day Paul took the four men and did as he was asked to do, spreading the news of the completing of the days of purification until the sacrifice was brought for each of them. As Paul told the Corinthians, to the Jews he became as a Jew and to those under the Law he became as under the Law (1 Corinthians 9:20).[6]

Asian Jews Cause a Riot (21:27-30)

> [27]And when the seven days were almost ended, the Jews which were of Asia, when they saw him in the temple, stirred up all the people, and laid hands on him, [28]crying out, Men of Israel help: This is the man, that teacheth all *men* every where against the people, and the law, and this place: and further brought Greeks also into the temple, and hath polluted this holy place. [29](For they had seen before with him in the city Trophimus an Ephesian, whom they supposed that Paul had brought into the temple.) [30]And all the city was moved, and the people ran together: and they took Paul, and drew him out of the temple: and forthwith the doors were shut (Acts 21:27-30).

The plan of the Jerusalem church elders failed. Instead of satisfying the Jews, the opposite happened when the seven days of purification were almost completed. Jews from the Roman province of Asia were in Jerusalem for the Feast of Pentecost. They saw him in the Temple and threw the whole crowd into confusion. Then they laid violent hands on Paul.

They had seen Paul in the city with Trophimus, a Gentile believer from Ephesus. They jumped to the false conclusion that

[6]Cf. Hackett, *op. cit.*, pp. 249, 251. Paul knew that these Jewish ceremonies had no value as far as our salvation is concerned. But he did recognize that they had a symbolic or teaching value for Jewish believers. They carried out these things not to gain salvation, not to get in right relation with God, but to express a dedication to God that was already settled in their hearts through Christ and their acceptance of His work on the cross.

Paul had brought him into the Temple.[7] Then they shouted that Paul taught everyone everywhere against the people (the Jews) and against the Law, and had now defiled the Temple by bringing in Greeks (Gentiles).

At this the whole city of Jerusalem was stirred up. (Most of them were probably already in the Temple at this time.) The Jews ran together from all directions, seized Paul, and dragged him out of the Temple, beating him as they did so. Immediately the great doors to the Temple court of the women were shut so the mob would not desecrate the Temple. No one seemed to notice that Paul had no Gentiles with him, however.

Paul Rescued by the Romans (21:31-40)

[31]And as they went about to kill him, tidings came unto the chief captain of the band, that all Jerusalem was in an uproar: [32]who immediately took soldiers and centurions, and ran down unto them: and when they saw the chief captain and the soldiers, they left beating of Paul. [33]Then the chief captain came near, and took him, and commanded *him* to be bound with two chains; and demanded who he was, and what he had done. [34]And some cried one thing, some another, among the multitude: and when he could not know the certainty for the tumult, he commanded him to be carried into the castle. [35]And when he came upon the stairs, so it was, that he was borne of the soldiers for the violence of the people. [36]For the multitude of the people followed after, crying, Away with him.

[37]And as Paul was to be led into the castle, he said unto the chief captain, May I speak unto thee? Who said, Canst thou speak Greek? [38]Art not thou that Egyptian, which before these days madest an uproar, and leddest out into the wilderness four thousand men that were murderers? [39]But Paul said, I am a man *which am* a Jew of Tarsus, *a city* in Cilicia, a citizen of no mean city: and, I beseech thee, suffer me to speak unto the people. [40]And when he had given him license, Paul stood on the stairs, and beckoned with the hand unto the people. And when there was made a great silence, he spake unto *them* in the Hebrew tongue, saying . . . (Acts 21:31-40).

---

[7]Archaeologists have found two of the inscriptions that warned Gentiles not to go any further than the court of the Gentiles. They read (in Greek), "No foreigner may enter within this barricade which surrounds the Temple and enclosure (its inner courts). Anyone caught doing so will have himself to blame for his ensuing death." Cf. John Rutherford, "Partition, the Middle Wall of" in *The International Standard Bible Encyclopedia* (Grand Rapids: Eerdmans, 1943), IV, 2253. Cf. Bruce, *op. cit.*, p. 434.

The mob was already seeking to kill Paul when information came up to the tribune (the officer over a cohort of 600-1,000 men stationed in the Tower [castle, fortress] of Antonia on the northwest overlooking the Temple area). They told him that all Jerusalem was in a state of confusion. Immediately the tribune took soldiers and centurions (officers over 100 infantry) and with quite a show of force ran down to them.

The sight of the tribune and all the soldiers made the mob stop beating Paul. Binding Paul with two chains, the tribune asked the Jews who he was and what he had done. Everyone began shouting different things at once. There was no way the tribune could be sure what was being said in all the hubbub. So he ordered the soldiers to take Paul into the castle (fortress, tower of Antonia).

The soldiers had to carry Paul up the flight of steps from the Temple area into the Tower of Antonia because of the pressure of the crowds. They were following them trying to pull Paul away and crying out (loudly shrieking again and again), "Away with him!" By this they meant they wanted him killed. In fact, they would have pulled him apart if the soldiers had not lifted him up and surrounded him.

The crowd dropped behind as the soldiers came to the top of the steps and were about to enter the fortress. So Paul spoke in Greek to the tribune. He seemed surprised that Paul knew Greek and asked Paul if he were not the Egyptian who turned things upside down (as a political revolutionist) and led out into the desert 4,000 fanatical Jews (*sicarii,* "dagger men") who were known to assassinate their opponents.

Paul answered by identifying himself as a Jew, a citizen of the important city of Tarsus. Then he asked permission to speak to the people. When this was given, he was allowed to stand on the stairs. Signaling his desire to speak, he got the attention of the crowd and there was sudden quiet. Then Paul began to speak to them in the Hebrew language.

This is generally taken to be Aramaic, the language the Jews brought back from Babylonia after their exile there in the sixth century B.C. But there is some evidence that Jerusalem Jews took pride in being able to use the old (Biblical) Hebrew. They also read the Bible first in Hebrew in the synagogues every week before paraphrasing it into Aramaic, so they would all be familiar with the Biblical Hebrew. But, since they would understand both, it is not clear which is meant here. In some New Testament passages "Hebrew" is used to designate the closely related language of Aramaic which was used in most Palestinian homes.

ACTS

CHAPTER 22

This defense given on the stairs was the first of five that Paul was permitted to make. In it Paul emphasizes his heritage as a Jew and his encounter with Christ.

A Witness for Christ (22:1-21)

[1]Men, brethren, and fathers, hear ye my defense *which I make* now unto you. [2](And when they heard that he spake in the Hebrew tongue to them, they kept the more silence: and he saith,) [3]I am verily a man *which am* a Jew, born in Tarsus, *a city* in Cilicia, yet brought up in this city at the feet of Gamaliel, *and* taught according to the perfect manner of the law of the fathers, and was zealous toward God, as ye all are this day. [4]And I persecuted this way unto the death, binding and delivering into prisons both men and women. [5]As also the high priest doth bear me witness, and all the estate of the elders: from whom also I received letters unto the brethren, and went to Damascus, to bring them which were there bound unto Jerusalem, for to be punished.

[6]And it came to pass, that, as I made my journey, and was come nigh unto Damascus about noon, suddenly there shone from heaven a great light round about me. [7]And I fell unto the ground, and heard a voice saying unto me, Saul, Saul, why persecutest thou me? [8]And I answered, Who art thou, Lord? And he said unto me, I am Jesus of Nazareth, whom thou persecutest. [9]And they that were with me saw indeed the light, and were afraid; but they heard not the voice of him that spake to me. [10]And I said, What shall I do, Lord? And the Lord said unto me, Arise, and go into Damascus; and there it shall be told thee of all things which are appointed for thee to do. [11]And when I could not see for the glory of that light, being led by the hand of them that were with me, I came into Damascus.

[12]And one Ananias, a devout man according to the law, having a good report of all the Jews which dwelt *there,* [13]came unto me, and stood, and said unto me, Brother Saul, receive thy sight. And the same hour I looked up upon him. [14]And he said, The God of our fathers hath chosen thee, that thou shouldest know his will, and see that Just One,

and shouldest hear the voice of his mouth. [15]For thou shalt be his witness unto all men of what thou hast seen and heard. [16]And now why tarriest thou? arise, and be baptized, and wash away thy sins, calling on the name of the Lord.

[17]And it came to pass, that, when I was come again to Jerusalem, even while I prayed in the temple, I was in a trance; [18]and saw him saying unto me, Make haste, and get thee quickly out of Jerusalem: for they will not receive thy testimony concerning me. [19]And I said, Lord, they know that I imprisoned and beat in every synagogue them that believed on thee: [20]and when the blood of thy martyr Stephen was shed, I also was standing by, and consenting unto his death, and kept the raiment of them that slew him. [21]And he said unto me, Depart: for I will send thee far hence unto the Gentiles (Acts 22:1-21).

When the crowd recognized Paul was speaking in Hebrew, they were even more quiet (not because Hebrew was a sacred language, but because it made them realize he was a Jew, not a Gentile, for Gentiles carried on all their business with the Jews in the Greek language). Paul then proceeded to identify himself as a Jew born in Tarsus but brought up in Jerusalem at the feet of Gamaliel.[1] That is, his schooling was under that famous rabbi. By Gamaliel he was trained with strict attention to every detail of the law of the fathers (the Law of Moses with the addition of all the traditions of the scribes and Pharisees). He was also a zealot, eagerly devoted to God, just as all his audience was. Clearly, Paul was not blaming them for beating him. Once, in his zeal for God, he would have done the same thing.

In fact, Paul persecuted (pursued) this (Christian) Way up to the point of causing the death of the believers, binding many both men and women, and having them put in prison. The high priest was a witness to this, as were all the elders (of the Sanhedrin). From them he received letters to the Jews of Damascus and went there to bring the believers bound to Jerusalem to be punished.

Then Paul told the story of the light from heaven and the voice of Jesus which his companions did not hear (in the sense of understanding what was said). He also drew attention to the fact that Ananias of Damascus was a devout (God-fearing, godly) man according to the Law, that is, in the way he was careful to keep the Law. All the Jews who lived in Damascus bore favorable witness to him.

---

[1]This indicates Paul came to Jerusalem in his early youth, probably in his early teens. Cf. Hackett, *op. cit.,* p. 256 and R. N. Longenecker, *Paul, Apostle of Liberty* (Grand Rapids: Baker Book House, 1976 reprint from 1964), p. 27.

Paul then gave more details of what Ananias said to him after restoring his sight. Ananias told him that the God of their fathers (the God of Abraham, Isaac, and Jacob) had appointed (elected, selected) him to know (come to know, realize) His will, to see the Just One (the righteous Servant, that is, the Messiah), and to hear His voice, not from a distance, but from His mouth, face to face. God did this so he could be His witness to all men (all mankind) of what he had seen and heard.

Then Ananias had said, "Now what do you intend? Rise, be baptized, and wash away your sins, calling on His name." This was a call to express faith. The sins would be washed away through calling on the Lord's name, however, not by the water of baptism.[2] As Peter brings out, the waters of baptism cannot wash away any of the filthiness of the flesh (that is, of the old nature). Rather, they are an answer (appeal, pledge) of a good conscience that has already been cleansed by faith in the death and resurrection of Christ (1 Peter 3:20, 21; Romans 10:9, 10). Peter also compares this to Noah. That is, the fact that Noah came through the flood was a witness to the faith that caused him to build the ark before the flood (1 Peter 3:20; see Hebrews 11:7). So coming through the waters of baptism bears witness to the faith that believed in Christ and received the cleansing of His blood and of His Word before the baptism.

Paul then skipped over his experiences in Damascus and told how he returned to Jerusalem. There, praying in this very Temple, he was in a trance. This was not a trance in the modern or heathen sense, but a state where his mind was disturbed by the circumstances. Then he saw Jesus who told him to hurry out of Jerusalem, for the people of Jerusalem would not receive his witness to Him. Paul tried to argue that they knew what he had done in connection with the death of Stephen. He apparently felt that they would surely listen when they saw what a change had taken place in him. But Jesus again commanded him to leave. His purpose was to send him (as an apostle) far away to the Gentiles (the nations).

This appearance and command of Jesus was not explained in chapter 9. There the Jerusalem leaders, because of a Jerusalem

---

[2]Cf. Hackett, *op. cit.*, p. 258.

plot to kill Paul, sent him to Tarsus. But now it is clear that it took this appearance of Jesus to make him willing to go.

Born a Roman (22:22-30)

[22]And they gave him audience unto this word, and *then* lifted up their voices and said, Away with such a *fellow* from the earth: for it is not fit that he should live. [23]And as they cried out, and cast off *their* clothes, and threw dust into the air, [24]the chief captain commanded him to be brought into the castle, and bade that he should be examined by scourging; that he might know wherefore they cried so against him. [25]And as they bound him with thongs, Paul said unto the centurion that stood by, Is it lawful for you to scourge a man that is a Roman, and uncondemned? [26]When the centurion heard *that,* he went and told the chief captain, saying, Take heed what thou doest; for this man is a Roman.

[27]Then the chief captain came, and said unto him, Tell me, art thou a Roman? He said, Yea. [28]And the chief captain answered, With a great sum obtained I this freedom. And Paul said, But I was *free*-born. [29]Then straightway they departed from him which should have examined him: and the chief captain also was afraid, after he knew that he was a Roman, and because he had bound him.

[30]On the morrow, because he would have known the certainty wherefore he was accused of the Jews, he loosed him from *his* bands, and commanded the chief priests and all their council to appear, and brought Paul down, and set him before them (Acts 22:22-30).

The Jews in the courtyard below listened to Paul until he spoke of the command to go to the Gentiles. The truth that God cares about the Gentiles is clear in the Old Testament (Genesis 12:3). But Roman oppression had blinded their minds. Gentiles in their eyes were dogs, scavengers. Thus, in their prejudice, they began crying out again for Paul's death. They felt he was not worthy to live.

While they were shouting this, they were also throwing their outer garments around as an expression of their uncontrollable anger. At the same time they threw dust in the air as a symbol of their rejection of Paul and his message. No doubt they would have thrown mud if it had been available.

This caused the tribune to have Paul brought into the fortress. In order to find out why the Jews shouted so against him, the tribune also told the soldiers to examine him by scourging. That is, they were to question him while torturing him with a whip made of leather thongs with pieces of bone and metal sewn in them.

Paul had already been whipped by Jews five times and beaten with rods by Romans three times (2 Corinthians 11:24, 25). But this punishment by a Roman scourge was worse and often crippled or killed its victim.

To prepare Paul for the scourging, the soldiers made him bend over and stretch forward. They bound him in that position with thongs (leather straps) to receive the flogging. (Some writers believe the meaning is that he was hung by the thongs with his feet a few inches above the ground.)

At this point Paul asked the centurion who was supervising this if it was legal to scourge (whip, flog) a man who was a Roman and uncondemned (his case not even having been tried). This the centurion reported to the tribune. He came at once, asking Paul if he was a Roman. The tribune then remarked that he bought his Roman citizenship with a great sum of money.[3] But Paul replied that he was Roman born. His father or grandfather must have given unusual service to the Romans in Tarsus and been rewarded by Roman citizenship for himself and his family.[4]

The soldiers who were about to question and torture Paul quickly left. The tribune also was afraid. He knew that Paul, as a Roman citizen, had a right to bring charges against him for putting chains on him.

The tribune kept Paul in custody, however, though without the chains we can be sure. The next day, because he wanted to know for sure why the Jews were accusing Paul, he brought him out, ordered the chief priests and the Sanhedrin to assemble, and made Paul stand up before them.

[3]Roman citizenship was often sold in the reign of the Emperor Claudius, especially by his wife and other court favorites. It apparently became a means of lining their pockets. The tribune had used this as a means of gaining a higher commission in the Roman army.

[4]Some older commentaries say that the entire city of Tarsus was given Roman citizenship, but the historical evidence does not confirm this.

ACTS
CHAPTER
23

Paul, who was once a member of the Sanhedrin and had cast his vote to stone Stephen, now had to face this highest court of the Jews. Their council chamber was west of the Temple area; the Roman tribune brought him there.

THE HOPE OF THE RESURRECTION (23:1-10)

[1]And Paul, earnestly beholding the council, said, Men *and* brethren, I have lived in all good conscience before God until this day. [2]And the high priest Ananias commanded them that stood by him to smite him on the mouth. [3]Then said Paul unto him, God shall smite thee, *thou* whited wall: for sittest thou to judge me after the law, and commandest me to be smitten contrary to the law? [4]And they that stood by said, Revilest thou God's high priest? [5]Then said Paul, I wist not, brethren, that he was the high priest: for it is written, Thou shalt not speak evil of the ruler of thy people.

[6]But when Paul perceived that the one part were Sadducees, and the other Pharisees, he cried out in the council, Men *and* brethren, I am a Pharisee, the son of a Pharisee: of the hope and resurrection of the dead I am called in question. [7]And when he had so said, there arose a dissension between the Pharisees and the Sadducees: and the multitude was divided. [8]For the Sadducees say that there is no resurrection, neither angel, nor spirit: but the Pharisees confess both. [9]And there arose a great cry: and the scribes *that were* of the Pharisees' part arose, and strove, saying, We find no evil in this man: but if a spirit or an angel hath spoken to him, let us not fight against God.

[10]And when there arose a great dissension, the chief captain, fearing lest Paul should have been pulled in pieces of them, commanded the soldiers to go down, and to take him by force from among them, and to bring *him* into the castle (Acts 23:1-10).

Paul showed no fear or hesitation. He knew he was in the will of the Lord, and he had learned to depend on the Holy Spirit.

Fixing his eyes on the council, he declared that he had lived his life (and fulfilled his duties) before God with all good conscience up to that day. (See 1 Corinthians 4:4; Philippians 3:6, 9.)

At this the high priest, Ananias, ordered those standing by Paul to hit him on the mouth. Paul reacted to this because his sense of justice was aroused. "God will strike you, you whitewashed wall!"[1] Paul took him to be one of the members of the council that was sitting there to judge him according to the Law. Yet he had commanded him to be struck contrary to the Law. The Law treated a man as innocent until he was proved guilty.

Those who had struck Paul rebuked him for reviling (abusing, insulting) God's high priest. Paul quickly apologized. He did not know the one who gave the command was the high priest. Ananias was made high priest in A.D. 47 by Herod of Chalcis.[2] Paul had been in Jerusalem since then only a few times and for short periods, so it is not strange that he had not seen the high priest before. It is probable also that since the tribune assembled the Sanhedrin on this occasion the high priest was sitting among the other members of the court instead of presiding.

But though Paul did not know who the high priest was, he did know the Scriptures. His quotation of Exodus 22:28 shows the genuine humility of his spirit and his willingness to submit to the Law which his accusers claimed he had defied.

Then Paul realized that there was an issue he could declare. As he already knew, but now noticed again, part of the Sanhedrin were Sadducees, part Pharisees. The Sadducees rejected the idea of any resurrection. The Pharisees believed the hope of the resurrection was fundamental to the hope of Israel and necessary for the full realization of God's promise.

Paul, therefore, took advantage of that situation with courage. It was an opportunity to witness to the truth of resurrection and to the fact of the resurrection of Jesus; he was not out of order in

[1]That is, a wall whitewashed over to hide the fact it was crumbling or decaying. Some see also a reference to what Jesus said about whitewashed tombs (Matthew 23:27). Cf. Hackett, *op. cit.,* p. 263.

[2]Ananias was a very greedy and disgraceful excuse for a high priest. In A.D. 66 he was put to death by the Jews themselves. Cf. Bruce, *op. cit.,* pp. 449, 450. Some believe Paul knew he was the high priest but was sarcastic here. That is, they take it that Paul meant no true high priest would do what Ananias did. Cf. Packer, *op. cit.,* p. 187. It seems more likely that he actually did not know.

this. Even before his conversion, as a Pharisee he realized how deep and important the doctrine of future resurrection is. Crying out that he was a Pharisee, the son of Pharisees,[3] he declared that it was with respect to the hope and resurrection of the dead that he was being called into question.[4]

This split the council into two camps. As they talked to one another, the discord grew. They even went beyond the idea of resurrection and began arguing about the existence of angels and spirits, which the Sadducees also denied.

The result was a great outcry as they clamored against each other. Some of the scribes (experts in the interpretation of the Law) who were on the side of the Pharisees stood up and greatly strove in Paul's behalf. They found no evil (nothing bad) in him. They suggested that an angel or spirit may have spoken to him.

But the mention of angel and spirit must have stirred up the Sadducees. There was so much upheaval and discord that the tribune became afraid that Paul might be torn apart by them. So he ordered the soldiers to go down and snatch him out of their midst and bring him back into the Fortress of Antonia.

Encouraged by the Lord (23:11)

And the night following the Lord stood by him, and said, Be of good cheer, Paul: for as thou hast testified of me in Jerusalem, so must thou bear witness also at Rome (Acts 23:11).

It had been a hard day for Paul. But during the night following, the Lord Jesus suddenly stood by him and said, "Be of good cheer (be of good courage, cheer up and don't be afraid)." As Paul had testified (given a clear witness) for Christ in Jerusalem, so must he also witness (testify) in Rome. Paul's desire to go to Rome had seemed impossible when he was arrested. But Jesus now made it clear that a witness in Rome was still God's will for him. This

[3]Though he was not as strict as some, he could still consider himself a Pharisee. Cf. Longenecker, *op. cit.*, pp. 261, 262.

[4]The Jewish Mishnah (the traditions of the Pharisees, written down about A.D. 200 and made a basic part of the Talmud) states that those who deny the resurrection of the dead will have no part in the age to come. This became the orthodox Jewish belief and the doctrines of the Sadducees were rejected. Cf. Bruce, *op. cit.*, p. 454.

encouragement upheld Paul in the sufferings, trials, and difficulties that were still to come.

A Jewish Plot Discovered (23:12-22)

[12]And when it was day, certain of the Jews banded together, and bound themselves under a curse, saying that they would neither eat nor drink till they had killed Paul. [13]And they were more than forty which had made this conspiracy. [14]And they came to the chief priests and elders, and said, We have bound ourselves under a great curse, that we will eat nothing until we have slain Paul. [15]Now therefore ye with the council signify to the chief captain that he bring him down unto you tomorrow, as though ye would inquire something more perfectly concerning him: and we, or ever he come near, are ready to kill him.

[16]And when Paul's sister's son heard of their lying in wait, he went and entered into the castle, and told Paul. [17]Then Paul called one of the centurions unto *him*, and said, Bring this young man unto the chief captain: for he hath a certain thing to tell him. [18]So he took him, and brought *him* to the chief captain, and said, Paul the prisoner called me unto *him*, and prayed me to bring this young man unto thee, who hath something to say unto thee.

[19]Then the chief captain took him by the hand, and went *with him* aside privately, and asked *him*, What is that thou hast to tell me? [20]And he said, The Jews have agreed to desire thee that thou wouldest bring down Paul tomorrow into the council, as though they would inquire somewhat of him more perfectly. [21]But do not thou yield unto them: for there lie in wait for him of them more than forty men, which have bound themselves with an oath, that they will neither eat nor drink till they have killed him: and now are they ready, looking for a promise from thee. [22]So the chief captain *then* let the young man depart, and charged *him, See thou* tell no man that thou hast showed these things to me (Acts 23:12-22).

The next morning over 40 Jews held a meeting to plot Paul's death. In doing so they invoked a curse on themselves, saying they would neither eat nor drink until they had killed Paul. Then they went to the chief priests and elders and explained their plan. These elders were, no doubt, Sadducees who did not like what Paul said about the resurrection.

The conspirators asked these leaders to get the Sanhedrin to make an official request to the tribune to bring Paul down, as if they intended to determine more precisely the facts concerning him. Before he got near, they would be waiting, prepared to kill him. That is, they would ambush him on the way, so the Sanhedrin would not be held responsible for his death.

Paul's sister's son happened to come on the scene just at this time and he heard their plot.[5] So he went immediately to the Fortress of Antonia and told Paul. Paul then called a centurion and asked him to take the young man to the tribune. The tribune received him courteously, took him by the hand, and retired into a place where they could talk privately. Then he asked what he had to tell him.

The boy told him of the plot and warned him not to be persuaded by their request to bring Paul to them. The more than 40 men who had put themselves under a curse were prepared, waiting for the promise from the tribune. The tribune then let the boy go, after making him promise not to tell anyone that he had reported these things to him.

Paul Taken to Caesarea (23:23-35)

[23]And he called unto *him* two centurions, saying, Make ready two hundred soldiers to go to Caesarea, and horsemen threescore and ten, and spearmen two hundred, at the third hour of the night; [24]and provide *them* beasts, that they may set Paul on, and bring *him* safe unto Felix the governor. [25]And he wrote a letter after this manner:

[26]Claudius Lysias unto the most excellent governor Felix *sendeth* greeting. [27]This man was taken of the Jews, and should have been killed of them: then came I with an army, and rescued him, having understood that he was a Roman. [28]And when I would have known the cause wherefore they accused him, I brought him forth into their council: [29]whom I perceived to be accused of questions of their law, but to have nothing laid to his charge worthy of death or of bonds. [30]And when it was told me how that the Jews laid wait for the man, I sent straightway to thee, and gave commandment to his accusers also to say before thee what *they had* against him. Farewell.

[31]Then the soldiers, as it was commanded them, took Paul, and brought *him* by night to Antipatris. [32]On the morrow they left the horsemen to go with him, and returned to the castle: [33]who, when they came to Caesarea, and delivered the epistle to the governor, presented Paul also before him. [34]And when the governor had read *the letter,* he asked of what province he was. And when he understood that *he was* of Cilicia; [35]I will hear thee, said he, when thine accusers are also come. And he commanded him to be kept in Herod's judgment hall (Acts 23:23-35)

The tribune knew he would be held accountable for Paul, as a

---

[5]Some writers believe he had come to Jerusalem from Tarsus to be educated, just as Paul had. Cf. Bruce, *op. cit.,* p. 457.

Roman citizen in his custody, if Paul were assassinated. Therefore, he had two centurions get 200 foot soldiers ready to go to Caesarea, along with 70 cavalry and 200 soldiers of another class. (What class it was is debatable today.) They were to leave at the third hour of the night (about 9 p.m.). Horses also were to be provided for Paul to ride so that he might be brought safely to Felix, the Roman governor of the province.[6]

The tribune also wrote a letter to explain to the governor why he was sending Paul. Acts says it was "after this manner (type, pattern, copy)." Probably what is meant is that this is an actual copy of the letter.

In the letter the tribune named himself, Claudius Lysias. (Lysias was a Greek name, indicating his Greek background.) Then he explained how he rescued Paul from the Jews who were about to kill him. He put himself in a better light than was actually the case, however. He implied that the reason he rescued Paul was because he learned Paul was a Roman; we can give him credit, though, for trying to put Paul in a good light. He explained that the accusations were based on questions of Jewish law and that he found nothing worthy of death or bonds. Because of the plot, he sent Paul to the governor, commanding his accusers to bring their charges against Paul to him also.

We wonder if word of this got to the more than 40 conspirators before Paul was taken out of the city. But the tribune made sure that they had no chance to do anything to him. Picture Paul, surrounded by 400 soldiers and 70 cavalry, leaving Jerusalem at nine o'clock in the evening. Such a troop movement, even at night, must have attracted attention. Though it may not have been known that Paul was in the midst of them, someone surely must have investigated.

The Bible does not tell us what the conspirators did about their vow. Obviously they had to eat and drink before long. Probably they found some way to offer a sacrifice or offering to atone for their failure to keep the vow. (The Jewish Mishnah indicates there was such a provision.)

That night the soldiers brought Paul as far as Antipatris (where there was a Roman colony), about half way to Caesarea. In the

[6]Marcus Antonius Felix was procurator of Judea from before A.D. 52 until A.D. 59.

morning the foot soldiers returned to the Fortress of Antonia. The 60 cavalry conducted Paul the rest of the way to Caesarea, delivered the letter, and brought Paul before the governor.

After reading the letter, Felix asked Paul what province he was from, probably because only if Paul came from a Roman province could he, as a Roman, take charge of him on his own authority. Then he ordered that Paul be kept in Herod's praetorium, the palace built by Herod the Great where the procurator now had his residence.

ACTS

CHAPTER

24

Only once did the Jews bring formal charges against Paul. On this occasion they hired an orator, a professional public speaker, to act as counsel for the prosecution.

TERTULLUS ACCUSES PAUL (24:1-9)

[1]And after five days Ananias the high priest descended with the elders, and *with* a certain orator *named* Tertullus, who informed the governor against Paul.

[2]And when he was called forth, Tertullus began to accuse *him* saying, Seeing that by thee we enjoy great quietness, and that very worthy deeds are done unto this nation by thy providence, [3]we accept *it* always, and in all places, most noble Felix, with all thankfulness. [4]Notwithstanding, that I be not further tedious unto thee, I pray thee that thou wouldest hear us of thy clemency a few words. [5]For we have found this man *a* pestilent *fellow,* and a mover of sedition among all the Jews throughout the world, and a ringleader of the sect of the Nazarenes: [6]who also hath gone about to profane the temple: whom we took, and would have judged according to our law. [7]But the chief captain Lysias came *upon us,* and with great violence took *him* away out of our hands, [8]commanding his accusers to come unto thee: by examining of whom thyself mayest take knowledge of all these things, whereof we accuse him.

[9]And the Jews also assented, saying that these things were so (Acts 24:1-9).

After five days the high priest, Ananias, with some of the members of the Sanhedrin (undoubtedly those who were his Sadducean friends), arrived with the orator Tertullus and reported to the governor against Paul. Paul was then called, and Tertullus was given opportunity to present his accusation against him. He began by flattering the governor: Through him they had obtained much peace; reforms had come to the Jewish nation through his forethought; these things the Jews accepted in all ways and in all places with thankfulness. But that he might not hinder the governor more, Tertullus besought the governor to listen briefly in his forbearance (consideration, fairness).[1]

Tertullus then falsely accused Paul of being a pestilent fellow (a plague), one stirring up sedition (discord, revolution, riot) among all the Jews who are in all the inhabited world (that is, in the Roman Empire). Then he implicated all the Christians by calling Paul a ringleader of the sect of the Nazarenes (Greek, *nazoraion,* the followers of the Man of Nazareth).

Finally, after this general accusation, Tertullus gave the specific charge. Paul, he said, tried to profane the Temple. But they laid hold on him. That is, they caught him in the act and stopped him before he could profane it. This, of course, was false. Moreover, Tertullus did not tell how they had seized Paul and without any trial had begun to beat him to death as an act of mob violence. Instead, (as most ancient New Testament manuscripts indicate) he pretended that Paul was being judged properly by their Law when the tribune intervened with much force and commanded his accusers to appear before the governor.

Tertullus also confidently declared that by examining Paul himself the governor would be able to find out these things (these accusations against Paul) were true.[2] The Jews then joined in attacking Paul (joined in pressing charges against him), saying again and again that these things were so.

Paul's Answer (24:10-21)

[10]Then Paul, after that the governor had beckoned unto him to speak, answered, Forasmuch as I know that thou hast been of many years a judge unto this nation, I do the more cheerfully answer for myself: [11]because that thou mayest understand, that there are yet but twelve days since I went up to Jerusalem for to worship. [12]And they neither found me in the temple disputing with any man, neither raising up the people, neither in the synagogues, nor in the city: [13]neither can they prove the things whereof they now accuse me. [14]But this I confess unto thee, that after the way which they call heresy, so worship I the God of my fathers, believing all things which are written in the law and in the prophets:

[1]Secular history shows Felix was actually a violent, unfair man.

[2]Some ancient manuscripts of the New Testament indicate that Tertullus meant Lysias the tribune should be examined rather than Paul.

[15]and have hope toward God, which they themselves also allow, that there shall be a resurrection of the dead, both of the just and unjust. [16]And herein do I exercise myself, to have always a conscience void of offense toward God, and *toward* men.

[17]Now after many years I came to bring alms to my nation, and offerings. [18]Whereupon certain Jews from Asia found me purified in the temple, neither with multitude, nor with tumult. [19]Who ought to have been here before thee, and object, if they had aught against me. [20]Or else let these same *here* say, if they have found any evildoing in me, while I stood before the council, [21]except it be for this one voice, that I cried standing among them, Touching the resurrection of the dead I am called in question by you this day (Acts 24:10-21).

When the governor nodded to Paul, indicating that he should speak, Paul addressed the governor courteously, but without the flattery Tertullus used. Since Felix had been many years a judge of the Jews Paul felt he could make his defense with good courage (in a good or cheerful spirit).

Then he presented the facts which the governor could easily find out for himself. It was at that time not more than 12 days since Paul came up to worship in Jerusalem.[3] That is, he was there only seven days before he was seized by the mob. During those seven days they did not find him conversing (or preaching) to anyone. Nor did he stir up a crowd in the Temple, in the synagogues, or in the city. In no way could they prove any of their accusations.

Paul then proceeded with a public declaration or confession of his faith. According to the way called a sect (a self-chosen opinion), he continued to serve the God of his fathers (his ancestors, Abraham, Isaac, and Jacob). He also showed by the way he served God that he was still a believer in everything that was according to the Law and everything written in the Prophets.

By the Law and the Prophets he also had a hope in God, a hope that these Jews shared. This hope was for a resurrection of both the just and the unjust (Daniel 12:2; John 5:29). For this reason Paul exercised himself continually to have a conscience, free from causing offense to God and men.

After this discourse on the resurrection, Paul returned to recounting the facts of his case. Now after many years he came to

[3]Worship was an important part of Paul's purpose for coming to Jerusalem. See Acts 24:14. Cf. Longenecker, *op. cit.*, pp. 262, 263.

bring alms to his people and offerings to God. It was while presenting these offerings that they found Paul in the Temple, purified, with no crowd, nor with any disturbance. But there were certain Jews from Asia who falsely accused him. They were the real accusers, and it was really their duty to be the ones to come before Felix and make their accusation if they had anything against Paul.

Paul here was taking advantage of the Law's demand for witnesses to make the accusation. Then he made it clear that none of these priests and elders present were witnesses of what went on in the Temple. There was really only one thing of which these were witnesses. They were present when Paul stood before the Sanhedrin and cried out that it was with respect to the resurrection of the dead that he was called into question. He would willingly let them accuse him of saying that.

Felix Postpones Making a Decision (24:22-27)

[22]And when Felix heard these things, having more perfect knowledge of *that* way, he deferred them, and said, When Lysias the chief captain shall come down, I will know the uttermost of your matter. [23]And he commanded a centurion to keep Paul, and to let *him* have liberty, and that he should forbid none of his acquaintance to minister or come unto him.

[24]And after certain days, when Felix came with his wife Drusilla, which was a Jewess, he sent for Paul, and heard him concerning the faith in Christ. [25]And as he reasoned of righteousness, temperance, and judgment to come, Felix trembled, and answered, Go thy way for this time; when I have a convenient season, I will call for thee. [26]He hoped also that money should have been given him of Paul, that he might loose him: wherefore he sent for him the oftener, and communed with him. [27]But after two years Porcius Festus came into Felix' room: and Felix, willing to show the Jews a pleasure, left Paul bound (Acts 24:22-27).

Felix then postponed making a decision. He had been governor long enough to have a more accurate knowledge of the teachings and life-style of the tens of thousands of Christians in Judea than Tertullus and the Jews present gave him credit for. So he put them off, saying that when the tribune Lysias came down he would learn the details of the things that concerned them. There is no evidence, however, that he ever sent for Lysias.

Felix then commanded the centurion to guard (and protect) Paul. He must also give him indulgence (a considerable amount of freedom) and must not forbid any of his own people from ministering to him. That is, the Christians would be allowed to visit him, bring him food, and give him whatever else he needed.

After some days Felix, with his wife Drusilla, who was a Jewess,[4] came, summoned Paul, and listened to him tell of the faith in Christ Jesus (the "in Christ Jesus" faith; that is, the gospel).

Paul not only presented the facts and the theology, but as he did in all his epistles, he went on to discuss practical matters of righteousness, self-control, and the coming judgment. At this, Felix became terrified and told Paul to go for now. At a later time he would call him again.

At the same time Felix hoped that Paul would give him a great deal of money (riches).[5] Therefore, he sent for him more often and talked (conversed) with him.

This continued over a two year period. Then Felix was replaced by Porcius Festus, who arrived in A.D. 59 and remained in office until his death in A.D. 61. The date of Paul's arrest was thus A.D. 57.

Because Felix still wanted to seek favor with the Jews, he left Paul bound.

---

[4]She was the young daughter of Herod Agrippa I (Acts 12:1) and was the sister of Herod Agrippa II and Bernice. Felix had seduced her from her former husband, King Aziz of Emesa.

[5]Some writers believe Paul received an inheritance about this time, but it cannot be proved. Felix may have hoped Paul's many friends would present a bribe for his release.

ACTS

CHAPTER 25

The Jews in Jerusalem had not given up. They still considered Paul their archenemy and wanted his death. So they took advantage of the new governor, Festus, with the intent of seeking a new opportunity for carrying out their plots.

Trial Before Festus (25:1-8)

[1]Now when Festus was come into the province, after three days he ascended from Caesarea to Jerusalem. [2]Then the high priest and the chief of the Jews informed him against Paul, and besought him, [3]and desired favor against him, that he would send for him to Jerusalem, laying wait in the way to kill him. [4]But Festus answered, that Paul should be kept at Caesarea, and that he himself would depart shortly *thither.* [5]Let them therefore, said he, which among you are able, go down with *me,* and accuse this man, if there be any wickedness in him.

[6]And when he had tarried among them more than ten days, he went down unto Caesarea; and the next day sitting on the judgment seat commanded Paul to be brought. [7]And when he was come, the Jews which came down from Jerusalem stood round about, and laid many and grievous complaints against Paul, which they could not prove. [8]While he answered for himself, Neither against the law of the Jews, neither against the temple, nor yet against Caesar, have I offended any thing at all (Acts 25:1-8).

After Festus took office in Caesarea he rested a day and then went up to Jerusalem.[1] Immediately the chief priests and chief men of the Jews informed him of their charges against Paul. Then they urgently requested him to send for Paul and have him

[1]According to the Jewish way of counting, after three days means on the third day. Cf. Lenski, *op. cit.,* p. 987.

brought to Jerusalem. Again there was a plot to ambush and kill him along the road.

Festus must have been informed of their previous plot, so he replied that Paul was kept (guarded) in Caesarea where he would soon be going. He then suggested that persons of power (ability) go down with him. Then if there was anything wrong (out of place, improper) in Paul, let them accuse him.

After eight or ten days, Festus did go down to Caesarea. The next day he sat on the judgment seat (the judge's throne, the tribunal). That is, he called for a new official trial and had Paul brought in.

The Jerusalem Jews then stood around him, making many weighty charges against him. But they could prove none of them. Luke does not give any details here, but the charges were undoubtedly similar to those Tertullus brought before Felix. Luke also merely summarizes Paul's defense here. Paul contended that he had not sinned in any way against the Jewish Law, the Temple, nor against Caesar, that is, against the Roman government. Later Festus shows that Paul bore witness to Christ's death and resurrection as well (verse 19).

Paul Appeals to Caesar (25:9-12)

[9]But Festus, willing to do the Jews a pleasure, answered Paul, and said, Wilt thou go up to Jerusalem, and there be judged of these things before me? [10]Then said Paul, I stand at Caesar's judgment seat, where I ought to be judged: to the Jews have I done no wrong, as thou very well knowest. [11]For if I be an offender, or have committed any thing worthy of death, I refuse not to die: but if there be none of these things whereof these accuse me, no man may deliver me unto them. I appeal unto Caesar. [12]Then Festus, when he had conferred with the council, answered, Hast thou appealed unto Caesar? unto Caesar shalt thou go (Acts 25:9-12).

Festus, then, desiring to gain favor with the Jews, asked Paul if he would be willing to go up to Jerusalem for another trial before him. Paul, of course, knew what this would mean. Friends probably had informed him of the new plot to kill him on the way. Luke, at least, knew about it, and others must have.

Paul knew he had one recourse to keep out of the clutches of the Jewish leaders. Every Roman citizen had the right to appeal to Caesar. Paul recognized that the authority behind the judgment seat, or tribunal, where Festus sat was Caesar's. As a Roman citizen he was where he had a right to be judged. To the Jews he had done no harm or injury, as Festus well knew.

Paul then stated his case for his appeal to Caesar.[2] If he was unjust and had done anything worthy of death, he would not refuse to die (that is, he would not object to the death penalty). But since there was nothing to these things of which he was accused, no one was able (had the power) to turn him over to the Jews as a favor to them.

Festus talked this over with his provincial council. But there was really nothing he could do. Paul had appealed to Caesar; to Caesar he must go. Probably Festus was glad the case was now out of his hands.

Festus Presents Paul's Case to Agrippa (25:13-22)

[13]And after certain days king Agrippa and Bernice came unto Caesarea to salute Festus. [14]And when they had been there many days, Festus declared Paul's cause unto the king, saying, There is a certain man left in bonds by Felix: [15]about whom, when I was at Jerusalem, the chief priests and the elders of the Jews informed *me,* desiring *to have* judgment against him. [16]To whom I answered, It is not the manner of the Romans to deliver any man to die, before that he which is accused have the accusers face to face, and have license to answer for himself concerning the crime laid against him.

[17]Therefore, when they were come hither, without any delay on the morrow I sat on the judgment seat, and commanded the man to be brought forth. [18]Against whom when the accusers stood up, they brought none accusation of such things as I supposed: [19]but had certain questions against him of their own superstition, and of one Jesus, which was dead, whom Paul affirmed to be alive. [20]And because I doubted of such manner of questions, I asked *him* whether he would go to Jerusalem, and there be judged of these matters. [21]But when Paul had appealed to be reserved unto the hearing of Augustus, I commanded him to be kept till I might send him to Caesar. [22]Then Agrippa said unto Festus, I will also hear the man myself. Tomorrow, said he, thou shalt hear him (Acts 25:13-22).

Some days later, King Agrippa (Herod Agrippa II, also known as M. Julius Agrippa II, son of the Herod of Acts 12), with his widowed sister Bernice, came to Caesarea to pay his respects to the new governor of Judea. Agrippa II had been made king of

[2]Nero was the Caesar. Up to this point Nero had good advisers, and Paul had every reason to be confident he would get a fair trial in Rome.

Chalcis between the Lebanon and Antilebanon mountains in A.D. 48. Later (A.D. 53) he became king of the tetrarchy of Philip east of the Sea of Galilee, and of Lysanius west and northwest of Damascus. In A.D. 56, Nero added cities around the Sea of Galilee.

Since they were there many days Festus laid Paul's case before Agrippa, desiring to consult with him about it. After relating how the Jews in Jerusalem informed (brought charges) against Paul and asked for a sentence of condemnation, he told how he refused to give them Paul as a favor and how he brought them together and put Paul on trial. Then, as a Roman he was surprised that they did not charge Paul with any of the evil things he supposed they would. Instead, they had questions against him of what Festus, as a Roman pagan, called "their superstition," and also of Jesus who was put to death, but whom Paul alleged to live.

Festus, however, did not admit that it was because he wanted to seek favor with the Jews that he asked Paul to go to Jerusalem. Instead, he told Agrippa he was at his wits' end concerning how to search out these things. Then, because Paul refused to go to Jerusalem and appealed to be kept for the decision of the emperor (the Augustus, a title meaning "worthy to be reverenced" used here of the emperor Nero), Festus commanded that he be kept under guard until he could send him to Caesar.

Agrippa responded by saying he himself wished to hear Paul. This pleased Festus, and he set the time for the next day.

Festus Presents His Case (25:23-27)

23And on the morrow, when Agrippa was come, and Bernice, with great pomp, and was entered into the place of hearing, with the chief captains, and principal men of the city, at Festus' commandment Paul was brought forth. 24And Festus said, King Agrippa, and all men which are here present with us, ye see this man, about whom all the multitude of the Jews have dealt with me, both at Jerusalem, and *also* here, crying that he ought not to live any longer. 25But when I found that he had committed nothing worthy of death, and that he himself hath appealed to Augustus, I have determined to send him. 26Of whom I have no certain thing to write unto my lord. Wherefore I have brought him forth before you, and specially before thee, O king Agrippa, that, after examination had, I might have somewhat to write. 27For it seemeth to me unreasonable to send a prisoner, and not withal to signify the crimes *laid* against him (Acts 25:23-27).

The next day Agrippa and Bernice arrived with a great display of pomp, that is, in all their royal robes and with all their attendants. The tribunes and the prominent men of Caesarea came too.

After Paul was brought in, Festus addressed King Agrippa and the others who were present, calling on them to look at this man about whom the whole multitude of the (Jerusalem) Jews petitioned, crying out that he must not live any longer. Again Festus declared he found that Paul had done nothing worthy of death. But since he appealed to Caesar, Festus decided to send him. His problem was he had nothing reliable (trustworthy) to write to his lord (Caesar). He hoped that after this examination before Agrippa he would have something to write. It seemed unreasonable to send a prisoner without pointing out in a letter the charge against him.

ACTS

CHAPTER

26

In the final hearing before Agrippa the Book of Acts records for the third time the account of Paul's conversion, giving some details not previously recorded.

PAUL THE PHARISEE (26:1-11)

[1]Then Agrippa said unto Paul, Thou art permitted to speak for thyself. Then Paul stretched forth the hand, and answered for himself:

[2]I think myself happy, king Agrippa, because I shall answer for myself this day before thee touching all the things whereof I am accused of the Jews: [3]especially *because I know* thee to be expert in all customs and questions which are among the Jews: wherefore I beseech thee to hear me patiently.

[4]My manner of life from my youth, which was at the first among mine own nation at Jerusalem, know all the Jews; [5]which knew me from the beginning, if they would testify, that after the most straitest sect of our religion I lived a Pharisee. [6]And now I stand and am judged for the hope of the promise made of God unto our fathers: [7]unto which *promise* our twelve tribes, instantly serving *God* day and night, hope to come. For which hope's sake, king Agrippa, I am accused of the Jews. [8]Why should it be thought a thing incredible with you, that God should raise the dead?

[9]I verily thought with myself, that I ought to do many things contrary to the name of Jesus of Nazareth. [10]Which thing I also did in Jerusalem: and many of the saints did I shut up in prison, having received authority from the chief priests; and when they were put to death, I gave my voice against *them.* [11]And I punished them oft in every synagogue, and compelled *them* to blaspheme; and being exceedingly mad against them, I persecuted *them* even unto strange cities (Acts 26:1-11).

With Agrippa's permission to speak for himself, Paul stretched out his hand and proceeded to make his defense. He counted himself happy to make a defense before Agrippa because Agrippa was especially expert in all the things concerning Jewish customs and questions. Therefore he begged him to listen patiently. Actually, Agrippa was a Jew by religion and could be expected to have a concern about these things.

Paul pointed out first that all the Jews knew his manner of life in Tarsus as well as in Jerusalem. They knew he lived a Pharisee, following the teachings of this strictest of Jewish sects. (See 2 Corinthians 11:22; Galatians 1:13; Philippians 3:5.)

Now Paul stood there being judged because of the hope of the promise God made to the patriarchs (Abraham, Isaac, and Jacob, and possibly other ancesters of Israel). This promise, Paul said, "our twelve tribes"[1] in earnestness served (worshiped) God day and night hoping to attain (reach as their God-given destination). The Jews' accusation against him concerned this hope. Why would the king judge it incredible if God raises the dead? That is, especially now that God has raised Jesus from the dead.

Paul himself had thought it necessary to do many things against the name (character, nature, and authority) of Jesus of Nazareth; he had put many of the saints (the believers set apart for God) in prisons. When they were put to death, he had cast his vote against them.[2] Going from synagogue to synagogue, he had often punished the believers, trying to compel them to blaspheme (that is, to blaspheme the name of Jesus). The Greek implies, however, that he was not able to make them do it.

So exceedingly and madly enraged had he been against them that he had pursued them even to foreign cities. Later, in 1 Timothy 1:13, Paul points out that he acted in ignorance of truth.

CONVERTED AND COMMISSIONED (26:12-18)

[12]Whereupon as I went to Damascus with authority and commission from the chief priests, [13]at midday, O king, I saw in the way a light from heaven, above the brightness of the sun, shining round about me and them which journeyed with me. [14]And when we were all fallen to the earth, I heard a voice speaking unto me, and saying in the Hebrew

---

[1]Note that Paul recognized that the Jews of his day included all 12 tribes. He was of the tribe of Benjamin. Anna, Luke 2:36, was of the tribe of Asher, one of the 10 northern tribes. The Jews at that time knew what tribe they belonged to. The 10 tribes were obviously never lost.

[2]It is on this basis that we must believe Paul was a member of the Sanhedrin. He did more than hold the clothes of the witnesses against Stephen. He cast his vote against him and many other Christians, a vote that called for the death penalty.

tongue, Saul, Saul, why persecutest thou me? *it is* hard for thee to kick against the pricks.

[15]And I said, Who art thou, Lord? And he said, I am Jesus whom thou persecutest. [16]But rise, and stand upon thy feet: for I have appeared unto thee for this purpose, to make thee a minister and a witness both of these things which thou hast seen, and of those things in the which I will appear unto thee; [17]delivering thee from the people, and *from* the Gentiles, unto whom now I send thee, [18]to open their eyes, *and* to turn *them* from darkness to light, and *from* the power of Satan unto God, that they may receive forgiveness of sins, and inheritance among them which are sanctified by faith that is in me (Acts 26:12-18).

Paul then recounted the story of his conversion on the Damascus road. The phrase, "It is hard for you to kick against the goads" was a common phrase used to express opposition to God.[3]

Beginning at verse 16, Paul gave Christ's commission in greater detail. Jesus said he appeared to Paul to appoint him for the important task of being a minister (a servant) and a witness "both of these things which you have seen and of those things in the which I will appear unto you," rescuing you from the people (the Jews) and from the Gentiles (the nations) to whom I send you to open their eyes and to turn them from darkness to light and from the authority of Satan to the (true) God, that they might receive the forgiveness of sins.

With their forgiveness they would receive an inheritance among those who are sanctified (treated as holy, set apart to God as His people to do His will) by faith in Christ. ("Faith in me" means the kind of faith that is fixed in me.)

Thus Paul showed that Jesus himself gave him a commission to carry out His work, as prophesied by Isaiah 42:6, 7 and 61:1, 2. That is, he would be sharing in the work of Christ.

Paul's Faithful Witness (26:19-23)

[19]Whereupon, O king Agrippa, I was not disobedient unto the heavenly vision: [20]but showed first unto them of Damascus, and at Jerusalem, and throughout all the coasts of Judea, and *then* to the Gentiles, that they should repent and turn to God, and do works meet for repentance. [21]For these causes the Jews caught me in the temple, and went about to kill *me*. [22]Having therefore obtained help of God, I continue unto this day, witnessing both to small and great, saying none other

[3]This identified the voice from heaven as divine. See Longenecker, *op. cit.*, pp. 98-100.

things than those which the prophets and Moses did say should come: [23]that Christ should suffer, *and* that he should be the first that should rise from the dead, and should show light unto the people, and to the Gentiles (Acts 26:19-23).

Paul then declared he was not disobedient to the heavenly vision (appearance). The word "vision" here does not mean a dream-type vision, but an actual appearance where Jesus in person spoke to him.

His obedience was shown in the way he declared to the Jews at Damascus, Jerusalem, all Judea, and also to the Gentiles, that they should repent (change their minds and fundamental attitudes), turn to God, and then do works worthy of their repentance. It was because of this message (which included blessings for the Gentiles) that the Jews seized Paul in the Temple and attempted to kill him.

Then Paul again began to bear witness to Christ. By the help of God he was standing to this day, testifying both to small and great. The great, of course, included King Agrippa.

Paul's witness was not limited to his own experience, however. Everything he said was only what the prophets and Moses had already said would come. In other words, his total message was based on the Scriptures: They declared that the Christ (the Messiah) must suffer; they showed how He, as the first of the resurrection from the dead, would proclaim light to the people (the Jews) and to the Gentiles (the nations).

Festus and Agrippa Reject the Gospel (26:24-29)

[24]And as he thus spake for himself, Festus said with a loud voice, Paul, thou art beside thyself; much learning doth make thee mad. [25]But he said, I am not mad, most noble Festus; but speak forth the words of truth and soberness. [26]For the king knoweth of these things, before whom also I speak freely: for I am persuaded that none of these things are hidden from him; for this thing was not done in a corner. [27]King Agrippa, believest thou the prophets? I know that thou believest. [28]Then Agrippa said unto Paul, Almost thou persuadest me to be a Christian. [29]And Paul said, I would to God, that not only thou, but also all that hear me this day, were both almost, and altogether such as I am, except these bonds (Acts 26:24-29).

This was powerful preaching. Festus felt its conviction and reacted against it by interrupting Paul. Shouting out loudly, he said, "You are raving mad, Paul. Your much learning is turning you into a raving madman." By "much learning" he meant "many writings," that is, the Scriptures Paul had been talking about.

Paul gently and courteously replied, "I do not speak as a madman, most excellent Festus, but I utter forth (anointed by the Spirit) words (Greek, *rhemata)* of truth and sound good sense." The king knew of these things. That is, the king could verify them if he wished to do so.

With this, Paul turned his attention again to the king. Paul could speak boldly (and freely) to him, for he was persuaded that none of these things were hidden to him (or had escaped his notice), for this (the facts of Christ's death and resurrection, the events of the gospel) had not been done in a corner; they were done publicly and were publicly known. Then, addressing Agrippa, Paul asked him if he believed the prophets. Without waiting for an answer, he added that he knew he believed.

Suddenly, and with surprise, Agrippa realized Paul was trying to convert him. By saying Agrippa believed the prophets, Paul was implying that he would therefore have to believe what they said about the Messiah, and this should cause him to believe what Paul said about Jesus. But it seems Agrippa was not willing to say he did believe the prophets; neither was he willing to say he believed Paul.

Agrippa's reply has been translated and interpreted in a number of ways. Some ancient manuscripts read literally, "In (by) a little, you seek to persuade me to become a Christian." The King James Version takes this to be an admission that he felt the force of Paul's arguments and Paul was almost persuading him to be a Christian.[4]

Other ancient manuscripts read, "In (by) a little, you seek to persuade me to act a Christian," that is, act the part of the Christian. Many writers take this as a rejection. He did not want Paul to use him to corroborate the gospel.

"In (by) a little" could mean "in brief" or "in a few words." Or it may mean "in a very short time." Thus, some say Agrippa meant "In brief, you are seeking to persuade me to become a Christian," and they interpret this simply as an expression of surprise. Others interpret the reply as irony: "In so short a time do you really think

---

[4]Thomas, *op cit.,* p. 435, upholds this view, citing Stier.

you can persuade me to become a Christian (or act, or live like a Christian)?" Still others take it to be a sharp rejection, "In brief, you are trying to persuade me to act (play the part of) a Christian." Whatever the translation, it is clear Agrippa was rejecting Paul's efforts to convert him.

Paul, however, refused to be discouraged. He replied, "I pray to God that both in brief or at length (or in a great degree), not only you, but all who are listening to me today might become such as I am (that is, a Christian like me), except for these chains." It is possible that Paul held up his hands to show the chains on his wrists at this point.

AGRIPPA RECOGNIZES PAUL'S INNOCENCE (26:30-32)

[30]And when he had thus spoken, the king rose up, and the governor, and Bernice, and they that sat with them: [31]and when they were gone aside, they talked between themselves, saying, This man doeth nothing worthy of death or of bonds. [32]Then said Agrippa unto Festus, This man might have been set at liberty, if he had not appealed unto Caesar (Acts 26:30-32).

Agrippa had heard enough. By standing up, he indicated the hearing was over. Then they all went out and discussed the hearing. All agreed that Paul had done nothing worthy of death or imprisonment; nothing in Roman law could hold him guilty. Then Agrippa told Festus that Paul might have been set free if he had not appealed to Caesar.

It is implied also that the emperor would see Paul's innocence and would have to set him free. Though Nero was the emperor in A.D. 59, he had not yet embarked on any campaign against the Christians. Under Roman law at this time it was not a crime to be a Christian. Not until Paul's second imprisonment, which is reflected in 2 Timothy, did it become dangerous under the Romans to be a Christian.

ACTS

CHAPTER 27

This account of Paul's journey to Rome gives us one of the most interesting and factual accounts of a sea voyage and a shipwreck to be found anywhere in ancient literature. Luke uses "we" throughout the passage, so it is clear he was an eyewitness.

CONTRARY WINDS (27:1-8)

[1]And when it was determined that we should sail into Italy, they delivered Paul and certain other prisoners unto *one* named Julius, a centurion of Augustus' band. [2]And entering into a ship of Adramyttium, we launched, meaning to sail by the coasts of Asia; *one* Aristarchus, a Macedonian of Thessalonica, being with us. [3]And the next *day* we touched at Sidon. And Julius courteously entreated Paul, and gave *him* liberty to go unto his friends to refresh himself. [4]And when we had launched from thence, we sailed under Cyprus, because the winds were contrary.

[5]And when we had sailed over the sea of Cilicia and Pamphylia, we came to Myra, *a city* of Lycia. [6]And there the centurion found a ship of Alexandria sailing into Italy; and he put us therein. [7]And when we had sailed slowly many days, and scarce were come over against Cnidus, the wind not suffering us, we sailed under Crete, over against Salmone; [8]and, hardly passing it, came unto a place which is called the Fair Havens; nigh whereunto was the city *of* Lasea (Acts 27:1-8).

For the trip from Caesarea to Italy, Paul and other prisoners were turned over to a centurion named Julius who belonged to the cohort of Augustus.[1] They first took passage on a ship belonging to Adramyttium, a port of Mysia, southeast of Troas. It was headed up the coast of Asia Minor.

[1]A cohort directly responsible to the emperor. "Cohort I Augustus" had its headquarters in Bananaea in northeast Palestine, east of the southern end of the Sea of Galilee, in the territory of Agrippa II.

Luke took passage on this ship to be with Paul. So did Aristarchus, a Macedonian believer from Thessalonica. They went along to help him and serve him in every way they could. Thus, Paul did not travel as an ordinary prisoner. He had friends.[2]

The next day at Sidon, Julius, treating Paul with humanitarian kindness, permitted him to go to his friends there to obtain care. Then, battling contrary westerly winds, they sailed east and north of Cyprus to Myra in Lycia, the southernmost part of the province of Asia.

At Myra, the centurion transferred Paul and his friends to a ship from Alexandria that was sailing for Italy with a cargo of wheat. (See verse 38.) Egypt was the chief source of wheat for the city of Rome, and these ships that carried wheat were considered very important.

The winds continued to be contrary, and they sailed very slowly trying to reach Cnidus on the coast of Coria in southwest Asia Minor. But the northwest winds did not let them get there. They were driven under the lee of Crete, that is along its east coast. Then they struggled along its south coast until they reached Fair Havens ("Good Harbors").

Caught in a Storm (27:9-20)

[9]Now when much time was spent, and when sailing was now dangerous, because the fast was now already past, Paul admonished *them,* [10]and said unto them, Sirs, I perceive that this voyage will be with hurt and much damage, not only of the lading and ship, but also of our lives. [11]Nevertheless the centurion believed the master and the owner of the ship, more than those things which were spoken by Paul. [12]And because the haven was not commodious to winter in, the more part advised to depart thence also, if by any means they might attain to Phoenix, *and there* to winter; *which is* a haven of Crete, and lieth toward the southwest and northwest.

[13]And when the south wind blew softly, supposing that they had obtained *their* purpose, loosing *thence,* they sailed close by Crete. [14]But not long after there arose against it a tempestuous wind, called Euroclydon. [15]And when the ship was caught, and could not bear up into the wind, we let *her* drive. [16]And running under a certain island which is called Clauda, we had much work to come by the boat: [17]which when they had taken up, they used helps, undergirding the ship; and, fearing lest

[2]Sir William Ramsay speculates that Luke and Aristarchus took passage as Paul's slaves, thus giving Paul more prestige in the eyes of the centurion. Cited by Bruce, *op. cit.,* p. 501.

they should fall into the quicksands, struck sail, and so were driven. [18]And we being exceedingly tossed with a tempest, the next *day* they lightened the ship; [19]and the third *day* we cast out with our own hands the tackling of the ship. [20]And when neither sun nor stars in many days appeared, and no small tempest lay on *us*, all hope that we should be saved was then taken away (Acts 27:9-20).

Because a considerable time had passed and the fast (the Day of Atonement, which in A.D. 59 was on October 5) had gone by, Paul recognized that it would be dangerous to continue their voyage. He had been in three shipwrecks already (2 Corinthians 11:25), and he knew how dangerous winter storms could be. So he went to those in charge of the ship and advised them of the certainty of injury and great loss to the ship and its cargo, as well as of their lives.

The centurion, however, was persuaded by the pilot and the captain (owner) of the ship to keep going. The harbor was unsuitable to spend the winter in, so the majority gave counsel to try to reach Phoenix (modern Phinika), a harbor further west which was better located whether the winds came from the northwest or the southwest.

A gentle south wind persuaded the centurion and the others that they could make it to Phoenix, so they sailed west, keeping close to the south coast of Crete. It was not long, however, before Paul's prediction came true. A vehement, turbulent wind called Euroclydon suddenly rushed against them from the east northeast. It caught the ship in its grip and drove it away from the shores of Crete. The sailors tried to face it into the land, but the wind was too strong. So they had to give way and let the wind carry the ship where it would.

The lee (south side) of a small island, Clauda, gave them a little temporary relief. Even then it was with difficulty that they regained control over the small boat that was towed behind. After they hoisted the boat onto the deck, they used helps to undergird the ship. That is, they fastened cables vertically around the ship to try to keep the timbers from straining too much or giving way.

Then, afraid they would be driven off their course into Syrtis, a quicksand off the coast of North Africa west of Cyrene, they slackened their tackle (or possibly, the topsail) and so were carried along by the wind.

The next day, because they were still in the grip of the storm, they began to throw things overboard to lighten the ship. Usually this would mean throwing part of the cargo overboard. But this ship's cargo of wheat was so important to Rome that it was the last thing they would get rid of. They probably began with personal baggage and cabin furniture.

The third day (according to their way of counting, the day after they began throwing things overboard), with their own hands they tossed overboard the ship's tackle (probably including the main yard).

The storm continued many days (probably 11, see verse 20). Without any sighting of the sun, moon, or stars, they had no way of knowing where they were. Finally, as this great winter storm continued to press upon them, all hope of rescue was stripped away.

Paul's Vision and Courage (27:21-37)

[21]But after long abstinence, Paul stood forth in the midst of them, and said, Sirs, ye should have hearkened unto me, and not have loosed from Crete, and to have gained this harm and loss. [22]And now I exhort you to be of good cheer: for there shall be no loss of *any man's* life among you, but of the ship. [23]For there stood by me this night the angel of God, whose I am, and whom I serve, [24]saying, Fear not, Paul; thou must be brought before Caesar: and, lo, God hath given thee all them that sail with thee. [25]Wherefore, sirs, be of good cheer: for I believe God, that it shall be even as it was told me. [26]Howbeit we must be cast upon a certain island.

[27]But when the fourteenth night was come, as we were driven up and down in Adria, about midnight the shipmen deemed that they drew near to some country; [28]and sounded, and found *it* twenty fathoms: and when they had gone a little further, they sounded again, and found *it* fifteen fathoms. [29]Then fearing lest we should have fallen upon rocks, they cast four anchors out of the stern, and wished for the day. [30]And as the shipmen were about to flee out of the ship, when they had let down the boat into the sea, under color as though they would have cast anchors out of the foreship, [31]Paul said to the centurion and to the soldiers, Except these abide in the ship, ye cannot be saved. [32]Then the soldiers cut off the ropes of the boat, and let her fall off.

[33]And while the day was coming on, Paul besought *them* all to take meat, saying, This day is the fourteenth day that ye have tarried and continued fasting, having taken nothing. [34]Wherefore I pray you to take *some* meat; for this is for your health: for there shall not a hair fall from the head of any of you. [35]And when he had thus spoken, he took bread, and gave thanks to God in presence of them all; and when he had broken *it,* he began to eat. [36]Then were they all of good cheer, and they also took

some meat. [37]And we were in all in the ship two hundred threescore and sixteen souls (Acts 27:21-37).

For a long time the 276 people on the ship (see verse 37) abstained from food. The Greek word could mean they lacked food, but in verses 34-36 we see they still had food on board. The word can also mean abstinence from food because of loss of appetite or from seasickness. Because of the storm many must have been seasick. Even if a person is not seasick himself, the sight and odor of seasickness in others is enough to cause a well person to lose his appetite.[3]

Then one night an angel appeared and encouraged Paul by telling him to stop being afraid. It was necessary (by the divine plan) for him to come before Caesar, and God also had graciously given him all those who were sailing with him. There would be no loss of life, only of the ship.

Before Paul told the others of this God-given assurance, he reminded them of his warnings given before they left Crete. He was not simply saying, "I told you so!" He remembered that they had refused to listen to him before; he wanted to be sure they would listen to him now. So he caught their attention by getting them to admit (in their minds) that he was right.

Then he gave the glory to God "whose I am, and whom I serve." Notice also that he began by encouraging them to be of good cheer (be of good courage and keep up their spirits). He concluded in the same way. But the grounds for their courage was Paul's faith in God.

What a picture this was! Paul the prisoner communicating his faith: "Sirs, I believe God." But he added they would be shipwrecked on an island.

On the fourteenth night they were still being driven by the wind, in whatever direction it blew, across the Sea of Adria (the Mediterranean Sea southeast of Italy, not the Adriatic Sea). About midnight the sailors supposed (had a suspicion) they were approaching land.[4] So they threw out a weighted rope to sound the depth and found it 20 fathoms (120 feet). A little later,

[3]The author speaks from experience.

[4]Some ancient manuscripts read that the land was resounding. In other words, they thought they could hear waves breaking on the shore.

possibly after about a half hour, they sounded again and found the depth to be 15 fathoms (90 feet).

Because they were afraid the ship might run aground on the rocks and break up before they could escape, they tossed out four sea anchors from the stern and wished (Greek, prayed) for the day to come. That is, they prayed that day would come before the ship ran aground.

The sailors decided it would be dangerous to wait until then, so they sought to flee from the ship. When they were discovered, they had lowered the small boat under the pretense of putting out anchors from the prow (bow) of the ship. Paul then told the centurion that unless these sailors stayed with the ship they could not be saved. As it turned out, they were needed to get the ship to go aground in the best place.

The soldiers under the centurion then cut the rope holding the small boat and let if fall off into the sea. Paul the prisoner, because of the need, had taken command of the situation.

Still in command of the situation, Paul took charge and encouraged every one to take food for their own bodily health and welfare. He assured them that not a hair would be lost from anyone's head. Not only would they be saved, there would be no injuries. Then he set them an example by taking a loaf of bread, giving thanks to God before them all, and beginning to eat. At that, all 275 of the others took courage, were inspired with hope, and they too took nourishment.

The Shipwreck (27:38-44)

[38]And when they had eaten enough, they lightened the ship, and cast out the wheat into the sea. [39]And when it was day, they knew not the land: but they discovered a certain creek with a shore, into the which they were minded, if it were possible, to thrust in the ship. [40]And when they had taken up the anchors, they committed *themselves* unto the sea, and loosed the rudder bands, and hoisted up the mainsail to the wind, and made toward shore. [41]And falling into a place where two seas met, they ran the ship aground; and the forepart stuck fast, and remained unmovable, but the hinder part was broken with the violence of the waves.

[42]And the soldiers' counsel was to kill the prisoners, lest any of them should swim out, and escape. [43]But the centurion, willing to save Paul, kept them from *their* purpose; and commanded that they which could swim should cast *themselves* first *into the sea,* and get to land: [44]and the rest, some on boards, and some on *broken pieces* of the ship. And so it came to pass, that they escaped all safe to land (Acts 27:38-44).

After they were all satisfied with food, they threw out the cargo of wheat so the ship would ride higher. This would help them get closer to the shore.

When daylight came they did not recognize the land. But they noticed a bay and decided that if they were able they would run the ship aground on the beach. St. Paul's bay, as it is called today, fits exactly the things recorded in this chapter.

Releasing the anchors, they left them in the sea, because this also would lighten the ship. At the same time they unfastened the rudder (or steering paddle), raised the foresail (set on the bow) to catch the wind, and headed for the beach.

Instead of reaching the beach, they accidently came to a place between two seas, a narrow, shallow channel. The bow of the ship ran aground in mud and clay, while the stern began breaking up because of the force (violence) of the waves.

The soldiers then conferred with one another and their counsel was to kill the prisoners lest they swim away and escape. But the centurion wanted to save Paul, so he prevented them from carrying out this purpose. Then he commanded all who could swim to jump overboard first and get to the land. The rest followed, some on planks (boards from the ship) and others on whatever they could find that would float. Thus all were brought safely to the land. But as Paul warned, the ship was a total loss.

ACTS
CHAPTER
28

The Lord had assured Paul that he must go to Rome. He had also promised to give him the lives of all the 275 others who were on board. He did as He had promised.

MIRACLES AT MELITA (28:1-10)

[1]And when they were escaped, then they knew that the island was called Melita. [2]And the barbarous people showed us no little kindness: for they kindled a fire, and received us every one, because of the present rain, and because of the cold. [3]And when Paul had gathered a bundle of sticks, and laid *them* on the fire, there came a viper out of the heat, and fastened on his hand. [4]And when the barbarians saw the *venomous* beast hang on his hand, they said among themselves, No doubt this man is a murderer, whom, though he hath escaped the sea, yet vengeance suffereth not to live. [5]And he shook off the beast into the fire, and felt no harm. [6]Howbeit they looked when he should have swollen, or fallen down dead suddenly: but after they had looked a great while, and saw no harm come to him, they changed their minds, and said that he was a god.

[7]In the same quarters were possessions of the chief man of the island, whose name was Publius; who received us, and lodged us three days courteously. [8]And it came to pass, that the father of Publius lay sick of a fever and of a bloody flux: to whom Paul entered in, and prayed, and laid his hands on him, and healed him. [9]So when this was done, others also, which had diseases in the island, came, and were healed: [10]who also honored us with many honors; and when we departed, they laded *us* with such things as were necessary (Acts 28:1-10).

After arriving safe on land they found out the island was called Melita (Phoenician or Canaanite for "refuge"), now called Malta. It was south of Sicily and its people were descended from Phoenician colonists who probably spoke a dialect closely related to Hebrew.

Throughout this passage Luke calls the local people barbarians. But he does not mean that they were degraded or uncivilized. To the Greeks any foreigner who could not speak Greek was a barbarian. Later they gave the Romans a little leeway by including among the barbarians those who could not speak Greek or Latin.

It is easy to see that the citizens of Malta were good people even if they could not speak Greek. Their kindness went beyond the ordinary. They lit a fire and welcomed all 276 of these strangers who had escaped the wrecked ship. Because of the rain and the cold, the fire was an act of great kindness and must have been a welcome sight to all from the ship.

A little later, Paul gathered a large bundle of brushwood and put it on the fire. The heat brought out a viper that had been picked up with the wood, and it fastened on his hand (that is, bit him). Many writers take notice of the fact that there are no vipers on Malta today. But it is a small island and the people eventually got rid of them after Paul's day.

When the people of Malta saw the wild creature bite Paul, they jumped to the conclusion that Paul must be a murderer, whom, though he escaped safely from the sea, vengeance ("the Justice") had not let live. By "the Justice" they may have meant their heathen goddess of justice.

Paul simply shook the beast off into the fire and suffered no harm. (See Luke 10:19; Mark 16:18.) The local people had seen others bitten by the same kind of vipers; so they expected Paul to swell up or drop dead. For a long time they waited and watched, but nothing unusual happened to him. So they changed their minds and said he was a god.

Nearby were fields (lands, properties) belonging to the chief man (the governor) of the island, whose name was Publius. He welcomed them with kindness and for three days entertained them with friendly thoughtfulness.

Then it happened that the father of Publius lay sick, suffering from fevers (a recurring fever) and dysentery. Paul came in, prayed for him, and laid hands on him, and God healed him. Then the rest of the people of the island who had illnesses came and were healed.

We can be sure Paul kept ministering to them during the three winter months that followed. As a result, the people honored Paul and his friends with many honors (probably including gifts of money to help them stay alive during the winter months). When Paul and the others set sail in the spring, the people placed on board the things they needed for the journey. Apparently, they provided not only for Paul, but for all 276 of those who were shipwrecked.

Arriving in Rome (28:11-16)

[11]And after three months we departed in a ship of Alexandria, which had wintered in the isle, whose sign was Castor and Pollux. [12]And landing at Syracuse, we tarried *there* three days. [13]And from thence we fetched a compass, and came to Rhegium: and after one day the south wind blew, and we came the next day to Puteoli: [14]where we found brethren, and were desired to tarry with them seven days: and so we went toward Rome. [15]And from thence, when the brethren heard of us, they came to meet us as far as Appii Forum, and the Three Taverns; whom when Paul saw, he thanked God, and took courage. [16]And when we came to Rome, the centurion delivered the prisoners to the captain of the guard: but Paul was suffered to dwell by himself with a soldier that kept him (Acts 28:11-16).

The rest of the journey to Italy took place on another ship of Alexandria that wintered in Malta, probably at the good harbor of Valetta. Its figurehead was the Discuri (the boys of Zeus, that is, Castor and Pollux, who in Greek mythology were the sons of Zeus and Leda and were considered patrons of sailors).

The ship stopped three days at Syracuse in eastern Sicily, then made a circuit (tacked against the wind) to Rhegium in the toe of Italy's "boot." After another day the wind changed and it took them only one more day to reach Puteoli (modern Pozzuoli) on the bay of Naples. There they found Christian brethren who successfully urged them to stay seven days. Clearly, the centurion who was responsible for Paul recognized that God was with him and did not oppose anything Paul desired.[1]

From Puteoli they went on to Rome by land, taking the famous Roman road, the Appian way. At Appii Forum (Appius' Market Town), 43 Roman miles (39.15 English miles) south of Rome, and again at the village of Three Taverns (Three Shops), about 33

[1]Some writers speculate that the centurion had business in Puteoli which kept him there a week.

Roman miles (30.3 miles) from Rome, delegations of Roman believers met Paul and proceeded with him and his friends back to Rome in a procession whose numbers would have done credit to a visiting monarch. Actually, it was a custom when an emperor visited a city for the people to go out and meet him and escort him back into the city.

Each time the delegations met Paul there must have been a time of shouting and rejoicing. All this was an unexpected surprise to Paul. When he saw them he gave thanks to God and took courage. Surely God would give him a ministry in Rome as he desired (Romans 1:11, 12). Though Luke does not mention it, we can be sure also that the church had received the Epistle to the Romans, studied it with appreciation, and felt like they already knew Paul.

At Rome Paul was handed over to the commander of Nero's praetorian guard. But he was permitted to live by himself, lightly chained by the wrist to a soldier who guarded him. As verse 30 indicates, he was able to rent an apartment and keep it for the two years he was in Rome. Luke and Aristarchus also remained in Rome to help him during this period (Colossians 4:10, 14; Philemon 24). Fortunately, the apartment was large enough for a considerable number of people to gather, as verses 23-25 indicate.

Paul Meets the Jewish Leaders (28:17-22)

[17]And it came to pass, that after three days Paul called the chief of the Jews together: and when they were come together, he said unto them, Men *and* brethren, though I have committed nothing against the people, or customs of our fathers, yet was I delivered prisoner from Jerusalem into the hands of the Romans: [18]who, when they had examined me, would have let *me* go, because there was no cause of death in me. [19]But when the Jews spake against *it,* I was constrained to appeal unto Caesar; not that I had aught to accuse my nation of. [20]For this cause therefore have I called for you, to see *you,* and to speak with *you:* because that for the hope of Israel I am bound with this chain.

[21]And they said unto him, We neither received letters out of Judea concerning thee, neither any of the brethren that came showed or spake any harm of thee. [22]But we desire to hear of thee what thou thinkest: for as concerning this sect, we know that every where it is spoken against (Acts 28:17-22).

After three days Paul called together (invited) the Jewish leaders in Rome to his apartment. Ancient Roman inscriptions show there were several Jewish synagogues in Rome at this time. Paul then told them how he came to be in Rome as a prisoner. He emphasized his innocence and explained why he appealed to Caesar, being careful not to put any blame on the Jewish nation (people) as a whole.

Paul's purpose, however, was to do more than explain why he was there. He wanted to testify to the fact it was for the hope of Israel he was bound by a chain.

The Jewish leaders replied that no letters had come from Judea, nor had anyone brought a report of Paul's trial or spoken anything bad concerning him. Then they expressed a desire to hear Paul tell what he had in his mind.

They were not complimentary to the Christians, however, for they called Christianity a sect that everywhere was opposed (spoken against, debated about). Paul's epistle to the Romans shows that the church in Rome was already well established by A.D. 57 and probably long before that. Apparently, these Jewish leaders had listened to the critics and had never bothered to investigate for themselves.

Paul Preaches to Jews in Rome (28:23-28)

[23]And when they had appointed him a day, there came many to him into *his* lodging; to whom he expounded and testified the kingdom of God, persuading them concerning Jesus, both out of the law of Moses, and *out of* the prophets, from morning till evening. [24]And some believed the things which were spoken, and some believed not.

[25]And when they agreed not among themselves, they departed, after that Paul had spoken one word, Well spake the Holy Ghost by Isaiah the prophet unto our fathers, [26]saying, Go unto this people, and say, Hearing ye shall hear, and shall not understand; and seeing ye shall see, and not perceive: [27]for the heart of this people is waxed gross, and their ears are dull of hearing, and their eyes have they closed; lest they should see with *their* eyes, and hear with *their* ears, and understand with *their* heart, and should be converted, and I should heal them. [29]Be it known therefore unto you, that the salvation of God is sent unto the Gentiles, and *that* they will hear it (Acts 28:23-28).

The Jews set a date among themselves and came to Paul's apartment in considerable numbers. To these he gave explanation of what was in his mind by bearing solemn witness to the kingdom (rule) of God. As he always did in the synagogues, he used the books of Moses and the prophets to teach the gospel and to try to persuade them that Jesus is truly the Messiah.

He continued this teaching and preaching from early morning until evening. Some were persuaded. That is, they believed and obeyed Paul's message and exhortation. Some disbelieved.

Because they were in disagreement they left, but not before Paul had one final word. He quoted for them what the Holy Spirit in Isaiah 6:9, 10 said to their ancestors. Then he added that God's salvation was also sent to the Gentiles (a reference to his own call). They (emphatic) would also hear (and obey).

Two Years of Opportunity (28:29-31)

[29]And when he had said these words, the Jews departed, and had great reasoning among themselves. [30]And Paul dwelt two whole years in his own hired house, and received all that came in unto him, [31]preaching the kingdom of God, and teaching those things which concern the Lord Jesus Christ, with all confidence, no man forbidding him (Acts 28:29-31).

This was not Paul's last opportunity. For two whole years he was able to preach and teach boldly and freely, welcoming all who came into his apartment. This was an answer to his requests for prayer sent to some of the churches he had founded (Ephesians 6:19, 20; Colossians 4:3, 4). Even some from Caesar's household were converted (Philippians 4:22). This probably came about through the witness of soldiers made to the whole praetorian guard ("palace") (Philippians 1:13).[2]

Luke breaks off suddenly. There is no formal conclusion to this Book.

The Book of Acts goes on today.[3]

---

[2]The praetorian guard was the emperor's own guard and its officers who would be in contact with Paul on the emperor's behalf when his appeal was presented.

[3]Some believe Paul was released after two years when he was called before the emperor because the Jews had sent no accusation. Others believe the case was automatically dismissed at the end of the two years because no charges were presented. Philemon 22 shows Paul expected to be released.

First Timothy shows he was indeed released and went to the Roman province of Asia. Ancient tradition says he did go to Spain also. This was followed by Paul's second imprisonment and death. Second Timothy 4:13 indicates he left his cloak at Troas, possibly because of a sudden arrest. Second Timothy also shows conditions in Rome during Paul's second imprisonment. Nero was blaming the Christians for the fire in Rome, and it had become a crime to be a Christian.

Subject Index

Scripture Index

Old Testament

SCRIPTURE INDEX

NEW TESTAMENT

ROMANS

1 CORINTHIANS

2 CORINTHIANS

GALATIANS

EPHESIANS

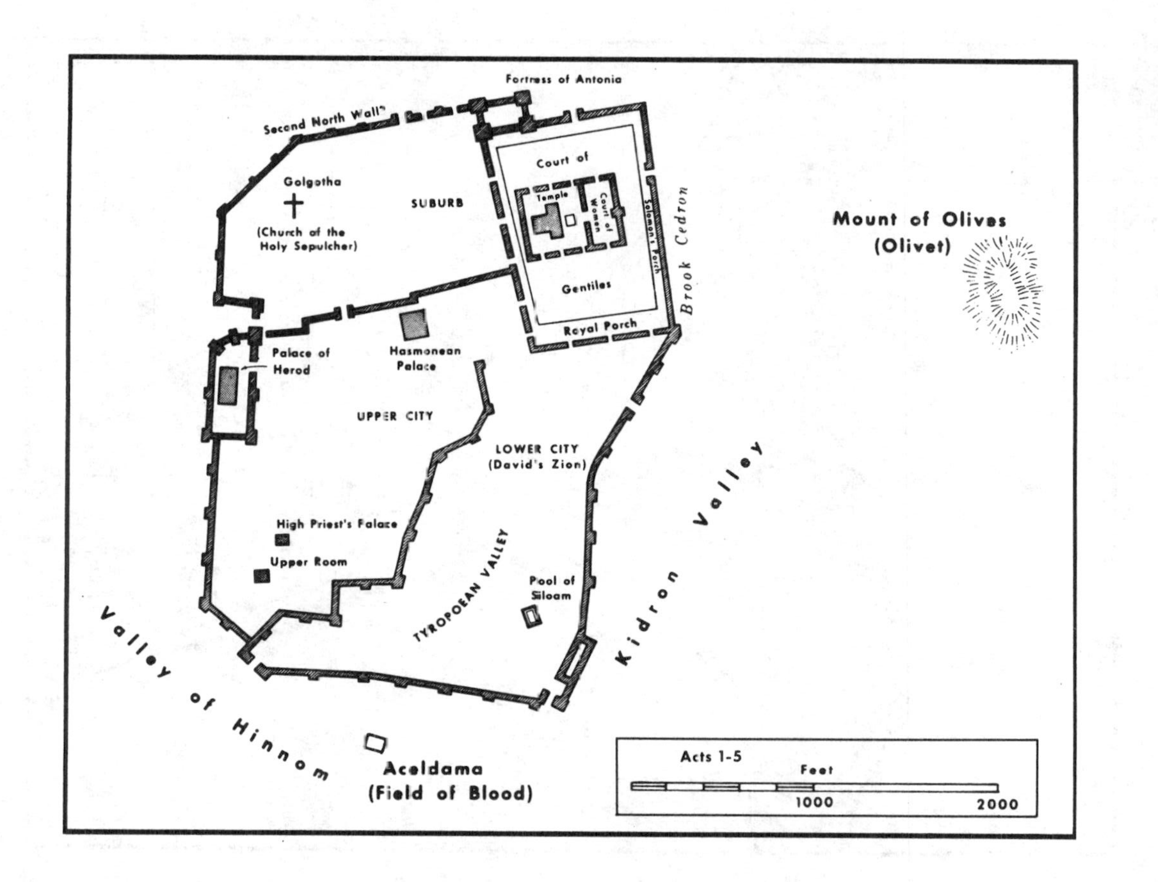

Fortress of Antonia
Second North Wall
Golgotha
(Church of the Holy Sepulcher)
SUBURB
Court of
Temple
Court of Women
Gentiles
Solomon's Porch
Royal Porch
Brook Cedron
Mount of Olives
(Olivet)
Palace of Herod
Hasmonean Palace
UPPER CITY
LOWER CITY
(David's Zion)
High Priest's Palace
Upper Room
TYROPOEAN VALLEY
Pool of Siloam
Kidron Valley
Valley of Hinnom
Aceldama
(Field of Blood)
Acts 1-5
Feet
1000
2000

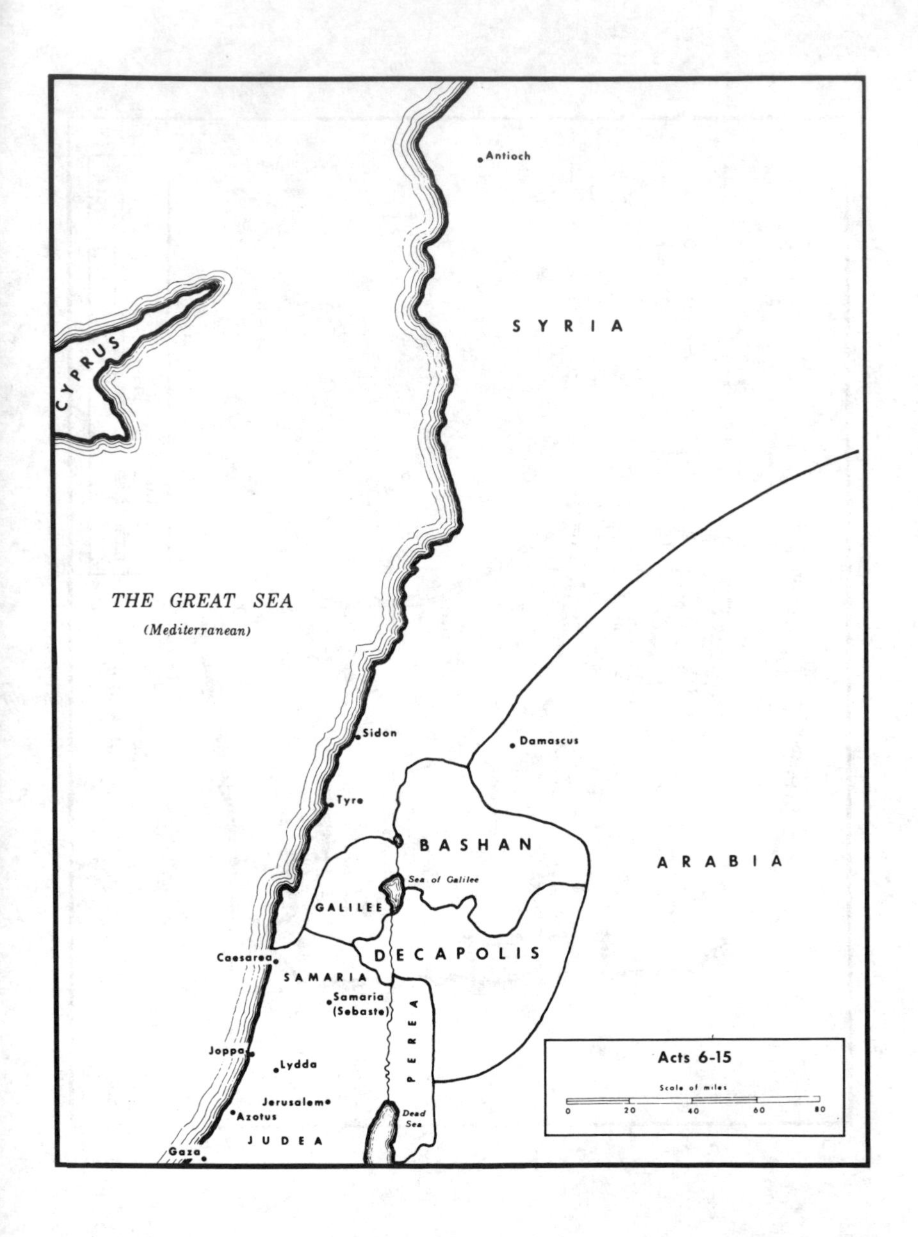
Antioch
SYRIA
CYPRUS
THE GREAT SEA
(Mediterranean)
Sidon
Damascus
Tyre
BASHAN
ARABIA
Sea of Galilee
GALILEE
DECAPOLIS
Caesarea
SAMARIA
Samaria
(Sebaste)
PEREA
Joppa
Lydda
Jerusalem
Azotus
Dead Sea
JUDEA
Gaza
Acts 6-15
Scale of miles
0
20
40
60
80

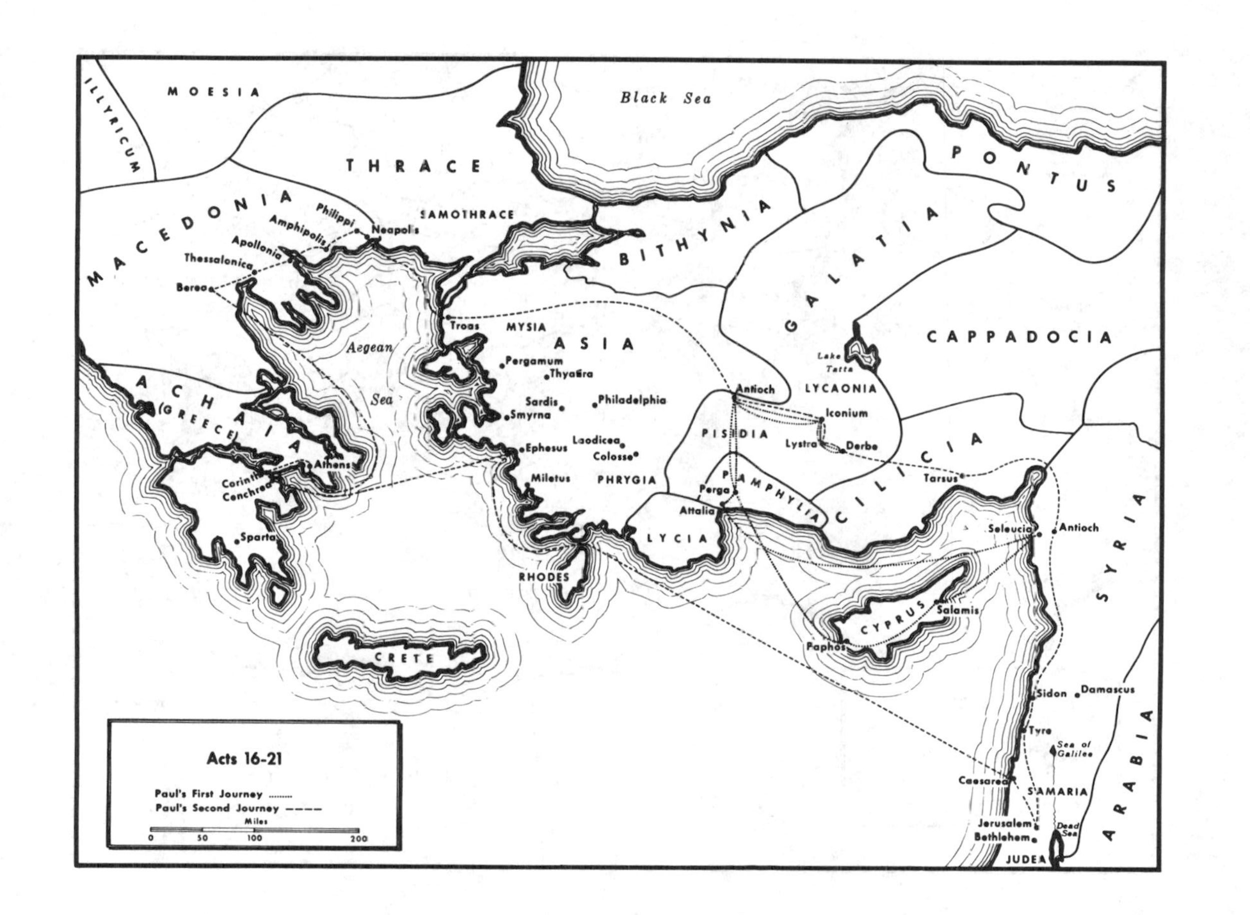
MOESIA
ILLYRICUM
THRACE
Black Sea
PONTUS
MACEDONIA
Philippi
Amphipolis
Neapolis
SAMOTHRACE
Apollonia
Thessalonica
Berea
BITHYNIA
GALATIA
CAPPADOCIA
Troas
MYSIA
ASIA
Aegean
Sea
Pergamum
Thyatira
Sardis
Smyrna
Philadelphia
Lake Tatta
Antioch
LYCAONIA
Iconium
ACHAIA
(GREECE)
PISIDIA
Lystra
Derbe
Ephesus
Laodicea
Colosse
Athens
Corinth
Cenchrea
Miletus
PHRYGIA
CILICIA
Tarsus
PAMPHYLIA
Perga
Attalia
LYCIA
Sparta
Seleucia
Antioch
SYRIA
RHODES
CYPRUS
Salamis
Paphos
CRETE
Sidon
Damascus
Tyre
Sea of Galilee
Caesarea
SAMARIA
ARABIA
Jerusalem
Bethlehem
Dead Sea
JUDEA
Acts 16-21
Paul's First Journey
Paul's Second Journey
Miles
0
50
100
200

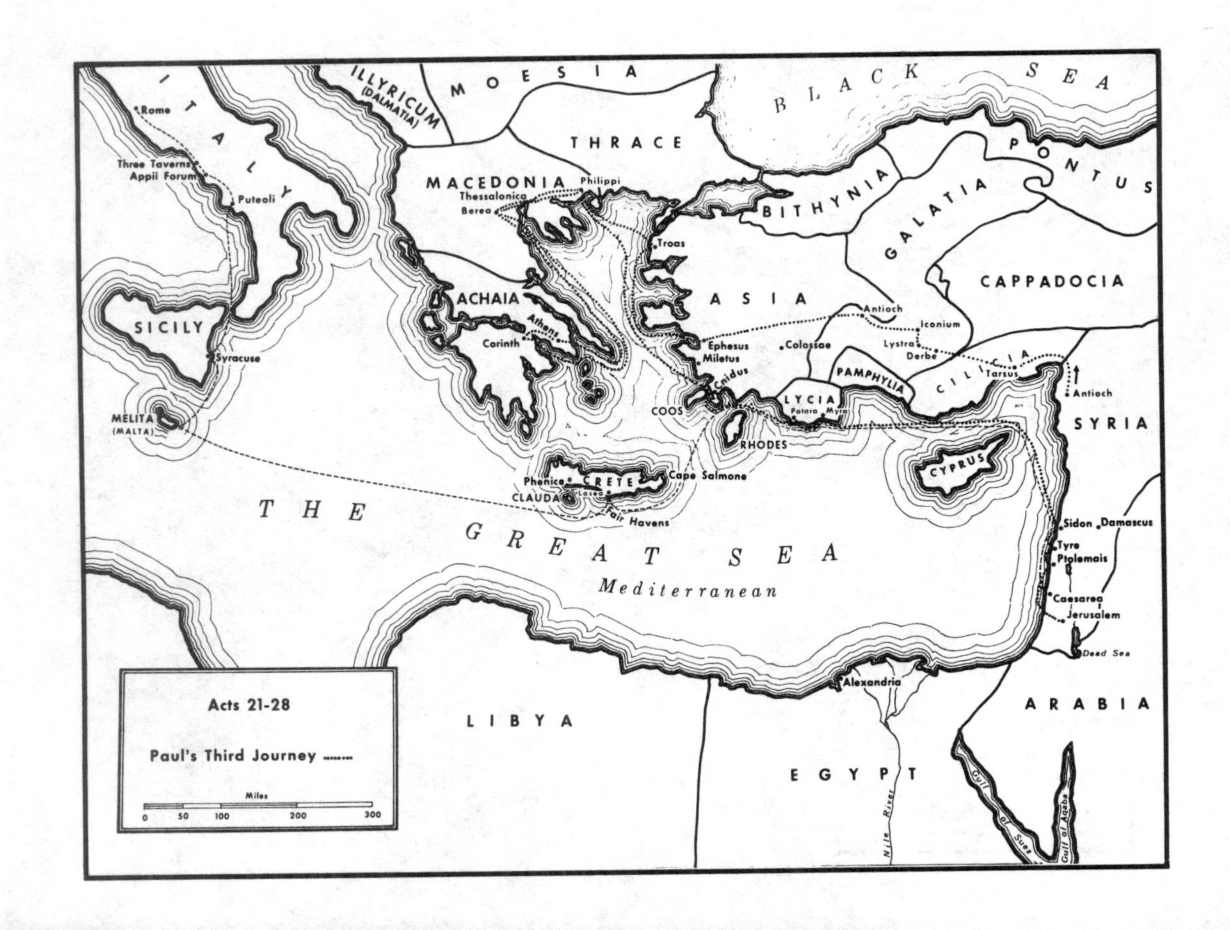
ITALY
Rome
Three Taverns
Appii Forum
Puteoli
SICILY
Syracuse
MELITA
(MALTA)
ILLYRICUM
(DALMATIA)
MOESIA
THRACE
MACEDONIA
Philippi
Thessalonica
Berea
ACHAIA
Athens
Corinth
BLACK SEA
BITHYNIA
PONTUS
GALATIA
CAPPADOCIA
Troas
ASIA
Antioch
Iconium
Lystra
Derbe
Ephesus
Miletus
Colossae
Cnidus
COOS
RHODES
LYCIA
Patara
Myra
PAMPHYLIA
CILICIA
Tarsus
Antioch
SYRIA
CYPRUS
Phenice
CRETE
Cape Salmone
CLAUDA
Lasea
Fair Havens
THE GREAT SEA
Mediterranean
Sidon
Damascus
Tyre
Ptolemais
Caesarea
Jerusalem
Dead Sea
Alexandria
LIBYA
EGYPT
Nile River
ARABIA
Gulf of Suez
Gulf of Aqaba
Acts 21-28
Paul's Third Journey
Miles
0
50
100
200
300